The Roman Cult of Salus

Martin A. Marwood

BAR International Series 465
1988

B.A.R.

5, Centremead, Osney Mead, Oxford OX2 0DQ, England.

GENERAL EDITORS

A.R. Hands, B.Sc., M.A., D.Phil.
D.R. Walker, M.A.

BAR -S465, 1988: 'The Roman Cult of Salus'

Price £11.00 post free throughout the world. Payments made in dollars must be calculated at the current rate of exchange and $8.00 added to cover exchange charges. Cheques should be made payable to B.A.R. and sent to the above address.

© Martin A. Marwood, 1988

ISBN 0 86054 596 2

For details of all new B.A.R. publications in print please write to the above address. Information on new titles is sent regularly on request, with no obligation to purchase.

Volumes are distributed from the publisher. All B.A.R. prices are inclusive of postage by surface mail anywhere in the world.

Printed in Great Britain

CONTENTS

		Page
Bibliography and Abbreviations		iii
Introduction		x
Chapter One:	The Ancient Literary Evidence	1
Chapter Two:	The Evidence of the Coinage	21
Chapter Three:	The Evidence of the Acts of the Arval Brothers	37
Chapter Four:	The Evidence of the Calendars, the Menologia Rustica and the Feriale Duranum	53
Chapter Five:	The Military Dedications, I: The Dedications of the Equites Singulares Augusti	62
Chapter Six:	The Military Dedications, II: Dedications other than those of the Equites Singulares Augusti	71
Chapter Seven:	The Epigraphic Evidence for the Civilian Cult excluding that of the Arval Brothers and that of the Calendars	85
Chapter Eight:	Conclusion	147
Addendum:	The Mainz Jupiter Column	157

BIBLIOGRAPHY AND ABBREVIATIONS

AE   L'année épigraphique, for 1988 ff., Paris.

AFA   W. Henzen, Acta Fratrum Arvalium Quae Supersunt, Berlin, 1874.

ANRW   H. Temporini, W. Haase (ed.), Aufstieg und Niedergang der römischen Welt, Berlin and New York, 1972 ff.

Alföldy   G. Alföldy, Noricum, London, 1974.

Axtell   H.L. Axtell, The Deification of Abstract Ideas in Roman Literature and Inscriptions, published Ph.D. dissertation, University of Chicago, 1907.

BCH   Bulletin de correspondance hellénique, Athens and Paris, 1877, ff. (1893-1952, Paris only).

BM   The Coins of the Roman Empire in the British Museum, H. Mattingly, R.A.G. Carson, P.V. Hill (ed.), I-VI, London, 1923 ff. (Vol. VI, 2nd ed., 1975) (cited by page then coin number).

Bauchhenss, 1984a. G. Bauchhenss, Die grosse Jupiter-Säule aus Mainz (CSIR, Deutschland II.2), Mainz, 1984.

Bauchhenss, 1984b. G. Bauchhenss, Denkmäler des Juppiterkultes aus Mainz und Umgebung (CSIR, Deutschland II.3), Mainz, 1984.

Birley, 1953. E. Birley, Roman Britain and the Roman Army, Collected Papers, Kendal, 1953.

Birley, 1978. E. Birley, 'The Religion of the Roman Army: 1895-1977', ANRW, II. 16. 2 (1978), 1506-1541.

Birley, Deities. E. Birley, 'The Deities of Roman Britain', ANRW, II.18.1 (1986), 3-112.

A.R. Birley, 1979. A.R. Birley, The People of Roman Britain, London, 1979.

A.R. Birley, 1981. A.R. Birley, The 'Fasti' of Roman Britain, Oxford, 1981.

CAH   The Cambridge Ancient History, Cambridge, 1923 ff.

CIL   Corpus Inscriptionum Latinarum, I-XVI, Berlin, 1863 ff.

CPIL   R. Hurtado de San Antonio (ed.), Corpus provincial de inscripciones latinas, Cáceres, (Diputacion provincial de Cáceres, servicios culturales) Cáceres, 1977.

CSIR	Corpus Signorum Imperii Romani (country, volume and fascicule indicated), several places of publication by various institutions, 1967 ff.
Cagnat	R. Cagnat, Cours d'épigraphie latine, 4th ed., Paris, 1914.
Crawford	M.H. Crawford, Roman Republican Coinage, (2 vols.) Cambridge, 1974 (cited by page then coin number).
Davies, 1969.	R.W. Davies, 'The Medici of the Roman Armed Forces', ES, VIII (1969), 83-99.
Davies, 1970.	R.W. Davies, 'The Roman Military Medical Service', Saalburg - Jahrbuch, XXVII (1970), 84-104.
Davies, 1972.	R.W. Davies, 'Some More Military Medici', ES, IX (1972), 1-11.
Domaszewski	A. von Domaszewski, 'Die Religion des römischen Heeres', Westdeutsche Zeitschrift für Geschichte und Kunst, XIV (Trier, 1895), 1-128 (reprinted separately, New York, 1975).
Dumézil	G. Dumézil, Archaic Roman Religion, (2 vols.) Chicago, 1970 (translated from French edition of 1966).
Dura V	A. Perkins (ed.), The Excavations at Dura-Europos conducted by Yale University and the French Academy of Inscriptions and Letters: Final Report V, Part 1. The Parchments and Papyri (ed. C.B. Welles, R.O. Fink, J.F. Gilliam), New Haven, 1959.
EE	Ephemeris Epigraphica, CIL Supplementum, I-IX, Rome and Berlin (IX, Berlin only), 1872-1903.
EPROER	M.J. Vermaseren (ed.), Études préliminaires aux religions orientales dans l'empire romaine, Leiden, 1961 ff.
ES	Epigraphische Studien, Köln/Düsseldorf, 1967 ff.
Edelstein	E.J. and L. Edelstein, Asclepius: A Collection and Interpretation of the Testimonies, (2 vols.) Baltimore, 1945.
FD	A.S. Hoey, R.O. Fink, W.F. Snyder, 'The Feriale Duranum', YCS, VII (1940), 1-222.
Fears	J.R. Fears, 'The Cult of Virtues and Roman Imperial Ideology', ANRW, II. 17. 2 (1981), 827-948.
Ferguson	J. Ferguson, The Religions of the Roman Empire, London, 1970.

Gordon   A.E. and J.S. Gordon, <u>Album of Dated Latin Inscriptions</u>, (4 vols.) Berkeley, 1958-1965 (cited by inscription number).

Grant   M. Grant, <u>From 'Imperium' to 'Auctoritas', A Historical Study of 'Aes' Coinage in the Roman Empire, 49 BC - AD 14</u>, Cambridge, 1946.

HC   A.S. Robertson, <u>Roman Imperial Coins in the Hunter Coin Cabinet, University of Glasgow</u>, I-V, Oxford, 1962-1982 (cited by page then coin number).

Harris   E. and J.R. Harris, <u>The Oriental Cults in Roman Britain</u>, EPROER, 6, Leiden, 1965.

M. Henig,   <u>Religion in Roman Britain</u>, London, 1984.

Holder   A. Holder, <u>Alt-celtischer Sprachschatz</u>, (3 vols.) Leipzig, 1896-1913.

IDR   D.M. Pippidi, I.I. Russu (ed.), <u>Inscriptiones Daciae et Scythiae Minoris Antiquae</u>, 1st series: <u>Inscriptiones Daciae Romanae</u>, I-III, I.I. Russu <u>et alii</u> (ed.), Bucharest, 1975 ff.

II   <u>Inscriptiones Italiae</u>, I-XIII, Rome (except III, Helsinki), 1931 ff.

ILER   J. Vives (ed.), <u>Inscripciones latinas de las España romana</u>, (2 vols.) Barcelona, 1971, 1972.

ILLRP   A. Degrassi (ed.), <u>Inscriptiones Latinae Liberae Rei Publicae</u>, I, II, Firenze, 1963 (II), 1965 (I, 2nd ed.) (numbered continuously).

ILS   H. Dessau (ed.), <u>Inscriptiones Latinae Selectae</u>, I-III, Berlin, 1892-1916.

Imagines   A. Degrassi (ed.), <u>Inscriptiones Latinae Liberae Rei Publicae, Imagines</u>, Berlin, 1965.

Instinsky, 1959. H.U. Instinsky, 'Kaiser Nero und die Mainzer Jupitersäule', <u>Jahrbuch des römisch-germanischen Zentralmuseums Mainz</u>, 6 (1959), 128-141.

Instinsky, 1963. H.U. Instinsky, <u>Die alte Kirche und das Heil des Staates</u>, München, 1963.

<u>JRS</u>   <u>The Journal of Roman Studies</u>, London, 1911 ff.

Jolliffe   N. Jolliffe, 'Dea Brigantia', <u>The Archaeological Journal</u>, XCVIII (1941), 36-61.

Jones, LRE	A.H.M. Jones, *The Later Roman Empire, 284-602: A Social, Economic and Administrative Survey*, Oxford, 1964 (reprint of 1973, in 2 vols. with pagination continuous).
KP	*Der Kleine Pauly*, I-V, K. Ziegler, W. Sontheimer, H. Gärtner (ed.), Stuttgart (I-III), München (IV, V), 1964-1975.
Kajanto	I. Kajanto, *The Latin 'Cognomina'*, Helsinki, 1965.
Latte	K. Latte, *Römische Religionsgeschichte* (Handbuch der Altertumswissenschaft, fortgeführt von H. Bengtson, V. 4), München, 1960.
Lex	W.H. Roscher (ed.), *Ausfuhrliches Lexikon griechischen und römischen Mythologie*, I-VI, Leipzig, 1884-1937 (Leipzig and Berlin, 1924-1937).
Liebeschuetz	J.H.W.G. Liebeschuetz, *Continuity and Change in Roman Religion*, Oxford, 1979.
Marwood	M.A. Marwood, 'A Reappraisal of the Altar of Julius Apolinaris at Corbridge, Northumberland', *Latomus, revue d'études latines*, XLIII (1984), 316-335.
Mattingly	H. Mattingly, *Roman Coins*, 2nd ed., London, 1962.
Meiggs	R. Meiggs, *Roman Ostia*, 1st ed., Oxford, 1960.
Merlat	P. Merlat, *Répertoire des inscriptions et monuments figures du culte de Jupiter Dolichenus*, Paris and Rennes, 1951.
Michels	A.K. Michels, *The Calendar of the Roman Republic*, Princeton, 1967.
Mócsy	A. Mócsy, *Pannonia and Upper Moesia: A History of the Middle Danube Provinces of the Roman Empire*, London, 1974.
Mundle	I. Mundle, 'Dea Caelestis in der Religionspolitik des Septimius Severus und der Julia Domna', *Historia* (Wiesbaden), X (1961), 228-237.
NS	*Notizie degli scavi di antichita*, Rome/Milan, 1876 ff.
Norden	E. Norden, *Aus altrömischen Priesterbüchern*, Lund and Leipzig, 1939.
OCD^2	N.G.L. Hammond, H.H. Scullard, *The Oxford Classical Dictionary*, 2nd ed., Oxford, 1970.

ORLR	E. Fabricius, F. Hettner, O. von Sarwey (ed.), *Der obergermanisch-raetische Limes des Römerreiches im Auftrage der Reichs-Limeskommission*, Heidelberg, 1914-1915, Berlin and Leipzig, 1929-1937.
Oliva	P. Oliva, *Pannonia and the Onset of Crisis in the Roman Empire*, Prague, 1962.
Olshausen	E. Olshausen, '"Über die römischen Ackerbrüder". Geschichte eines Kultes', *ANRW*, II.16.1 (1978), 820-832.
PIR[1]	*Prosopographia Imperii Romani Saec. I.II.III*, I-III, E. Klebs, H. Dessau, P. de Rohden (ed.), Berlin, 1897-1898.
PIR[2]	*Prosopographia Imperii Romani Saec. I.II.III*, I-V, E. Groag, A. Stein, L. Petersen (ed.), Berlin, 1933 ff.
PBSR	*Papers of the British School at Rome*, London, 1902 ff.
Palmer	R.E.A. Palmer, *Roman Religion and Roman Empire*, Philadelphia, 1974.
Pflaum	H.-G. Pflaum, *Les carrières procuratoriennes équestres sous le haut-empire romain*, (4 vols.) Paris, 1960, 1961 (*Supplément*: 1982).
Phillips	E.J. Phillips, *Corbridge, Hadrian's Wall East of the North Tyne* (*CSIR*, Great Britain I.1), Oxford, 1977.
Platner-Ashby	S.B. Platner, T. Ashby, *A Topographical Dictionary of Ancient Rome*, London, 1929.
Pulgram	E. Pulgram, *Italic, Latin, Italian, 600 BC to AD 1260: Texts and Commentaries*, Heidelberg, 1978.
RC	N. Lewis, M. Reinhold (ed.), *Roman Civilization*, I, II, New York, 1951, 1954.
RE	*Paulys Real-Encyclopädie der classischen Altertumswissenschaft, Neue Bearbeitung*, G. Wissowa, W. Kroll *et alii* (ed.), Stuttgart, 1893-1970, München, 1973 ff.
RIB	R.G. Collingwood, R.P. Wright (ed.), *The Roman Inscriptions of Britain*, I, Oxford, 1965. (R. Goodburn, H. Waugh, *Epigraphic Indexes*, Gloucester, 1983).
RIC	H. Mattingly, E.A. Sydenham, C.H.V. Sutherland, R.A.G. Carson (ed.), *The Roman Imperial Coinage*, I-IX, London, 1923 ff. (cited by page then coin number).

RIU	L. Barkóczi, A. Mócsy (ed.), *Die römischen Inschriften Ungarns*, I-III, Amsterdam, 1972 ff.
RR	C. Daicoviciu, H. Daicoviciu, R. Florescu (ed.), *Römer in Rumänien*, (Ausstellung des römisch-germanischen Museums Köln und des historischen Museums Cluj: exhibition catalogue) Köln, 1969.
Richmond	I.A. Richmond, 'Roman Legionaries at Corbridge, Their Supply-Base, Temples and Religious Cults', *Archaeologia Aeliana*, 4th series, XXI (1943), 127-224.
Ryberg	I.S. Ryberg, *An Archaeological Record of Rome from the Seventh to the Second Century BC* (*Studies and Documents*, XIII, 1), London and Philadelphia, 1940.
Schwarte	K.H. Schwarte, 'Salus Augusta Publica: Domitian und Trajan als Heilbringer der Staates', *Bonner Festgabe Johannes Straub (Beihefte der bonner Jahrbucher*, 39), A. Lippold, N. Himmelman (ed.), Bonn, 1977.
Scullard	H.H. Scullard, *Festivals and Ceremonies of the Roman Republic*, London, 1981.
Solin	H. Solin, *Die griechischen Personennamen in Rom: ein Namenbuch*, I-III, Berlin and New York, 1982.
Speidel, 1965.	M.P. Speidel, *Die Equites singulares Augusti: Begleittruppe der römischen Kaiser der zweiten und dritten Jahrhunderts* (*Antiquitas*, Reihe 1: *Abhandlungen zur alten Geschichte*, 2), Bonn, 1965.
Speidel	M.P. Speidel, *The Religion of Jupiter Dolichenus in the Roman Army*, *EPROER*, 63, Leiden, 1978.
Stern	H. Stern, *Le calendrier de 354: étude sur son texte et ses illustrations*, Paris, 1953.
Thulin	C. Thulin, 'Salus', *RE*, I.A.2 (1920), 2057-2059.
Waltzing	J.P. Waltzing, *Étude historique sur les corporations professionnelles chez les Romains depuis les origines jusqu'à la chute de l'empire d'occident*, I-IV, Louvain, 1895-1900.
Webster	G.A. Webster, *The Roman Imperial Army of the First and Second Centuries AD*, 2nd ed., London, 1979.
Weinstock	S. Weinstock, *Divus Julius*, Oxford, 1971.
Wilkes	J.J. Wilkes, *Dalmatia*, London, 1969.

Wissowa, Lex   G. Wissowa, 'Salus', Lex, IV (1909-1915), 295-301.

Wissowa, RK   G. Wissowa, Religion und Kultus der Römer (Handbuch der klassischen Altertums-wissenschaft, ed. I. von Müller, V, 4), 2nd ed., München, 1912.

YCS   Yale Classical Studies, New Haven, 1928 ff.

Note on Citation

Abbreviations such as p. and nr. are used only where necessary in order to avoid possible ambiguity; for instance, where the normal method of citation from a particular work is departed from (for example where pages are cited in CIL).

INTRODUCTION

This study aims to present and discuss the evidence for the cult of one of the most important of the deified 'virtues' worshipped by the Romans. Salus was important both as an object of piety, both public and personal, and as a political and social concept: both cult and concept came to be of great significance in imperial ideology and propaganda.[1]

The fullest overall summary has hitherto been that of G. Wissowa in Roscher's Lexikon (1909).[2] Even briefer was the treatment by C. Thulin in RE (1920).[3] Wissowa, again, and, more recently, K. Latte (1960) have provided outlines within general works on Roman religion.[4] In works on the deified 'virtues' as a body, there are the section in H.L. Axtell's monograph and the remarks passim in J.R. Fears' seminal article.[5] Especially valuable among treatments of particular aspects of the cult are: that by Fears on the influence of Greek practices and concepts on the early cult; that by S. Weinstock on the developments towards the establishment of a cult of Salus Caesaris and on the establishment of the cults of Salus Augusta and Salus Augusti; and that by Schwarte on the development of imperial ideology with respect to the concept of the imperial salus under Domitian and Trajan, as manifested in the Arval records, in the Panegyricus and letters of the younger Pliny and in the coin-issues.[6] On the early cult there is the section in G. Radke's, Die Götter Altitaliens.[7]

The purpose of this study is to indicate, present or summarize, as appropriate as well to discuss, the evidence, to date, explicitly relating to the Roman cult of Salus. Thus, it has been necessary to restrict the essential scope of the study to the evidence for Salus where the deity is named as such. To have included all the evidence for Hygieia would have enlarged the study unduly (and impracticably) beyond its envisaged scope. Evidence relating to Salus where she is perceived or depicted as Hygieia but where she is named as Salus has, of course, been included.[8]

Nearly all the epigraphic evidence is presented verbatim (Chapters Three to Seven). The evidence of the Arval records (Chapter Three), though indicated in its entirety, is sometimes presented verbatim, sometimes in reported form. In Chapter One the literary evidence is indicated and discussed (though not cited verbatim) under headings which refer to aspects of the cult or to aspects of the development of salus as a social and political concept. The evidence of the coin-issues is necessarily presented (in chronological order) in summary form (Chapter Two). Cross-references indicate to a certain extent where a particular aspect of the cult is manifested in the different categories of evidence, and Chapter Eight presents the chief conclusions deriving from the evidence as a whole. It is intended that the nature and scope of the evidence will be readily discernible whatever interpretation is here placed upon it.

The critical signs employed in presenting the epigraphic texts are essentially those used in RIB,[9] though deliberate erasures are indicated as such verbally after the text. Defective letters which are, however, restorable with certainty are not indicated as such. Doubtful lettters are indicated by subscript dots. Abbreviations are only expanded where required to make clear the significance of the text for the cult of Salus or where their expansion is not obvious.

This study originated as a thesis submitted to the University of Manchester following research carried out whilst the author was a student in the Department of Archaeology. I am most grateful to my former supervisor Dr. J.P. Wild for his invaluable guidance and encouragement, without which the original thesis would not have been completed. I owe a great debt of gratitude to both Professor G.D.B. Jones and Professor A.R. Birley for their encouragement, their understanding and many kindnesses. Dr. A.K. Jackson has been a great source of encouragement. Dr. G.P. Burton generously assisted in the translation of the Gabii inscription, and Dr. P.A. Holder has given me generous assistance on many points of information and interpretation for which I am most grateful. In the process of modifying the original work I have incurred further substantial debts which it is a pleasure to acknowledge. I am enormously grateful to Dr. V.A. Maxfield of the Department of History and Archaeology at the University of Exeter for her most generous and detailed scrutiny of the original work and for her many invaluable suggestions and points of information. Professor Birley has again supplied most valued advice and drawn attention to several errors. Dr. G.A. Webster has provided inspirational encouragement. I am most grateful to the editor of this series, Dr. A.R. Hands, for his greatly appreciated and patient efforts in bringing this volume to fruition. Mrs. B. Atherton and Ms. J. Goodwin have helped enormously by the speed and efficiency with which they have undertaken the typing. The opinions expressed below together with any remaining errors and inadequacies are entirely my own responsibility.

I am most grateful to the Department of Education and Science for the award of a state studentship for 1975 to 1976 and to the University of Manchester for the award of a university research scholarship for 1976 to 1977.

Manchester, April 1988   M.A.M.

NOTES

1. The principal ordinary meanings of salus were those of 'welfare', 'safety' (incolumitas), 'salvation' (personal and universal), 'deliverance' and 'health' (valetudo): for the meanings of 'Salus' as deity, below, 1-2, 6-8, 12-14, 21-25, 30, 87, 147-149, 152.

2. Wissowa, Lex, 295-301.

3. Thulin, 2057-2059. Cf. also L. Deubner, Lex, III.i, 2161 ('Personifikationen abstrakter Begriffe').

4. Wissowa, RK, 131-133, 306-309; Latte, 51, 234, 300, 322. Cf. also Scullard, 170 and H. Mattingly, OCD^2, 948 ('Salus').

5. Axtell, 13-15; Fears, passim and especially 859-862, 882-883, 887-888 (note.284), 915, 917, 919, 929-930, 934, 937.

6. Fears, 859-862; Weinstock, 163-174; Schwarte, 225-246; cf. also Instinsky, 1963, 21-39.

7. Münster, 1965, 277-278. Cf. also Norden, 212-216 and L. Preller, Römische Mythologie, II, 3rd ed. (H. Jordan), Berlin, 1883, 234-237.

8. Thus, I have not systematically considered the engraved gems. These, of course, can be understood as evidence for cult and may imply that individuals, in wearing them, were putting themselves under the protection of the deity depicted, but where Salus may be considered to be depicted on gems it is always as Hygieia: e.g., M. Henig, A Corpus of Roman Engraved Gemstones from British Sites, British Archaeological Reports, 8(i and ii), Oxford, 1974, i, 91 and ii, nos. 285, 286; G.M.A. Richter, The Engraved Gems of the Greeks and Romans, London, 1968 (I) and 1971 (II), nos. 128, 129; E. Zwierlein-Diehl, Die antiken Gemmen des kunsthistorischen Museums in Wien, München, 1973 (I) and 1979 (II), I, nr. 207 and II, nos. 1200, 1573-1576.

9. RIB, pp. xv, xxxiv.

CHAPTER ONE: THE ANCIENT LITERARY EVIDENCE

A. Introduction

The chief purpose of this chapter is to present and discuss the evidence of ancient authors concerning the cult of Salus. The references will be arranged under headings which, it is hoped, will provide a useful framework whilst at the same time allow the nature of the evidence to be readily discernible. It is appropriate to include here some discussion of literary and other evidence which has seemed necessary to an understanding of certain aspects of the cult of Salus but which itself is not directly related to a cult.

This latter purpose will involve: evidence for the swearing of oaths, private and public, by the _salus_ of Julius Caesar and by that of the emperors; a review of the literary manifestations of the tendency, beginning, among certain groups in Roman society, around the late second century BC, to conflate, in a hitherto unprecedented way, the welfare of the state with that of outstanding individuals; finally, and in connection with this latter tendency, a brief treatment of the influence of ideas and practices deriving from the Hellenistic east whereby Roman Salus came to assume the associations of the Greek idea of _soter_.[1a] In much of this I shall depend upon recent and detailed treatments of these issues which render a detailed rehearsal of the relevant evidence, and of the minutiae of the arguments, already inappropriate in the present context, unnecessary.

Some of the issues raised by the literary evidence are not discussed fully or, in some cases at all, in this chapter, but, rather, reference is made to the appropriate sections in succeeding chapters where it has been thought more appropriate to locate the relevant discussion.

The direct and indirect literary evidence seems to indicate four aspects to the nature of Roman Salus and an initial statement of these at the outset will assist in a fuller appreciation of both the significance of the evidence and its presentation here. Firstly, there is the aspect of Salus as a state deity with a major temple on the Quirinal Hill and who is later called Salus Publica. Secondly, but perhaps of a more ancient origin, there is a personal Salus. Thirdly, there is Salus as the Romanized Hygieia. This Salus seems to have had a Latin equivalent both as a simple condition and, though rarely found, as a deity in _valetudo_.[1] Finally, there is the aspect, reflected chiefly in the literary evidence, which was not at first expressed as a cult, that of _salus_ as the equivalent of the Greek _soter_. This aspect is manifested in cult form at the earliest during the dicatatorship of Julius Caesar, though this conclusion relies upon circumstantial evidence, and comes to be of paramount importance in imperial ideology and propaganda as Salus Augusti.

These different aspects are, of course, interrelated in the evidence, and it seems likely that elements of more than one of these aspects of Salus the deity and salus the condition may, on occasion, be present in the minds of the authors referred to below. Perhaps only in the minds of those in official circles, motivated not by religious conviction but by a desire to form public opinion and to disseminate propaganda, would there have been a clear idea of what message it was intended to convey in the public cult-acts and of the range of connotations attaching to the various aspects of Salus at any particular time.

The passages referring to the cult of Salus will be numbered consecutively throughout the chapter regardless of headings.

B. Salus and the Quirinal Temple

1 and 2 : Livy, IX.43.25 and X.1.9 (reign of Augustus)

The first passage records the beginning of the building of the temple in 306 BC by C. Junius Bubulcus, then censor. It refers to his vow, as consul in 313 BC, during the last phase of the Second Samnite War, to build the temple. The second passage records that Bubulcus, this time as dictator, dedicated the temple (thus fulfilling the vow) in 302 BC.

The circumstances of the vowing of the temple become familiar from a study of the establishment of the cults of 'virtues' at Rome: most of those thus celebrated in the republican period were so as a result of vota made during wars. The period of and after the Second Samnite War marked the beginning of a period of just over a century (in political terms until the defeat of Antiochus III in 188 BC) which saw the establishment of cults of many of the important 'virtues', partly as the response, in the sphere of state religion, to the social and political demands imposed by wars, in Italy, with Carthage and in the east.[2] As requires no further emphasis here, the votive offering, both public and private, is "the touchstone of piety in antiquity",[3] and this must have been an important stage in the development of the cult of Salus: the beginning of the temple in 306 BC implies that Salus was deemed to have fulfilled her part of the bargain implicit in the votive process and thus to have preserved the welfare of the state. Henceforth, Salus was definitely a state-cult, though that she may have been previously is not excluded by the fact of the vowing of this temple in 313 BC.[4]

Here ought to be mentioned a central problem with regard to our understanding of the establishment of the cults of 'virtues' at Rome in this period: the question of to what extent they were innovations brought about through the influence of Greek political and religious practices and ideas - an influence likely to have been greatly increased in the course of and subsequent to the Samnite Wars which brought Rome into increased contact with the Greek cities of southern Italy - as opposed to their being primarily a native Roman or Italic development. This problem, though a relevant consideration with regard to the establishment of the cult of Salus, cannot be more than summarily addressed in the present context, partly for reasons of space, but more so because it properly would require account to be taken of the relevant evidence for the 'virtues' as a whole, and further, because a full review of the question is included in J.R. Fears' lengthy and recent article.[5] In any case, whatever conclusion might tentatively be reached in this respect, it is difficult to do more than make vague suggestions concerning a possible primitive Italic nature for Salus. (The types of some imperial coin-issues may hint at an older conception of Salus.[6]) As in the case of other deified 'virtues' as well as of the anthropomorphic deities, even where, in the case of the latter, we are sure of a primitive Italic origin, the transformation wrought under Greek influences almost completely obscures any primitive aspects which had survived until the time of our earliest sources. In the case of Salus the evidence of Livy provides our earliest certain knowledge of the cult. The contemporary literary evidence begins with that of Plautus in the early second century BC (see below), whilst none of the scarce early epigraphic evidence definitely belongs to the fourth century (and only that from Horta may). The earliest coin-issue is that of 91 BC.[7]

3 : Cicero, Pro Publio Sestio, 131 (56 BC);
4 : Cicero, Epistulae ad Atticum, IV.2.4 (57 BC)

From the evidence of the calendars we know that the anniversary or natalis of the Quirinal temple fell on August 5. In both of these passages Cicero remarks on the coincidence of the birthday of his daughter with that of the colony of Brundisium and that of the temple of Salus on August 5, the day of his arrival at Brundisium in 57 BC.

5 : Pliny the Elder, Naturalis Historia, XXXV.19 (AD 77);
6 : Valerius Maximus, VIII.14.6 (reign of Tiberius)

Both passages inform us that a clan of the Fabii received the cognomen 'Pictor' because the first holder of the name, C. Fabius Pictor, earned it by his painting the temple of Salus. Pliny provides a date of 304 BC (thus during the building of the temple) and informs us that both painting and temple were destroyed by fire in the reign of Claudius.

7 and 8 : Tacitus, Annales, XV.53.2 and XV.74.1 (early second century AD)

Though the first does not and the second may not refer to the Quirinal temple, it is appropriate to deal with these passages here. Tacitus, referring to AD 65, records that the Senate voted the building of a temple to Salus in gratitude for Nero's safe deliverance from the Pisonian conspiracy. The place specified for the temple (nr. 8) was that at which Scaevinus had kept the dagger. The first passage tells us that this was (depending upon the source), either in an existing temple of Salus 'in Etruria', or in a temple of Fortuna at Ferentinum (itself in Etruria). 'In Etruria' is a late addition to the manuscript[8]: however, for Ferentinum there is epigraphic evidence for the existence of a temple.[9] It has been suggested that there are words missing from the manuscript of the second passage which may have recorded the building of a second temple to Salus, this time at Rome.[10] It is noteworthy then, that, according to Pliny, the Quirinal temple had been destroyed in the previous reign.[11] The gold and silver coins of Nero with a type and legend of Salus are thought to celebrate the same deliverance.[12]

9: Varro, De Lingua Latina, V.52 (c.43 BC);
10: Paulus Diaconus (c. AD 725 - c. AD 799), Exerpta Pauli ex Librorum Pompei de Verborum Significatu, p. 437 (ed. W. Lindsay, Hildesheim, 1965)

These two passages, widely separated in time, inform us that the presence of the aedem Salutis had given rise to the application of the epithet 'Salutaris' to the Collis Salutaris (Varro) and to the nearby Salutaris Porta (Paulus).

Varro is actually quoting verbatim from a religious document entitled the Sacra Argeorum which comprised a list of sacraria or shrines visited in the archaic 'Procession of the Argives' through the four Servian regions of the city. From this passage it appears that the fourth shrine was opposite the temple of Apollo and near an aedem Salutis. Varro is demonstrating that, before the name 'Quirinalis' became more widely applied, there had been separate hill-names, among them Collis Salutaris.

The details and meaning, to the extent that this is understood, of the two annual ceremonies of the Argei do not concern us as such.[13] However, the reference in the document referred to by Varro to the Collis Salutaris and indeed to a temple of Salus has been taken to indicate a considerable antiquity for the site, as a centre for a cult of Salus, and, indeed, for the cult generally. Thus it has been suggested that a less pretentious shrine or fanum preceded Bubulcus' obviously imposing building.[14] Corroborative evidence has been cited in the inscriptions from Pisaurum and Praeneste and in the dipinto from Horta. However, none of these needs to be older than the third century, though the dipinto may belong to the fourth. The Praeneste pillar, however, (first half of second century or earlier) is interesting in this respect as it refers to an obviously old and revered 'altar of Salus', the canon governing the cult of which, had already gained enough respect to be adopted as a model for other cults.[15] The ceremonies of the Argei themselves are now thought to be undoubtedly of greater antiquity than the third century BC, possibly even dating from the sixth century, but the relevant consideration here is that of the date of the document referred to by Varro, and concerning this there can only be supposition. A further corroboration for the argument in favour of an archaic cult-site of Salus on the Quirinal has been the association of Salus with Semo Sancus Dius Fidius whose cult had a centre on the neighbouring Collis Mucialis and from whose name may be derived that of the Porta Sanqualis which is the gate in the city wall next to the Porta Salutaris.[16]

The evidence is inconclusive concerning this aspect, and, since J.R. Fears' study, it can no longer be assumed that Salus, as well as some other deified 'virtues', had a primitive Roman or Italic, possibly pre-urban, origin. This is still a possibility but it is also at least possible that the cult of Salus owes its establishment to the vow of Bubulcus made in a war-time crisis. This was precisely the kind of raison d'être of other such cults: a divine force, being first recognised as operating, is then placated and won over for the good of the Roman state.[17]

11 : Orosius (c. AD 380 - c. AD 420), Historiae Adversum Paganos, IV.4.1;
12 : Livy, XXVIII.11.4-5 (reign of Augustus);
13-15: Obsequens (probably fourth century AD), Prodigiorum Liber, 12 [71]; 38 [98]; 43[103] (ed. O. Rossbach, 1910, Leipzig)

The passages record or purport to record omens involving the temple: Livy, Orosius and Obsequens (nr. 13) tell of lightning striking the temple in, respectively, 275 BC, 206 BC, and 166 BC, the language used being notably similar.

The second Obsequens passage (his work is in justification of paganism and based on an epitomized Livian tradition) is interesting: an 'ara Salutis' is destroyed (again de caelo tacta) in 113 BC. We may note the suggestion that it was this altar whose canon was used as a model for the cult of Hercules at Praeneste in the third or early second century BC.[18] The third passage of Obsequens records the settling of a swarm of bees in front of the temple in 104 BC, which, if reliable, would indicate at least the temple's existence at that time.

Two remaining passages which certainly relate to the Quirinal temple are treated as part of the next section (nos. 16 and 17).

C. The Cult of Salus Caesaris: 'Soter' and 'Soteria'

16 : Plutarch, Vitae Parallelae, Cato Maior, XIX.4 (c. AD 100-120);
17 : Cicero, Epistulae ad Atticum, XII.45.3 (May, 45 BC)

Plutarch tells us that a statue of Cato was erected by the people (at an unspecified date[19]) in the temple of Salus (Ὑγιείας) in commemoration of his censorship (of 184 BC). The dedication as translated by Plutarch recorded the fact "that when the Roman state was tottering to its fall, he was made censor, and by helpful guidance ... restored it again".[20]

S. Weinstock argues firmly against the notion that this honour can be regarded as a precedent for the later honour apparently proposed for Julius Caesar; Cato having no share in the cult in contrast to the situation with respect to Caesar.[21]

Cicero, addressing Atticus, refers to Caesar as 'your neighbour': this alludes to the fact that Atticus' house was on the Quirinal Hill and that a statue of Caesar was to be, or had recently been, erected in the temple of Quirinus, bearing the dedication Deo Invicto.[22] Cicero's statement that he would rather see Caesar sharing the temple of Quirinus rather than that of Salus (eum σύνναον Quirini malo quam Salutis) could imply that there had been an original intention to erect the statue in the temple of Salus. Weinstock suggests that the intention was changed because of the fortuitous coincidence of the festival of the Parilia in April (45 BC) when advantage was taken of the fact to further enhance the image, already cultivated, of Caesar as the new Romulus.[23] If Caesar's statue was to have been erected in the temple of Salus, then it would have been an unprecedented honour. For though, as in the case of Cato, statues of outstanding men had previously been erected in state temples at Rome, none can be shown to have had a cultic significance.[24]

There may then have been an intention to institute a cult of Salus Caesaris, parallels for which may be seen in the cults of Clementia Caesaris and Victoria Caesaris.[25] Weinstock argues that the relevant precedents for Caesar's honour are the Hellenistic practices whereby statues of kings and generals (including Roman generals) could be erected in temples, the individual thus becoming a σύνναος θεός.[26]

We know from Dio's explicit statement, referring to 44 BC, that among the honours decreed for Caesar was the institution of an official oath by his health (ὑγίειαν). This then is the precedent for the later oaths by the salus Augusti. Weinstock argues for the existence of an unofficial fore-runner of this oath in use among Caesar's followers as early as the beginning of the Civil War.[27] In this connection he notes the possibility that Salus, as Salus Semonia, had an ancient function in overseeing oaths.[28]

As discussed below, a private cult of Salus is at least as old as the comedies of Plautus (early second century BC), and, in a revealing development of this cult, individuals came to address each other as 'mea salus'. Furthermore, for comic effect an individual could pose as another's Salus in the divine sense.[29] This aspect of Salus, which Weinstock suggests would have been much older than the public Salus, institutionalized in 302 BC, became the first Roman equivalent of the Greek 'soter'.[30] It is clear, even in a comic context, that this Salus is a deity of general welfare and so is quite distinct from the conception of Salus, well recognised by 180 BC, as the Roman Hygieia.[31]

J.R. Fears argues that it may have been partly due to the influence of contemporary Hellenistic "religio-political" concepts acting upon an inherently Roman instinct to deify abstract ideas, when the need was perceived, that Salus received her public cult,[32] and I shall discuss briefly below the possible influence of Greek practices upon the development of the private cult of Salus, a development which seems to lead to Salus Caesaris and Salus Augusti.

However, an inherently Roman tendency is also recognisable in the processes leading towards the probable institution of a cult of Salus Caesaris: this may be seen in the practice of awarding the corona civica. By the beginning of the first century BC, but, Weinstock argues, not long before this, a change in attitude is apparent among the ruling class at Rome whereby, henceforth, a man could be considered eligible for the award for a general act of salvation benefitting the citizen body as a whole, and not necessarily involving personal bravery in battle. Thus it was that Caesar received the corona civica in the significant year of 45 BC.[33]

Despite the comic play made of the private cult of Salus and the use of salus as a term of endearment in the comedies of Plautus,[34] there was a serious development in the concept of personal salus, chiefly manifested in the writings of Cicero, whereby an individual could, as an expression of great gratitude or hope, call upon another as his salus. Thus, in 57 BC Cicero spoke of the man who arranged his return from exile as, "parens, deus, salus nostrae vitae, fortunae, memoriae nominis".[35] In 70 BC in his attack upon Verres he recalled that he himself was salus to a woman whose son had been murdered by Verres: "ita me suam salutem appellans".[36] In the public sphere also there is evidence that outstanding figures were regarded by their followers as saviours and hailed as their 'salus'.[37]

Cicero provides many instances of his regarding outstanding figures as individuals upon whom the salus of the state rested: himself, Scipio the Younger, Pompey, Marius and, finally, and insistently, Caesar.[38] (It is interesting to note his statement, in a different vein, of the opposite, perhaps more traditional view: "omnes omnium ordinum homines in salute rei publicae salutem suam repositam esse arbitrabantur".[39]) This attitude only becomes significant, with respect to the cult of Salus, with the actions taken by Caesar and by his supporters. In addition to the oath by the health of Caesar and the planned statue in the temple of Salus, we know from Cassius Dio that in 44 BC annual public vota were instituted on his behalf, perhaps in the form 'pro salute rei publicae et Caesaris' and thus echoing the vota made each year by the incoming consuls on January 1 and fore-shadowing the vota for the safety of the emperors.[40]

There had been extraordinary instances of similar vows for the recovery from illness of outstanding individuals, in 91 BC for Livius Drusus and in 50 BC for Pompey.[41] However, these, though public, did not take place at Rome. Furthermore, Caesar's vota were to be annual state events. We may note, finally, in connection with this argument for a cult of Salus Caesaris, Weinstock's suggestion that the cult-statue intended for the temple of Salus was to have been a temporary measure and that the ultimate aim was for a temple of Salus Caesaris.[42]

The foregoing discussion is important because, even though the establishment of a cult of Salus Caesaris cannot be regarded as certain, the developments toward that end provide the context for the cults of Salus Augusta and Salus Augusti established early in the Principate if not under Augustus.

The influence of contemporary Hellenistic 'religio-political' concepts and practices was of great significance for these developments: firstly, this influence provided the inspiration and model for the transformation of the native cult of Salus into the public cult of 302 BC (if it does not entirely account for it);

secondly, this influence may also have transformed the private cult of Salus and, perhaps, may also have encouraged the idea of the state's dependence upon outstanding individuals.

A significant piece of evidence for the effect of this influence is the statement by Cicero in his speech against Verres in 70 BC, "is est nimirum soter qui salutem dedit", which shows salus to be the earliest rendering of the Greek title soter.[43]

Besides the title soter there were Greek festivals called soteria held in honour of particular gods, and in Achaea there is attested the cult of a personification in her own right, Soteria (Σωτηρία). Our evidence for these concepts, considerable in scope, is chiefly of the Hellenistic period and chiefly relates to the festivals and to the assumption of the title by Hellenistic rulers. Deities were called theoi soteres who had demonstrated their ability to save individuals and communities from both natural and man-made dangers. The soteria celebrated either the fact of salvation or the expectation of it, and individual occurrences are attested, in honour of the saving gods concerned, in Greece in the fifth century.[44]

The earliest attested annual soteria dates from 297 BC. J.R. Fears sees a Roman parallel to the Greek practice of commemorating an act of salvation in the very foundation of Salus as a state cult at Rome in that this commemorated a specific instance of divine salvation of the state during the Second Samnite War.[45] The significant difference is that at Rome, henceforth definitely, there was, as part of state religion, the cult of a deity whose sole concern was the welfare of the state. However, it is just possible that the personified Soteria already had a cult at Metapontum in Greek southern Italy in the late fourth century which could have provided the model and direct inspiration for the Roman act and which could have been brought to Roman attention in the context of the Samnite Wars. An alternative explanation is that the Romans themselves personified the concept of salvation inherent in the Greek soteria festivals. A coin-series of Metapontum, an Achaean colony, bears the legend ΣΩΤΗΡΙΑ and could either commemorate the earliest regular festival held in honour of the female deity whose head is depicted, or celebrate Soteria, the divine personification, a possibility enhanced by the fact of the city's connection with Achaea where there was a cult of Soteria.[46]

The title soter is at least as old as the fifth century and came to be applied to both gods and mortals. In the Hellenistic period it became a frequent epithet of rulers and others and was bestowed by those enjoying material benefits or salvation from political oppression or from the threat of barbarian invasion. It could imply a kind of deification, but not necessarily the existence of a cult:[47] an aspect of the tradition of the ruler-cult in the Greek east which continued into the period of the Christian empire.[48]

Fears suggests that again the "latter part of the Second Samnite War provides a suitable historical context for the introduction to Rome of the political imagery inherent in the Greek title Soter". The practice had long been known in the Greek cities of southern Italy, and Fears suggests that "it may have been her Greek allies who introduced Rome to the concept of soter, celebrating the Romans as saviours against the barbarous Samnites".[49]

Whether or not this last suggestion is correct, in later periods this practice of the Greek east must have extended a considerable influence upon Roman political and religious thought and practice. Among Roman generals thus honoured by the Greeks was T. Quinctius Flamininus whose proclamation of the freedom of Greece at Corinth in 196 BC led to his being called <u>soter</u>.[50] In 167 BC King Prusias of Bithynia greeted Roman senators as <u>theoi soteres</u>.[51] Among several similar inscriptions at Rome[52] erected on behalf of cities of the Greek east, there is a bilingual dedication from the Quirinal Hill recording in Latin and Greek the gratitude of the people of Laodicea ad Lycum to the <u>populum Romanum, quei sibei salutei fuit, benefici ergo, quae sibei benigne fecit</u> ('Ρωμαίων γεγονότα ἐ[αυτῶι] σωτῆρα καὶ εὐεργέτην).[53] It is thought to relate to the end of the first war with Mithridates, around 86 to 84 BC, when the Greek cities of Asia Minor, having initially welcomed the king as a liberator (from the Romans), were now seeking, or giving thanks for, salvation from the king's oppression.[54]

Another dedication from the Quirinal echoes the sentiment on behalf of the people of Ephesus. Whilst at Ephesus itself an inscribed decree of 87 or 86 BC, declaring war on Mithridates, refers to the "Romans, the saviours of all".[55]

Caesar too was hailed, on inscriptions, as <u>soter</u> by several Greek cities and explicitly as a god at Ephesus.[56]

D. <u>The Importance of the Imperial Salus</u>

The circumstantial evidence for a cult of Salus Augusti or of Salus Augusta under Augustus is compelling.[57] We know from the numismatic and epigraphic evidence of a cult of Salus Augusta under Tiberius.[58] The earliest certain manifestation of Salus Augusti is on the coins of Galba, although the Ostia dedication may be earlier than this.[59] Here I intend to indicate briefly the circumstantial evidence for the developing significance of the <u>salus</u> of the emperor and thus provide the context for an understanding of the early development of these cults.[60]

The <u>Institutes</u> of Justinian (AD 533) provide evidence of an official oath by the <u>salus</u> of Augustus, and the <u>Codex Theodosianus</u> (AD 395) attests that an oath by the <u>salutem principum</u> (Arcadius and Honorius) was still in use in the late fourth century: the latter certainly did not refer to a deity.[61] Two statements of Tertullian (c. AD 197) provide clear evidence that Christians regarded the oath by the emperor's <u>salus</u> as acceptable (in contrast to that by his <u>genius</u>), because no deity was involved, and that they were happy to pray (to the Christian god) for his <u>salus</u>.[62] Indeed this became a duty after the Edict of Toleration.[63]

The oath of allegiance to a new emperor, which later became a formalized annual event, became an occasion for proclaiming the paramountcy of the emperor's <u>salus</u>. An early example, recorded in stone, of AD 37, is the oath of the citizens of Aritium Vetus in Lusitania affirming their allegiance on the accession of Gaius: it asserts that the swearers will be the enemies of any who bring danger to Gaius or his salus and that they will hold neither themselves nor their children dearer than his salus ('eius saluti').[64]

In his Panegyricus Pliny states that Nerva's adoption of Trajan was the foundation for the state's libertas, salus and securitas and that at Trajan's accession people prayed for his salus and thereby ensured their own. Later he approves the bargain struck by the state with the gods, whereby the gods will preserve Trajan while he does the same for everyone else, and he asserts that vows offered for the salus of the emperor will ensure the eternity of the empire.[65] He finishes by addressing a prayer to Jupiter in which he does not burden the god with vows nor asks for pax, concordia, securitas, ops or honores, but simplex cunctaque ista complexum omnium votum est, salus principis.[66]

The message is, significantly though less extravagantly, conveyed in his letters to Trajan while governor of Bithynia-Pontus (c. AD 112). In one, Trajan's salus is sanctissima.[67] In the letter reporting the vows and oath of allegiance on the occasion of Trajan's dies imperii he says, precati deos ut te generi humano, cuius tutela et securitas saluti tuae innisa est, incolumen florentemque praestarent.[68]

Vows pro salute imperatoris, taken by the priesthoods on behalf of the Roman people, had become annual events, fixed eventually on January 3, at some time between AD 14 and 38.[69]

K.H. Schwarte has shown that the letters of Pliny attest changes under Trajan concerning the vota of January 3 and, probably also, the vota and oath of allegiance on the dies imperii: there is a continuation but also a development of Domitianic policy. The little, but presumably deliberate, ambiguity which remained following the changes culminating in the form of the vota of January 3, AD 91,[70] regarding the independent and direct operation of Salus Publica has disappeared:[71] in terms of imperial ideology, the welfare of the empire, citizens and others, now depends entirely upon that of the emperor who is the medium through which salvation is effected.

By, if not in, the reign of Trajan, the celebration of the dies imperii had become a formalized annual event including both vota and oaths of allegiance, and, moreover and importantly, if they had not been so previously, now the non-citizen provincials were involved in the ceremonies. A further development under Trajan, which appears to have taken place in about AD 112, was, significantly, the involvement of the provincials in the January 3 vota. Thus, according to Schwarte, Trajan brought about a change already signalled as inevitable by the developments under Domitian: the vota of January 3, once a concern only of the Roman people, are now performed by all the people of the empire.[72]

These changes can be seen as complementary to the ideological changes, manifested in the Arval records and in the reports of Pliny, whereby upon the safety of the emperor depended not only that of the Roman people but that of the whole world. Thus, a phrase in the letters of Pliny reporting the dies imperii corresponds almost exactly with the legend of the aureus commemorating Trajan's tenth dies imperii (AD 108) which proclaims the SALUS GENERIS HUMANI.[73]

E. Augustus and Salus Publica: The Association of Salus, Concordia and Pax

18 : Suetonius, Divus Augustus, LVII.1 (c. AD 120);
19 : Cassius Dio, LIV.35.2 (c. AD 220);
20 : Ovid, Fasti, III.881-2 (c. AD 17)

Suetonius tells us that people "of all sorts", each year, in fulfilment of vows "pro salute eius", threw coins into the Lacus Curtius and on January 1 brought gifts to the Capitol for Augustus. With these gifts he dedicated statues to certain gods. From Dio we learn that the citizens were frequently making these collections and bringing them to him on January 1 and that on one occasion (in 11 BC) the Senate and people had contributed money meant for statues of Augustus. Instead he erected statues to Salus Publica (Ὑγιείας δὲ δημοσίας), Concordia and Pax.

The lines of Ovid, written much nearer to the time, may refer to the same act. He gives March 30 as a date for worshipping Janus, Concordia, "Romana Salus" and an "altar of Pax". J.G. Frazer suggested that the three deities had a combined cult in a temple, dedicated on March 30, in which stood an altar of Pax.[74]

The association of Concordia and Salus finds articulation elsewhere in a way which may suggest a special relationship. The formula salutis concordia occurs on an aureus associated with the revolt of Civilis (AD 69-70).[75] However, the same two 'virtues' with the same difference of case occur on the local aes coins of the Roman colony of Buthrotum in Epirus perhaps dating from the years 10 to 1 BC. M. Grant has suggested that the legends are likely to refer to Augustus' act of 11 BC.[76] They may imply a local cult of Salus.[77]

Concordia and Salus occur together in Cicero's list of deified "utilitates" and in that of Arnobius.[78] Concordia and pax are among the divine benefits listed by Pliny as subsumed under the salus principis.[79]

F. Salus Semonia

21 : Festus (late second century, epitomizing Verrius Flaccus of the Augustan period), De Significatu Verborum, p. 404 (ed. W. Lindsay, Hildesheim, 1965);

22 : Macrobius, Saturnalia, I.16.8 (c. AD 400);
23 : Varro, De Lingua Latina, V.74 (c. 43 BC)

Macrobius refers to Salus with this epithet and the fragmentary text of Festus implies a relationship with 'Semonia'. Varro here lists Salus with Pales, Vesta, Fortuna, Fons and Fides as deities whose cults were, he believes, Sabine in origin. Salus Semonia, the question of her possible relationship with a deity of oath, Semo Sancus Dius Fidius, and that of a Sabine origin for Salus are discussed in the context of the Rome inscription naming Salus Semonia.[80]

G. **Salus as The Deity of Personal Salvation and Welfare: The Association of Salus and Fortuna**

24 : Cicero, Oratio pro M. Fonteio, X.21 (69 BC);
25 : Cicero, Actio in Verrem, II.iii.131 (70 BC);
26-34 : Plautus: Asinaria, 712; 727; Captivi, 529; 863; Casina, 801; Cistellaria, 644; 742; Mostellaria, 351; Poenulus, 128 (205-190 BC);
35 : Pseudacronis, Scholia in Horatium Vetustiora, Expositio in Horatium Carmina, II.17.31 (fifth century AD);
36 : Terentius, Adelphoe, 761 (160 BC)

These passages all indicate more or less unambiguously Salus as a personal deity of general welfare. In some of the Plautus passages there are individuals who refer to themselves or others as salus for rhetorical effect, but always in such a way that the indirect allusion is clearly to the deity. Despite the comic contexts the Plautus passages are significant not least because of their early date (late third to early second centuries BC). I shall note below the association with Spes in Mostellaria.[81]

The passages from the Pseudacron, from Asinaria (712) and from Captivi (863) refer to cult acts. The Pseudacron (fifth century AD, but perhaps with Acron material of the second century) in commenting on Horace (Carmina, II.xvii.31) refers to the fulfilment of a vow to Salus in which an aedem has been promised in return for escape from an implied danger or predicament.

Despite the comic hyperbole, these two Plautus passages perhaps reflect an observed commonplace in the contemporary Hellenistic world: si quidem mihi statuam et aram statuis atque ut deo mi hic immolas bovem: nam ego tibi Salus sum, (Asinaria, 712). The thought "bespeaks the very foundation of the ruler-cult in the Greco-Roman world".[82]

Additionally, we must simply note the association of Salus and Fortuna, in Captivi, 863, and Asinaria, 727, which may have significance in the light of the association manifested in some coin-issues and in the epigraphic evidence.[83]

H. **'Salus' used as a Term of Endearment or of a Personal Human Saviour: The Association with Spes**

37 : Cicero, Actio in Verrem, II.v.129 (70 BC);
38-42 : Plautus: Casina, 801; Poenulus, 421; Bacchides, 879; Pseudole, 709; Mercator, 867 (205-190 BC)

All these are instances of someone calling another his salus because of a capacity to act as a saviour. The Cicero passage, much later in date, is mentioned above.[84]

The *Pseudole* and *Mercator* passages and that from *Mostellaria* (above, nr. 33) seem to indicate more than a casual relationship between Salus and Spes: an association attested epigraphically, in the imperial period as a joint cult at Gabii, and in some coin issues.[85] On the basis of the *Mercator* line Fears suggests a "beneficient triad" with Victoria forming a third element and that the "hellenizing context of Plautine comedy will suggest the source by which this formula entered Rome".[86] Later, Velleius Paterculus combines *salus* and *spes* in his description of the day on which Tiberius was adopted by Augustus: *certa spes ... omnibus nominibus salutis.*[87]

I. Salus as the Goddess of Health (Hygieia)

43 : Apuleius, *Metamorphoseon*, X.25 (c. AD 160-180);
44 : Augustine, *De Civitate Dei Contra Paganos*, III.25 (AD 413-426);
45 : Macrobius, *Saturnalia*, I.201 (c. AD 400);
46 : Vitruvius, *De Architectura*, I.2.7 (c. 27-13 BC);
47 : Livy, XL.37.2-3 (reign of Augustus);
48 : Terentius, *Hecyra*, 338 (165 BC)

The contexts of these passages make it plain that Salus as the Roman equivalent of Hygieia is intended.

The passage from Apuleius' novel tells of a doctor who prepares a poison sacred to Proserpina as opposed to a healthy drink *sacra Saluti*. Augustine, in the process of ridiculing a theory postulated by Labeo (Cornelius Labeo, a writer, perhaps of the later third century AD, on Romano-Etruscan religious lore[87a]) concerning the deification of opposites, refers to Labeo's observation at Rome of a temple to Febris (*numen* of Fever) as well as one to Salus (*Romae etiam Febri sicut Saluti templum constitutum*).

The Livy passage provides a *terminus ante quem* of 180 BC for the establishment at Rome of the "divine ministry of public health as it functioned in Epidaurus".[88] The snake, the manifestation of Asklepios, had been brought, in 292 BC, from Epidaurus to Rome where a temple on the Insula Tiberina was dedicated in 291 BC. This was the result of a consultation of the Sibylline Books in 293 BC at the height of an epidemic during the Third Samnite War.[89] Livy tells us that among the measures decreed to avert the epidemic of 180 BC was another consultation of the books by the *decemviri sacris faciundis* and the vowing of gifts and the giving of gilded statues to Apollo, Aesculapius and Salus by the consul.[90] This is the earliest attestation of the assimilation of Hygieia, the associate of Asklepios, to Salus.

However, fifteen years later, the passage from Terence's *Hecyra* (first published in 165 BC) provides a further contemporary manifestation. Vitruvius (writing c. 27-13 BC) provides practical advice for the siting of temples and in particular for those of Aesculapius and Salus, *ut eorum deorum, quorum plurimi medicinis aegri curari videntur*. He also emphasizes the importance of the presence of suitable springs.[91] Thus, he says, "the divinity from the nature of the site will gain a greater ... reputation and authority".[92]

Macrobius' explanation of the association of the snake with statues of Aesculapius and Salus involves his equation, of the former with the sun and of the latter with the moon, which reflects his particular notions of solar syncretism and the "common solar theology of the late pagan world".[93] Macrobius' theory concerning the snake - that it symbolizes rejuvenation and the shedding of infirmity by analogy with its own skin-shedding - is one of several ancient theories seeking to account for the snake's association with Asklepios. This problem is a difficult one: what matters for us is that by the time of the god's transplantation to Rome, the snake was universally known as the god's attribute, companion and indeed as his incarnation.[94] The evidence of the coinage amply shows that the snake also became the primary attribute of Salus.[95]

An ivory relief-tondo from Pompeii depicts Apollo facing a female figure, presumably Salus-Hygieia, who holds a _patera_ and a snake which coils towards the god's outstretched hand.[96]

J. A Stoic Definition and Christian Ridicule of Deified 'Virtues'

49 : Cicero, _De Deorum Natura_, II.60-62 (45 BC);
50 : Arnobius, _Adversus Nationes_, IV.1 (c. AD 297)

In his imaginary dialogue set in 77 or 76 BC Cicero provides an explicit definition of the phenomenon of the deification of qualities or conditions in the context of an exposition of Stoic theology: certain benefits are so important as, of necessity, to be of divine origin, and these '_utilitates_' themselves provide the deities' names.[97]

Arnobius' late third century Christian view reverses this logic by suggesting that such deities are so regarded simply because we desire the implied benefits so much. He seems to be assuming an inherent scepticism on the part of his pagan readers in his rhetorical question implying that their gods are brought into disrepute by the inclusion amongst them of _nullius substantiae nomina_. He notes that they receive _aras...cum magnificis exaedificatatas delubris._

Concordia and Salus are the only deities common to both lists.[98]

K. '_Romana Salus_'

51 : Claudian, _Carmina Minora_, XXX.189 (c. AD 395-404)

Claudian, pagan poet at the Christian court of Honorius and Stilicho, is addressing the latter's wife: "for you Roman Salus lights the torches and your marriage brings great garlands". Although he was the court poet of Honorius, Claudian himself remained pagan. The contemporary coinage shows Salus ('Reipublicae') as incorporated into the ideology of the Christian empire. The same epithet is used by Ovid.[99]

L. *Salus' Place in the Zodiac*

52: Martianus Capella, De Nuptiis Philologiae et Mercurii, I.45 (AD 410-439)

In his description of the summoning of the major deities to a council of the gods, Capella gives a catalogue of the divine inhabitants of each of the sixteen regions of the Zodiac. Salus, in the first region, is listed after Jupiter, the Dii Consentes and the Penates, and before the Lares, Ianus and the Favores opertanei Nocturnasque. The idea is thought to derive from Etruscan lore with Cornelius Labeo (perhaps of the later third century AD) or Varro being Capella's source.[100]

One of the few occurrences of the Dii Consentes on dedications is with Salus on the Sarmitzegetusa dedication.[101] Favor and the Penates occur with Salus on the Apulum dedication.[102]

NOTES

1a. "Saviour", below, 6, 8-9.

1. Cato 'Censorius', De Agri Cultura, CXLI.3; Latte, 227, note 3; below, 22.

2. Fears, 834, 846, 848-850, 866; Weinstock, 167.

3. A.D. Nock, CAH X (1934), 481.

4. Fears, 847, note 76.

5. Ibid., 849-869.

6. H. Mattingly, OCD^2, 948 ('Salus'); but cf. Schwarte, 244-5; below, 23, 27.

7. Epigraphic: below, 86-90; coin: below, 21.

8. H. Furneaux, The Annals of Tacitus, Oxford, 1907, II, 388, note to line 2.

9. Below, 111.

10. Furneaux, op.cit. (note 8), 414, note to line 3; cf. ed. E. Koestermann, Vol. I, Leipzig, 1965, 374, note to line 28.

11. Above, nr. 5.

12. Below, 22. The column dedicated to Jupiter O. M. for the welfare of Nero by the inhabitants of the canabae at Moguntiacum (Mainz), which may include Salus among its relief depictions of Roman state deities, may also be a manifestation of a general thanksgiving following the passing of this crisis: Instinsky, 1959, 131-139; below, 157 ff.

13. Scullard, 90-91, 120-121; Dumézil, 449-450; H.J. Rose, H.W. Parke, OCD^2, 104 ('Argei').

14. Wissowa, Lex, 296; Wissowa, RK, 132; Thulin, 2057.

15. Below, 89-90.

16. Below, 91-92; CIL, VI, 975 (AD 136) attests a Vicus Salutaris in both Regio X (Palatium) and Regio XIV (Trans Tiberim). There is no reason to deduce the existence of cult-centres in these vici; the epithet must be in the genetive form, indicating persons of that name: Wissowa, Lex, 297.

17. Fears, 828-869.

18. Below, 89.

19. Perhaps in 184 BC or after his death in 149 BC; Weinstock, 187.

20. B. Perrin, Plutarch's Lives (Loeb), London and New York, 1914, II, 359.

21. Weinstock, 171, note 3; 187.

22. Ibid., 186, 169.

23. Ibid., 169, 171, 184-186.

24. Ibid., 171, 186-188, 309.

25. Ibid., 111, 171, 241.

26. Ibid., 186, 187.

27. Cassius Dio, XLIV.50.1; Weinstock, 168, 172, 174, 212, 217.

28. Below, 91.

29. Below, 12.

30. Weinstock, 167; Fears, 861.

31. Below, 13.

32. Fears, 860-861.

33. Weinstock, 163-167. Perhaps a forerunner of this change in attitude with regard to the corona civica is the award of the corona obsidionalis, the siege crown, to Q. Fabius Maximus by the senate and people of Rome in recognition of his having saved Rome and Italy from the threat of Hannibal during the Second Punic War; V.A. Maxfield, The Military Decorations of the Roman Army, London, 1981, 68; Pliny, Nat. Hist., XXII.10.

34. Above, 6; below, 12.

35. Cicero, Oratio post Reditum ad Quirites, 11.

36. Cicero, Actio in Verrem, II.v.129; below, 8.

37. Silius Italicus, Punica, VII.734 and cf. 747, perhaps anachronistically: "Fabiumque salutem certatim" (Q. Fabius Maximus, 217 BC). Lucan, De Bello Civili, II.221: "salus rerum" (Sulla, c. 80 BC). For Caesar, Weinstock, 168, 212.

38. Weinstock, 166, 167, 169, 172; Instinsky, 1963, 31.

39. Cicero, Oratio pro Rabirio Perduellonis Reo ad Quitites, 20; Weinstock, 169, note 1.

40. Cassius Dio, XLIV.6.1; XLIV.50.1; Weinstock, 217-219; Schwarte, 226-229; below, 38-42.

41. Weinstock, 219; below, 21-22.

42. Weinstock, 171.

43. Cicero, Actio in Verrem, II.ii.154; Weinstock, 162; Fears, 861; cf. Instinsky, 1963, 28 and 71, note 11.

44. Fears, 859-860; OCD^2, 1005 ('Soteria')(unattributed).

45. Fears, 860.

46. Ibid., 860.

47. Ibid., 860-861; H.J. Rose, OCD^2, 1005 ('Soter'); A.D. Nock, CAH, X, (1934), 481-482; Instinsky, 1963, 25.

48. Cf. the inscribed "supplication and petition" to "the divine emperors, the saviours of the entire human race", Arycanda, Lycia/Pamphylia, AD 311/312; RC, II, 600-601.

49. Fears, 860.

50. Weinstock, 143, 164.

51. Ibid., 164; Fears, 861.

52. ILLRP, 174-181 and pp. 114-117.

53. ILLRP, 177; CIL, VI, 374; Weinstock, 164, 167; Fears, 853, 861.

54. ILLRP, pp. 119-120, notes to 176 and 177.

55. ILLRP, 176; RC, I, 201.

56. Weinstock, 166.

57. Weinstock, 171-173; circumstantial evidence: the special vows of 30 and 16 BC; Augustus' reception of the corona civica "a genere humano" (Pliny, Nat. Hist., XVI.8); Ovid's address: "patriae cura salusque tuae" (Tristia ex Ponto, II.574); the possibility of an official oath by his salus (below); the Alabanda inscription (Caria) in Greek attesting a municipal cult and priest of the "Hygieia and Soteria of the Emperor Caesar" (AE, 1934, 46). Weinstock also examines the indications for a cult of Salus Augusti under the subsequent Julio-Claudians; ibid.

58. Below, 22, 100-101; cf. Valerius Maximus, I. Praef., to Tiberius, "certissima salus patriae".

59. Below, 23, 102.

60. On the question of the distinction, if any, intended or perceived, between the genetival and adjectival forms of the epithet, generally and regarding Salus: Fears, 886-888; Weinstock, 111, 174; Schwarte, 240-246; below, 23, 24.

61. *Institutes*, 2.23.1; *Codex Theodosianus*, 2.9.3.

62. Tertullian, *Apologeticus*, 32.2; 30.1.

63. Lactantius, *De Mortibus Persecutorum*, 34.5 (c. AD 318).

64. *CIL*, II, 172; cf. the language of Cassius Dio, LIX.9.2 (AD 38).

65. Pliny, *Panegyricus*, 8.1; 23.5; 67.3-5.

66. *Ibid.*, 94.2.

67. Pliny, *Epistulae*, X.83.

68. *Ibid.*, X.52.

69. See the evidence of the Arvals, below, 38; Schwarte, 226-228; cf. Cassius Dio, LIX.3.4 (AD 37).

70. The Arval evidence, below, 40-41.

71. Schwarte, 233-238.

72. Cf: the Ptolemais inscription for a possible earlier indication, below, 110-111; *Acta S. Scillitanorum*, 3 and Tertullian, *Apologeticus*, 28, 1 (late 2nd c.) for compulsion to sacrifice *pro salute imperatoris*.

73. Below, 24; Pliny, *Epistulae*, X.52 (above, 10); X.102; cf. Elder Pliny, *Nat. Hist.*, XVI.8 (above, note 57); cf. Martial, *Epigrammaton Libri*, II.91.1-2, to Domitian: "*rerum certa salus, terrarum gloria, Caesar, sospite quo magnos credimus esse deos*".

74. J.G. Frazer, *The Fasti of Ovid*, London 1929, III, 158-159.

75. *BM*, I, p. 308; obv. SALUTIS with bust, rev. CONCORDIA with type.

76. Grant, 271-272, 281. Cf. the occurrence of Salus legends on local coins of cities in Spain, perhaps imitating Tiberius' SALUS AUGUSTA coins of AD 22/23, below, 22.

77. Weinstock, 172, note 5.

78. Below, 14.

79. Above, 10.

80. Below, 90-92; also 147.

81. Below, 13.

82. Fears, 861 (quotation), 862.

83. Below, 22-27, 71, 73-74, 98, 112-113.

84. Above, 7.

85. Below, 24-25, 28-30, 105; cf. also 55.

86. Fears, 862.

87. Vell.Pat., II.103.5.

87a. G. Wissowa, RE, IV.1 (1900), 1351-1355 ('Cornelius, 168'). Perhaps also a source for Martianus Capella (below, nr. 52).

88. Dumézil, 444.

89. Livy, X.47.7; XI. Periocha; Dumézil, 443.

90. Wissowa, Lex, 300, assumes the acts resulted from the consultation.

91. Below, 77-78, 93, 95-96, 105-106, 116-122, for epigraphic indications of the cult's association with water.

92. Edelstein, I, 370, nr. 707.

93. Ibid., II, 106; Ferguson, 218.

94. Edelstein, II, 226-231.

95. Below, 22-29; below, 102-103, for Glabrio's statue at Ostia probably portraying Salus holding a snake. The goddess accompanying Mercury in one of the relief panels of the Mainz Jupiter column, dating from the reign of Nero, may be an early representation of Salus, the state deity (implied by the context), with her snake (coiled around what may be an altar); Instinsky, 1959, 139; Bauchhenss, 1984a, 4, 14, 16 and Taf. 4; below, 157 ff.

96. H. von Hesberg, ANRW, II.17.2 (1981), 1156-1157, nr. 46B.

97. Fears, 828, 832-833.

98. Above, 11.

99. Above, nr. 20.

100. M. Grant, Greek and Latin Authors, 800 BC - AD 1000, New York, 1980, 275; Wissowa, Lex, 297. For Labeo as ridiculed by Augustine, above, nr. 44.

101. Below, 112-113.

102. Below, 73-74.

CHAPTER TWO: THE EVIDENCE OF THE COINAGE

A. Introduction

The aim of this chapter is to provide a summary of the evidence relating to the cult of Salus provided in Roman state coin-issues.

There are more than seven hundred and fifty issues bearing a Salus legend, a type of Salus or both. Thus, what follows is a selective treatment, including what seems, or seems as if it might be, significant. It is important to note that in most instances the footnotes provide examples for the points being made and not exhaustive lists.

The headings list the persons in whose names the coins discussed below the headings were struck. The dates contained in the headings, though usually corresponding to reigns, refer specifically to the periods to which particular groups of issues belong. Thus, for years not covered in the headings, no evidence for issues celebrating Salus has been discovered. Dates given in the text, similarly, always refer to particular issues or groups of issues.

After the *aureus* of Civilis (AD 69-70),[1a] all types and legends relating to Salus are borne on the reverses, and, with the exception of six issues of Probus,[2a] the obverse always bears at least the image and name of the person in whose name it was struck.

The goddess is always draped.

B. The Republican Coinage

The Coins of the Moneyer D. Junius Silanus L.F., 91 BC.[1]

The diademed head of Salus occurs on the obverse of six *denarii*, all but one of which bear SALUS as the accompanying legend. ROMA is part of the legend on two of the reverses, and on all of the reverses the type is that of Victoria in a chariot. It has long been considered likely that these issues represent the moneyer's celebration of his descent from C. Junius Bubulcus Brutus who was responsible for the foundation of the temple of Salus on the Quirinal Hill.[2] Issued at the beginning of the Social War, these coins combine in imagery and legend the themes of Salus, Victoria and Roma, and we may note J.R. Fears' observation that, in the context of the transformation then taking place in the function of the 'virtues' in Roman political life, "the preservation of the corporate body of the Roman people, personified in the figure of Roma, was still the context in which men commemorated Salus".[3] We shall simply note the possibility that these issues were connected with the vota performed for the health of M. Livius Drusus.[4]

The Coins of the Moneyer Mn. Acilius Glabrio, 49 BC

The obverse of these denarii bears the legend SALUTIS accompanying the laureate head of Salus, while the reverse depicts a standing goddess leaning on a column, holding a snake and identified by VALETU in the legend.[5]

Thus, Salus appears to be equated with Valetudo.[6] The moneyer is usually identified as the partisan of Julius Caesar. However, Fears regards this issue as celebrating Pompey's return to health, which was celebrated in all municipia, vows for his recovery having been made throughout Italy (50 BC):[7] "now ... the preservation of the great man provided the context in which men dedicated the coinage to the divine figure of Salus."[8]

C. The Imperial Coinage

Tiberius: AD 22 or 23

Salus first appears on a dupondius of Tiberius: the legend SALUS AUGUSTA accompanies the type of a bust thought to represent the deity with the features of Livia whose recovery from illness in AD 22 the issue is thought to commemorate.[9] Vows had been made for her recovery.[10]

Rather than referring to any significance with respect to Salus on the part of Tiberius, the epithet and portrait are perhaps to be interpreted rather, either as a reference to his membership of the house of Augustus, or as a compliment to Livia.[11]

This coin was apparently the stimulus for contemporary coin-issues in some Spanish colonies. Some aes issues of Emerita are thought to portray Livia's likeness (as may also an issue of Turiaso) along with the legend SALUS AUGUSTI, and SAL AUG is combined with the type of an altar on coins of Ilici.[12]

Nero: AD 65 - 68

A type of the goddess, enthroned and holding a patera, accompanies the simple legend SALUS on three gold and silver issues. Their striking is thought to have been among the acts celebrating Nero's escape from the Pisonian conspiracy.[13] At least one temple of Salus was also decreed.[14]

Galba: AD 68 - 69

These issues are important, as the Salus legends on them were to remain decisive for over a century. SALUS GENERIS HUMANI first appears on the unattributed issues, usually with a type of Victoria, and continues on the attributed issues with a type thought to be of Fortuna (goddess, standing sacrificing with patera, foot on globe, and holding rudder). The globe is the common feature of the two types. Thus, in an unprecedented way, is the destiny of the Roman people associated with that of the provinces.[15] An unattributed denarius of Galba combines, as obverse and reverse legends, SALUS PUBLIC(A) (with laureate bust of Salus) and ROMA VICTRIX, perhaps in deference to the Roman people.[16] SALUS AUGUSTA reappears, but now with a Salus type: goddess, enthroned, holding patera and sceptre.[17]

SALUS AUGUSTI appears for the first time, with a type recalling that of Glabrio's issues: goddess, standing, leaning on a column and holding and feeding a snake.[18] Both these issues are associated with Galba's titles and portrait on the obverses, but the types seem to clearly differentiate the two conceptions of the deity. Salus Augusti appears to be depicted as Roman Hygieia and so perhaps represents the 'Health of the Emperor'.[19]

SALUS GENERIS HUMANI echoes the words reported as used by Vindex in his letter appealing to Galba and in his speech to the Gauls launching his revolt.[20] There is also one dedication to Salus Generis Humani which is from Gaul.[21]

Vespasian, Titus, Domitian, Julia: AD 69 - 91

SALUS AUGUSTA continues with the same type on the sestertii of Vespasian and Titus Caesar until AD 78.[22] SALUS AUGUSTI with her type continues until AD 71 on the asses of Vespasian.[23] The abbreviated SALUS AUG now appears (AD 73) on the denarii of Vespasian and Titus Caesar with a type similar to that of Salus Augusta but lacking the sceptre: this continues under Titus on his coins and those of Domitian Caesar and Julia Augusta.[24]

Domitian's denarii under Vespasian and Titus, advertising his title PRINCEPS IUVENTUTIS, are accompanied by a type of Salus Augusti, but, interestingly, from 79 the type, now also on an aureus, includes for the first time the patera, an attribute of Salus Augusta, out of which the snake is fed.[25]

Under Titus (AD 80-81) a sestertius bearing SALUTI AUGUSTI, accompanying a type of an altar in the form of a temple, may commemorate the dedication of an altar to Salus by the Senate during an illness of Titus.[26] Remarkably, though, the type is continued by Domitian (AD 84-91), with the same legend with the dative of dedication (once as SALUTI AUGUST), and almost exclusively of any other Salus coins.[27]

The only other Salus issue of Domitian is a denarius bearing SALUS AUGUST accompanying a type like that of SALUS AUG (above) but with the patera replaced by corn-ears. This new attribute may recall an older conception of Salus, but K.H. Schwarte suggests a reference to Domitian's concern for Italian agriculture or for Rome's corn-supply.[28]

Nerva: AD 96 - 97

All of Nerva's Salus issues carry this type - enthroned goddess holding corn-ears - always accompanied by SALUS PUBLICA.[29]

Trajan: AD 98 - 117

Now the types of Salus Augusta (without sceptre) and Salus Augusti are completely fused, and an altar is added around which the snake coils whilst being fed from a patera by the enthroned goddess.

The type predominates throughout the reign: up to AD 115 or 116 with no Salus legend (usually with SPQR OPTIMO PRINCIPI),[30] and from then with the ambiguous SALUS AUG (as part of the reverse legend).[31]

The only other Salus coins are the aurei, probably commemorating Trajan's decennalia of AD 108, with their legend SALUS GENERIS HUMANI associated with a standing deity (perhaps Fortuna), foot on globe, sacrificing with a patera over an altar and holding a rudder, thus recalling Galba's coins.[32]

Hadrian and L. Aelius Caesar: AD 118 - 138

There appears now to be a further development with the new combined Salus-type, inherited from Trajan, being associated with the unambiguous SALUS AUGUSTI (a variation has Salus standing and in addition holding a sceptre). Thus, suggests Schwarte, is the beneficial power of the emperor unambiguously associated with the health of the emperor.[33]

SALUS PUBLICA reappears on a dupondius of 119-128 combined, perhaps significantly, with a type similar to that of Trajan's decennalia SALUS GENERIS HUMANI issue but without the altar.[34]

Most of Hadrian's issues bear SALUS AUG combined with one of a range of variations. When standing, Salus is either feeding her snake (sometimes coiled round an altar, sometimes held), or sacrificing with the patera and holding a sceptre. When the snake is not held, the free arm sometimes bears either a sceptre or a rudder on a globe.[35] When enthroned, Salus is usually feeding the snake coiled round the altar - once she holds a rudder on a globe as well, and once she simply sacrifices with the patera.[36] The snake is now almost invariably fed from the patera.

SALUS also occurs without epithet with the type of her enthroned and feeding the snake coiled round an altar.[37] A sestertius of L. Aelius Caesar (137-138) of this kind has the interesting addition of a statuette of Spes (perhaps the hope vested in the designated successor) on which Salus leans.[38] There are at least ten issues bearing only a type of Salus (combined with imperial titles).[39]

Antoninus Pius, Faustina I and II, Marcus Caesar: AD 138 - 161

Now for the first time the combined type introduced under Trajan, and much used under Hadrian, is associated with the legend SALUS PUBLICA, on sestertii of 140-144. Thus, according to Schwarte, are combined the different connotations of Salus Augusti, Salus Augusta and Salus Publica (the health of the emperor, the welfare-bringing power of the emperor and the general welfare which is a result of these two). He suggests that the delay in overtly stating this association in the coinage is indicative of the exceptional position of the concept of Salus Publica deriving from the republican tradition.[40]

Otherwise there is a considerable variety of types but only as regards details: all depict Salus, enthroned or standing, with <u>patera</u> feeding the snake whatever else they have. One exception is a <u>dupondius</u> of Faustina I (138-141) depicting Salus holding the snake and leaning against a tree. It is one of several issues bearing SALUTI AUG.[41] The dative also occurs as SALUTI AUGUSTAE on an issue of Faustina deified.[42] The tree recurs on one of the few issues with simple SALUS where the snake coils round it.[43] The rudder on the globe often replaces Salus' sceptre.[44] Of those issues bearing a legend as well as a type, SALUS AUG again predominates. Two issues have SALUS AUGUSTI.[45] About half of the Salus coins have no Salus legend.

Marcus Aurelius, Lucius Verus, Faustina II, Lucilla and Commodus: AD 161 - 180

In this period the nominative SALUS only occurs in the absence of a qualifying adjective or genetive and then only on the issues of the imperial women.[46] Until 164 SALUTI AUGUSTOR is the predominant legend.[47] From 168 to 171 several issues of Marcus carry SALUTI AUG.[48]

Some issues of Faustina II (161-176) bear the ambiguous SALUTI AUGUSTAE.[49] However, a <u>sestertius</u> of Marcus (170-171) also has this legend which, in this case, must be the adjectival form.[50]

Whereas, before 176 very few types are unaccompanied by a legend, after 176 none of the issues (and thus none of those of Commodus as co-emperor) bear legends. Most of the types of this period (176-180), of both Marcus and Commodus, exhibit one of two new variations on the traditional theme: that of Salus, enthroned, usually holding a branch over the snake which is coiling up either from the ground or from an altar.[51]

Before 176 variations of the established type, often with a sceptre but never with a rudder and globe, occur with all the legends.

A type of Juno appears with SALUS on an <u>aureus</u> of Faustina II.[52]

Commodus and Crispina: AD 180 - 192

The legends are now SALUS AUG, SALUS and SAL(US) GEN(ERIS) HUM(ANI). Again, types without legends account for about half of the Salus issues. The new variations of the previous reign do not continue: but there are innovations.

The types alone and those accompanying SAL AUG are variations on traditional forms.[53] Two of five issues bearing SALUS are the only coins (182-183) in the name of Crispina Augusta:[54] the other three (183-186) depict Salus enthroned and feeding the snake but in association with the figure of Spes as well as with a mass of symbolic detail including, variously, a statue of Bacchus, a griffin and a sphinx.[55]

The three issues bearing SAL(US) GEN(ERIS) HUM(ANI) (c. 191) all depict the standing goddess holding a snake-wreathed sceptre and raising a kneeling figure.[56]

The Civil Wars: Pescennius Niger and Clodius Albinus: AD 193 - 197

All of Niger's five denarii (193-194; from Antioch) employ the dative form, all with the imperial epithet abbreviated, except for the one issue with SALUTI AUGUSTI. On four of the denarii Salus is standing, holding and feeding the snake; the fifth bears a type of a goddess holding scales and cornucopiae.[57]

Albinus' two denarii (195-97) carry SALUTI AUG accompanying traditional types.[58]

Septimius Severus and Caracalla: AD 197 - 212

The legends are now SALUTI AUGG, SALUTI AUG and SAL(US) GEN(ERIS) HUM(ANI), with the first certainly representing the genetival form of the epithet.[59]

Among those bearing only a type, four exhibit a new variation: the snake coils up to be fed out of the lap of the enthroned goddess.[60] One of Severus' eastern issues has SALUTI AUG with the type of a lighted altar.[61] A denarius of Caracalla (211-212), the latest coin of these reigns, has a traditional type but with Salus also holding a cornucopiae.[62] A few issues of Caracalla (199-201) proclaim SAL(US) GEN(ERIS) HUM(ANI) accompanying the type associated with this legend under Commodus: Salus raising a kneeling figure and holding a snake-wreathed staff.[63]

Macrinus: AD 217 - 218

This short reign produced a relatively large number of issues celebrating Salus, and there is a distinct change of policy: the Salus legends are always SALUS PUBLICA (usually unabbreviated). The types are traditional, with a variation: Salus, always enthroned, feeds the snake coiled round an altar and either holds a sceptre or extends a hand to touch the snake's head.[64]

Elagabalus: AD 218 - 222

All but two of these issues proclaim the personalized SALUS ANTONINI AUG accompanying a type of Salus standing and holding the snake which she feeds with a cake (or out of a vessel).[65] The one instance of SALUS AUGUSTI accompanies a traditional type but with the goddess, for the first time since the reign of Antoninus Pius, resting an arm upon a rudder set on a globe.[66]

Severus Alexander: AD 222 - 235

The legends employed are SALUS PUBLICA (seven issues), SALUS AUGUSTI and SALUTI AUGUSTI (one issue each). This last, notably, with the dative of dedication, occurs on a bronze medallion (undated) and depicts, in addition to Salus, the emperor in military dress.[67] Otherwise the types, including those used without a Salus legend, are traditional as prior to Elagabalus - Salus, enthroned, apart from the SALUS AUGUSTI issue, and feeding the snake from a patera, not with cake.[68]

Maximinus: AD 235 - 238

The issues all bear the legend SALUS AUGUSTI in association with one traditional type: Salus enthroned feeds her snake, which is coiled round an altar, from a patera[69]

Gordian III: AD 238 - 241

All eight issues bear a legend, either SALUS AUGUSTI or SALUS AUG, accompanying one of two traditional types.[70]

Philippus I and Otacilia Severa: AD 244 - 249

The issues all bear a legend, either SALUS AUGG (after the elevation of Philip's son in 247) or SALUS AUG. Types are traditional, and Salus is always standing, and on those where the snake is coiling round an altar (thus freeing one hand), she holds a rudder (without globe).[71]

Hostilian (Reign of Trajan Decius), Trebonianus Gallus and Volusianus: AD 251 - 253

Again, all the issues bear a legend, usually SALUS AUGG, sometimes SALUS AUGUS. The types continue as in the previous reign but with the sceptre replacing the rudder as a held attribute when the snake is not held.[72]

Valerian, Gallienus and Salonina: AD 254 - 268

Under the joint reign (to 260) the types, always accompanied by a legend, continue as in the previous reign, with the exception of the one issue bearing SALUS ITAL which has Salus offering fruits to the emperor who holds a spear.[73] Otherwise, the legend is usually SALUS AUGG, but there are two instances each of SALUS PUBLICA (257) and SALUS AUG (258-259).[74]

There is both continuity and innovation under the reign of Gallienus. The types of Salus herself are traditional, though now with the enthroned goddess reintroduced on some issues. The legend is predominantly SALUS AUG (once SALUS AUGUSTI).[75] In addition there are

27

asses bearing OB CONSERVATIONEM SALUTIS (sometimes with AUGG); there is a silver medallion with the same (no AUGG) and one with OB CONSERVATIONEM PATRIAE; and there is an aureus bearing OB CONSERVAT SALUT.[76]

An aureus and three issues of antoniniani have SALUS AUG accompanied by a type of Aesculapius, and an antoninianus with this legend has a type of Apollo, thus completing "the divine ministry of public health".[77]

A silver medallion of Salonina has the legend PUDICITIAE AUGUSTAE accompanying a type depicting Pudicitia, Felicitas and Salus.[78]

Claudius II: AD 268 - 270

All the issues have SALUS AUG with one interesing exception: this has SPES PUBLICA with a type depicting Salus and Aesculapius.[79] The Salus types are traditional (and she is always standing), but most of the issues have non-Salus types, including those of Isis, Apollo, Apollo and Diana, and Aesculapius.[80]

The Gallic Empire: Postumus, Victorinus and the Tetrici: AD 259 - 274

Under Postumus (259-269) more new types are added, these now predominating over the traditional. Among the latter, the rudder appears once.[81] Types of Aesculapius predominate, accompanying most of the SALUS AUG legends, the one SALUS AUGUSTI and both SALUS EXERCITI legends.[82]

Two antoniniani and an aureus proclaiming the SALUS PROVINCIARUM accompany types depicting the personified River Rhine.[83]

One of the SALUS AUG sestertii depicts Salus holding a palm, and the personalized SALUS POSTUMI AUG occurs on an antoninianus and an aureus, the latter depicting both Salus and Aesculapius.[84]

Under Victorinus (268-270) orthodoxy returns, with traditional types accompanying SALUS AUG, with one exception: PAX AUG occurs on an irregular coin depicting Salus holding a spear![85]

PAX AUGG occurs under the Tetrici,[86] but, otherwise, all the issues (270-273/4) have Salus legends - SALUS AUGG, SALUS AUG and, once, SALUS EXERCITI. All except six have Salus types, though most of these, whilst basically of traditional conception, are modified by the addition of new attributes (sceptre and rudder are also present) - branch, anchor and wreath.[87] The non-Salus types include: Aesculapius, Victoria, pontifical implements and a soldier.[88]

Tacitus and Florian: AD 275 - 276

When the striking of Salus issues resumes, after a hiatus under Aurelian, the types are all traditional ones (Salus, standing, except for one issue, feeds her snake which is either held or coiling up from an altar), and are combined with either SALUS AUG or SALUS PUBLICA

(PUBLICA being sometimes abbreviated).[89]

Probus: AD 276 - 282

A similar situation obtains under Probus, though SALUS AUG now predominates over SALUS PUBLICA.[90] The one exceptional issue carries the legend SALUS MILITUM, though with a traditional type.[91]

Carus, Carinus, Numerianus and Magnia Urbica: AD 282 - 285

The situation remains the same in these reigns except for the appearance of SALUS AUGG under Carinus and Numerianus, the one issue bearing SALUS PUBLICA being that of Magnia Urbica.[92]

Diocletian, Maximian, Constantius, Severus Caesar, Licinius: AD 285 - 311

The types remain strictly traditional. Legends always accompany them, and, with one exception, these proclaim either SALUS AUGG or SALUS AUGG ET CAESS NN: Licinius' one issue has SALUS AUGG NN (308-311).[93]

The British Empire: Carausius and Allectus: AD 286 - 296

Whilst there are many idiosyncrasies in the Salus coinage of Carausius (286-293), especially in terms of attributes and associations, basically traditional (in terms of central imperial coinage) forms predominate. Of the large number of issues, leaving aside the blundered or otherwise not readily comprehensible, the legend is, with three exceptions, SALUS AUG or SALUS AUGGG (referring to Diocletian and Maximian): SALUS AUGG occurs once, and SALUS PUBLICA twice.[94] A type of Aesculapius occurs twice, and there is a pronounced association with Pax.[95] On several issues Salus holds a cornucopiae: on one, a globe.[96] On seven or more issues she sacrifices at an altar: a type not struck since the reign of Hadrian.[97]

Types of Salus are associated with the legends L(A)ETITIA AUG and VICTORIA AUG. SALUS AUG is once associated with a type of two draped figures holding wreaths and clasping hands.[98]

Under Allectus orthodoxy returns with all six issues (293-296) bearing SALUS AUG and traditional types.[99]

Constantine I, Fausta and Constantius Caesar: AD 315 - 335

A profound and permanent change now occurs in the issues celebrating Salus, as in the coinage generally, reflecting wider changes in the nature of the empire. From now onwards, except in the issues of Magnentius, Salus is associated less explicitly with the person of the emperor.[100] Types which may depict Salus only occur on the folles (324-327) of Fausta, accompanying the legend SALUS

REIPUBLICAE, where perhaps there is allowed to occur a confusion as to whether the draped and veiled female figure holding two children is that of Salus or that of the empress (and thus, in the latter case, designed to emphasize the dynastic principle).[101]

Salus Reipublicae is celebrated in the name of Constantine (and once in that of Constantius Caesar) only on medallions (gold, silver and aes), and then, with two exceptions, in the combination SALUS ET SPES REIPUBLICAE. The associated types glorify Constantine, some blatantly, in terms of his military victories, and some celebrate his establishment of a new imperial dynasty in their portrayal of his sons, in military dress, around him.[102] The gold medallion of 330 struck at Constantinople may celebrate Constantine's victory at Chrysopolis (324) and his subsequent restoration of Byzantium (the emperor, being crowned by Victoria, receives victory on a globe from a turreted female).[103] A silver medallion (with SALUS REIPUBLICAE only), thought to have been for circulation among senior army officers, depicts the chi-rho monogram on Constantine's helmet. At this date (315) this is less likely to be the Christian sign it was to become, than a personally adopted symbol of power.[104]

Constantius II, Constans, Magnentius and Decentius Caesar: AD 337 - 353

The one gold issue each of Constantius II and Constans (at Thessalonica, 337-340) continue the typology of the previous reign with SALUS ET SPES REIPUBLICAE accompanying a type of the three emperors (including Constantine II) in military dress.[105]

At his four Gallic mints, Magnentius and his Caesar Decentius struck several base billon and bronze issues with the legend SALUS DD NN AUG ET CAES accompanying a type of the chi-rho flanked by alpha and omega (351-353).[106] The legend is an appeal for recognition from Constantius: the type is thought to be an appeal, by the pagan Magnentius, for support among Christians.[107] There are also several problematic issues struck in 352 in the name of Constantius at Trier, which is thought to have been then under the control of Magnentius: their legend, the unique SALUS AUG NOSTRI, is combined with the Magnentian type of the chi-rho flanked by alpha and omega.[108]

Valentinian I and Valens: AD 364 - 367

Between 352 and 378, Salus Reipublicae appears only on these ten issues: six of gold with the abbreviated SALUS REIP accompanying a type of the emperor victorious and holding the labarum, standard of the Christian emperor;[109] and four of silver associating SALUS REIPUBLICAE with a type of four standards.[110]

Theodosius I, Flaccilla, Valentinian II, Arcadius, Honorius (: AD 379 - 408) and After

The SALUS REIPUBLICAE (always in full) carried by the issues of these reigns is part of the ideology of the Christian empire and of the policy of combining pagan concepts and imagery with Christian symbolism. However, in the case of Salus, the imagery has disappeared, no types of her having survived beyond the reign of Constantine I, if to that. There can be little doubt that Salus has ceased to have any pagan cultic significance.

She is now always 'Salus of the State', perhaps because the intimate association of a formerly pagan concept with, and dependent upon, the person of the emperor was now thought unsuitable for a Christian audience. The changed emphasis of the message conveyed by the imperial coinage is that the welfare of the state is dependent upon the glorious and constant victories of the army.[111]

On most of the Salus issues the legend is combined with types displaying the dramatic imagery of Victoria (usually combined with the chi-rho), the retention of which provides a stark example of the pragmatic adaptation of powerful pagan imagery by the Christian emperors.[112]

Issues (mainly aes) of the empress Flaccilla (379-388) combine the legend with types of Victoria inscribing the chi-rho upon a shield.[113] (A lesser number carry a type of the empress.[114]) The type and legend continue on the coins of empresses of the fifth century.[115]

The issues (all aes) of Theodosius I, Valentinan II, Arcadius and Honorius (383-408) bear a type of Victoria which, more dramatically and savagely than the Victoria types of Flaccilla, boasts of the military triumphs, portraying Victoria carrying a trophy and dragging by the hair a kneeling captive, the chi-rho being sometimes present in the field.[116]

A solidus of Theodosius II (425) combines the legend with a type of two togate (unusually) emperors each holding a globe bearing a cross.[117] Coins bearing SALUS REIPUBLICAE continue at least into the second half of the fifth century: a type borne on the solidus issues of Anthemius (467-472) depicts two emperors in military dress with, between them, a globe bearing a cross.[118]

Coins of Olybrius (472) proclaim the SALUS MUNDI and depict simply a cross.[119]

NOTES

1a. Above, 11.

2a. <u>RIC</u>, V, ii, 71, 500-501; obv. VIRTUS PROBI AUG.

1. Crawford, 337-339, 337, 2a - f.

2. Wissowa, <u>Lex</u>, 296; Latte, 234, note 1; above, 2.

3. Fears, 882; cf. Cicero's traditional view, above, 7.

4. Fears, 883, note 255; above 7; cf. the coins of Glabrio, next section.

5. Below, 102-103, for the supposed connection of the <u>gens Acilia</u> with the introduction of Greek medicine to Rome, and the statue of Salus at Ostia dedicated by a descendant of the <u>triumvir monetalis</u>; Crawford, 461, 442, 1a and 1b.

6. Above, 1.

7. Above, 7.

8. Fears, 882 (quoted), 883; cf. the coins of Silanus, previous section.

9. <u>BM</u>, I, 131, 81-84; Weinstock, 172; Fears 891.

10. Tacitus, <u>Annales</u>, III.64; 71.1.

11. Schwarte, 238-239; Grant, 271.

12. M. Grant, <u>Aspects of the Principate of Tiberius: Historical Comments on the Colonial Coinage Issued Outside Spain</u>, New York, 1950, 114, note 169; C.H.V. Sutherland, <u>JRS</u>, XXIV (1934), 36.

13. <u>BM</u>, I, 212-213, 87-100; Fears, 895; Weinstock, 173.

14. Above, 3-4; and below, 157, for the Mainz Jupiter column dedicated, perhaps now, <u>pro salute Neronis</u>, and perhaps depicting Salus.

15. <u>BM</u>, I, 297-298, 30-36; <u>RIC</u>, I, pp. 185-187, nos. 12, 13, 26, 29, 38; <u>BM</u>, I, 350, 230-231; Schwarte, 239.

16. <u>RIC</u>, I, 183, 20.

17. <u>BM</u>, I, 328, 119.

18. <u>BM</u>, I, 361, 265.

19. Schwarte, 240-241; Weinstock, 174; cf. Fears, 887, 888, note 284, who doubts the distinction.

20. Dio, LXIII.22.6; Suetonius, *Galba*, 9.2; above, 19, note 73, for echoes of the phrase in Pliny's reports to Trajan and in earlier literature.

21. Below, 122-123.

22. BM, II, 124, 574-575; 137, 624; 207, 827; RIC, II, 106, 774.

23. RIC, II, 63, 392; 74, note to 499.

24. BM, II, 16, 87-89; 264, 196; 247, 139; RIC, II, 138, 171; HC, I, 231, 6.

25. RIC, II, 42, 239; BM, II, 237, 84; Schwarte, 241.

26. RIC, II, 128, 105; Schwarte, 242; Weinstock, 174.

27. BM, II, 361, 291-293; RIC, II, 203, 396.

28. RIC, II, 158, 41; H. Mattingly, OCD^2, 948 ('Salus'); Schwarte, 244.

29. BM, II, 3, 19-21; Schwarte, 244-245.

30. BM, III, 198, 934.

31. HC, II, 35, 211.

32. BM, III, 87, 410; Fears, 922; on the epithet, above, 23 and note 20.

33. BM, III, 418, 1215; 440, 1348; Schwarte, 243.

34. BM, III, 421, 1237; Schwarte, 245.

35. BM, III, 279, 313; 440, 787; 476, 1555-1558.

36. BM, III, 279, 320; 331, 728; 477, note to 477.

37. HC, II, 155, 557.

38. BM, III, 545, note to 1926.

39. BM, III, 265, 207.

40. BM, IV, 209, 1310; Schwarte, 244, 246.

41. RIC, III, 160, 1095; BM, IV, 147, 987-992.

42. RIC, III, 169, 1200.

43. BM, IV, 855, *add.* to p. 169.

44. BM, IV, 209, 1308.

45. BM, IV, 216, 1352; 220, 1368.

46. BM, IV, 404, 147; HC, II, 392, 32-34.

47. BM, IV, 411, 198; 413, 208.

48. BM, IV, 455, 494-495.

49. HC, II, 359, 67-69.

50. RIC, III, 293, 1011.

51. BM, IV, 487, 696; HC, II, 399, 13.

52. BM, IV, 404, 146.

53. BM, IV, 704, 94-95; RIC, III, 412, 396; BM, IV, 776, 474.

54. BM, IV, 767, 423.

55. BM, IV, 799, 556; RIC, III, 416, 439; 421, 473; for association with Spes, above, 12-13.

56. BM, IV, 755, 358; 834, 682; RIC, III, 435, 606.

57. BM, V, 80, 312a-313.

58. RIC, IV, i, 49-50, 39-40.

59. BM, V, 61, 255-256.

60. BM, V, 357, 6-9.

61. RIC, IV, i, 163, 530.

62. BM, V, 438, 45-46.

63. BM, V, 187, 169-170.

64. BM, V, 507, 75-76; 513, 99.

65. BM, V, 547, 114-116; 592, 361.

66. BM, V, 553, 162-163.

67. BM, VI, 193, 783.

68. BM, VI, 160, 479; 118-119, 32-41; 214, 1014-1017.

69. BM, VI, 237, 175-180.

70. RIC, IV, iii, 28, 129a; 44, 261.

71. Ibid., 73, 47; 85, 141; 91, 188.

72. Ibid., 150, 224; 172, 123; 176, 152.

73. RIC, V, i, 99, 400.

74. Ibid., p. 57, nos. 250-251, 255; 99, 397-399; 114, 60.

75. Ibid., 155, 276.

76. Ibid., 135, 59; 142, 143-144; 168, 423.

77. Ibid., 136, 66; 176, 511-511b; 185, 610; above, 13-14.

78. Ibid., 111, 25.

79. Ibid., 230, 222.

80. Ibid., 218, 98-99; 224, 165-167; 229, 216-218; 230, 219-220.

81. RIC, V, ii, 344, 85.

82. Ibid., 351, 165; 363, 326-327; 368, 383.

83. Ibid., 340, 38; 344, 87; HC, IV, 90, 39-40.

84. RIC, V, ii, 251, 164; 360, 281; 363, 328.

85. Ibid., 393, 65-70; 398, 129.

86. Ibid., 409, 107-108.

87. Ibid., 410, 121-124 and 126-129; 412, 158; 423, 266-267.

88. Ibid., 423, 265; 425, 288 and 291.

89. Ibid., 331, 56 and 58; 358, 92.

90. Ibid., 76-77, 560-562 and 566-569.

91. Ibid., 28, 98.

92. Ibid., 136, 16; 185, 349; 166, 216-217; 194, 404.

93. RIC, V, ii, 229, 85-90; 268-269, 417-423; 298, 642-643; RIC, VI, 204, 628-629; 478, 194.

94. RIC, V, ii, 478, 165-166; 498, 404-405; 552, 13-14; 544, 32.

95. Ibid., 475, 136; 477, 160; 478, 163; 538, 929-933; 542, 996-997 and 999.

96. Ibid., 477, 158; 520, 662-663 and 665-666.

97. Ibid., 521, 671.

98. Ibid., 532, 831; 542, 1000; 544, 1026.

99. Ibid., 562, 42-44.

100. RIC, VII, pp. 46-56; Mattingly, 229-244.

101. RIC, VII, p. 53; 116, 300; 621, 130; 571, 12; 690, 76.

102. Ibid., 328, 280; 331, 298; 527, 204; 555, 99; 577, 44; 583, 8.

103. Ibid., pp. 54-55; 576, 43.

104. Ibid., pp. 62-64; 364, 36.

105. RIC., VIII, pp. 39-40; 403, 20-21.

106. Ibid., 123, 34-35; 163-164, 318-327a; 188-189, 153-176; 217, 188-202.

107. Ibid., p. 12; Mattingly, 231, note 1, and 239.

108. RIC, VIII, 165, 332-337.

109. RIC, IX, 145, 1a-b; 173-174, 1 and 3a-b.

110. Ibid., 43, 3a-b; 62, 3a-b.

111. Mattingly, 244.

112. Ibid., 241-242.

113. RIC, IX, 153, 34-35; 184, 46-47; 197, 23; 225, 48; 257, 28; 284, 43; reminiscent, perhaps, of the Victoria inscribing 'V' on a shield on the early SALUS GENERIS HUMANI issues of Galba.

114. Ibid., 197, 25; 233, 82; 245, 24.

115. HC, V, 479, 1-4; 487, 4.

116. RIC, IX, 133-134, 64a-e; 188, 65a-c; 195, 70a-c.

117. HC, V, 482, 10.

118. Ibid., 462, 1-2.

119. Mattingly, 240 and plate LXIII, 12.

CHAPTER THREE: THE EVIDENCE OF THE ACTS OF THE ARVAL BROTHERS

A. Introduction

The Fratres Arvales were an archaic priestly college dedicated to the cult of an agricultural deity, the Dea Dia. They were revived and enhanced in importance as part of the revival and reorganisation by Augustus of religious practices and priesthoods. Henceforth, as in the case of the other major priesthoods at Rome, their prime function was the petitioning and thanking of the gods (with vows and sacrifices) on behalf of the imperial family. Their membership of twelve, selected by co-optation, was restricted to a small group within the ruling class and always included the emperor.[1]

Our knowledge of them derives almost entirely from the records of their meetings and cult-acts. These records, inscribed on marble tablets,[1a] have survived in remarkable quantity and have been found in several places in Rome, but chiefly outside Rome at the Brothers' sacred grove at the fifth milestone on the Via Campana, and here, most notably, during the excavations of 1867-1871. The records cover the period from 21 BC to AD 241, though unevenly, as is also the case with regard to the fragments attesting the vows and sacrifices directed to Salus which date from the period AD 38 to 231. The cult-acts addressed to Salus took place in several locations but chiefly 'in Capitolio', which must refer to one of the successive temples of the Capitoline Triad on the Capitoline Hill. Interestingly, Salus is never honoured in her own prestigious temple on the Quirinal Hill, a fact which led W. Henzen to suggest that the Quirinal temple, burnt down in the reign of Claudius, was never rebuilt.[2]

We already know that public cult-acts were performed in the provinces on occasions such as those commemorated in the records of the Arvals, certainly on annual occasions such as the vota of January 3 and the dies imperii, but perhaps also on special occasions.[3] Fragments of inscriptions found at Cyrene and Ptolemais in Cyrenaica, and at Sarmizegetusa in Dacia, now seem to indicate that these acts may have been remarkably similar to those of the Arvals in terms of the formulae used and in the records made (and publicly displayed) of them.[4]

The evidence is described in categories determined by the type of occasion being celebrated: within these the arrangement is chronological.

B. **The Annual Vows for the Welfare of the Emperor on January 3**

1. AD 38

This is the earliest evidence for the establishment of annual vota for the welfare of the emperor on January 3.[5] The words of the actual vow, which would have been addressed in full to Jupiter, do not survive, but it is apparent from the words used in a further promise of gold and silver to him, that he had been promised a bos auratus. Using the actual words of address, which are an abbreviated version of, and refer to, the invocation to Jupiter Optimus Maximus, a bos aurata is then vowed in turn to both Juno Regina and Minerva:- (for example)

> Iuno Regina, quae in verba Iovi O M. bove aurato vovi esse futurum, quod hoc die vovi, ast tu ea ita faxis, tum tibi colle[gii] fratrum Arvalium nomine bove aurata voveo esse futuru[um].

Finally, the record changes to indirect reporting: in eadem verba vovit deae Diae, Saluti, Divo Augusto (the subject being the promagister of the college).[6]

2. AD 58

Fragments record the making of vows pro salute of Nero and Octavia and the sacrifices in fulfilment of the previous year's vows. They indicate that this year two victims were promised: to the Capitoline Triad, Saluti Publi[icae...], and to the three divi, Augustus, Livia and Claudius. The Dea Dia is an obvious omission from the list of 38.[7]

3. AD 59

The only notable change, evident from the records, which are almost complete, for this occasion, compared with the vota of the previous year, is that, whereas the Capitoline Triad and Salus Publica receive the vows in Capitolio, the divi receive their invocations in the new temple of Augustus. The magister of the College pronounces the words of the vow at the dictation of another brother (a consul).[8]

4. AD 60

Apart from minor changes in the wording and as regards the persons participating, the fulfilment and renewal of the vows for the salus of Nero and Octavia are recorded identically to those of AD 59.[9]

5. AD 69 (Galba)

The fragments referring to this year's vota indicate only two small changes compared with their performance in 59 and 60: now only single victims are vowed and Salus seems to be without her epithet.[10]

6. AD 77

The remaining fragment shows that the sacrifices in fulfilment of the previous year's <u>vota</u> are of two victims each to the members of the Capitoline Triad and Salus Publica, the <u>divi</u> no longer being honoured.[11]

7. AD 78

The complete record for this year shows that, after the fulfilment of the <u>vota</u> undertaken in 77, single victims were promised for the following year. The Capitoline temple is the one location in the absence of vows to, or sacrifices for, the <u>divi</u> (as in 77). Jupiter (Optimus Maximus) and Juno (Regina) now receive their epithets, though Salus does not. The list of recipients and victims is repeated pro T(ito)...Caesare.[12]

8. AD 81

The record, though now fragmentary, was apparently fuller than in previous years, where the records for the <u>vota</u> survive. After the vows of the previous year were fulfilled (in the Capitoline temple) with two victims each for the members of the Capitoline Triad and Salus Publica, vows were undertaken for the coming year on behalf of the emperor, of Domitian Caesar, and of Julia Augusta and her children.

The <u>magister</u> pronounced the new <u>vota</u> in terms dictated by another brother. For this year the address to the deities, in direct speech, is recorded with most of that to Jupiter surviving:

> <u>Iuppiter O.M., si imp(erator)... et Caesar ...
> Domitianus ... vivent domusque eorum incolumis
> erit a. d. III non. Ian., quae proximae p(opulo)
> R. Q(uiritium) rei p(ublicae) p. R. Q. [erunt,
> fuer]int, et eum eosque salvos servaveris ex
> periculis, ...[tunc tibi nom]ine collegi fratrum
> Arvalium bubus au[ratis II vovemus esse futuru]m.</u>[13]

The general form of the shortened address to the other deities, referring to the address to Jupiter, is indicated in the records for the <u>vota</u> of AD 38 (where the full address to Jupiter does not survive).[14]

9. AD 86

The <u>vota</u> for 86 (the next surviving after 81), though fragmentary, are essentially similar to those preceding. However, the sacrifices fulfilling the vows of 85 are of gilded oxen, and those promised for 87 (again for Domitian and the <u>Augustae</u>) are gilded and white oxen. The address to Salus can be restored from the surviving fragment and with reference to those to Juno and Minerva:-

> [Salus Pub]lica populi Romani Quiritium, quae in verba Iunoni Regin(ae) [bove femina au]rata vovi esse futurum, quod hodie vovi, ast tu ea ita fax(is), [tum tibi in eadem ver]ba nomine collegi fratrum Arvalium bove femin(a) [alba aurata voveo esse f]uturum.[15]

The address to Juno, in turn, refers to that to Jupiter.[16]

10. AD 87

This year's report is by far the fullest, both as originally recorded and as extant, with respect to both detail and language. There is also a significant development.

Firstly, there is a statement that, because the gods have responded favourably to the previous vota, the college has decreed the fulfilment and renewal of vows pro salute et incolumitate of Domitian, of the two Augustae and of the whole imperial house, to the Capitoline Triad and Salus Publica Populi Romani Quiritium. There is a remarkable departure, however, in that in the preamble the vows are called the vota orbis terra[rum]. The location is in Capitolio in pro[nao Iovis].[17]

There follows a detailed description of the performance of the sacrifices, announced above, by the acting magister: ture et vino in igne in foculo fecit immolavitq(ue) vino, mola cultroque Iovi ... (list of deities); exta aulicocta reddidit.[18] The victims are described simply as oxen (of appropriate sex) whereas in fact white and gilded ones had actually been promised.[19]

Lastly, the renewal of the vota is described with the address reproduced in direct speech and ending with that to Salus Publica Populi Romani Quiritium (her name in full and unabbreviated) which is essentially that of AD 86 (referring to the vow of Juno, which is shortened, in turn, by its reference to the vow to Jupiter). The victims vowed are all gilded oxen.[20]

11. AD 91

The record of this occasion, for which only parts of the new vows addressed to the deities survive, contains another[21] remarkable innovation. The address to Salus is complete and, essentially, is the same as that of 87 (except that the reference is made directly to the address to Jupiter). However, she is here, uniquely, called Salus Augusta P(ublica) p(opuli) R(omani) Q(uiritium).[22]

The change in perception of the well-being of the state implied by the change apparent in the vota of 91 seems to be manifested elsewhere in the records of the Arvals in the institution, in 86, of new annual vota on January 22 addressed only to Jupiter. In varying degrees of fullness they survive for 86, 87, 89 and 90, and there seems to be no other cause for these vota other than pro salute (et incolumitate in 87) of the emperor alone.[23]

In the vow (reported in full for 86, 87 and 90, and fully extant for 86), which is similar to that of January 3, Domitian is referred to as ex cuius incolumitate omnium salus constat.[24] The practice may have ceased after 90, the year before the exceptional vota of January 3, 91.

K.H. Schwarte suggests that the new vota of January 22 indicate that a reinterpretation of the relationship between the public well-being and that of the emperor had taken place.[25] Thus, in these new vota the welfare of all is stated explicitly to depend upon the person of the emperor. This, then, may indicate the significance of the phrase vota orbis terrarum of January 3, 87.[26] Schwarte suggests that this description and that of Domitian in the new vota are the indications of a policy designed to broaden the significance of the salus of the emperor by the designation of the emperor as the mediator of the welfare, not only of the Roman people, but of all the inhabitants of the empire. This process was carried further in the reign of Trajan, with regard to both the vota of January 3 and the oath of allegiance on the dies imperii,[27] and is perhaps reflected in the imperial coinage of Trajan, Hadrian and Antoninus Pius.[28]

The significance of the development of January 3, 91, is that now, in an unprecedented way, Salus Publica herself is explicitly associated with the person of the emperor (by the epithet Augusta): previously, the emperor's welfare had been sought from, among other deities, Salus Publica Populi Romani, the autonomous protector of the welfare of the whole Roman state. Now, the implication seems to be that the emperor is the mediator through which Salus Publica must act.

12. AD 169 to 177

Salus is attested only once on the few fragments belonging to the reign of Marcus Aurelius, and then on one of those three which probably relate to the vota on January 3.[29] From a composite reconstruction based on these three fragements, it seems likely that in this period the vota have undergone a change in form. In the address to Jupiter, the emperor's safety is sought but after that of the res publica ... imperium Romanum, exercitus, socii, nationes quae sub dicione populi Romani Q. sunt.[30] The fragment, dated between 169 and 177, attests the inclusion of Salus P[ublica]:[31] the names of Juno and Minerva have to be completely restored on all the fragments as do the victims, though it is clear that these are gilded and plural.

13. AD 183

From the fragment of the report, it is clear that, in contrast to the situation under Marcus, the safeguarding of the emperor's salus is the prime, indeed the only, objective: votorum solutorum et no[vorum] (or nu[ncupandorum]) causa pro salute imp. (in Capitolio).

Single oxen (of appropriate sex) were sacrificed to the members of the Capitoline Triad and [Sa]luti Publicae p(opuli) R(omani).[32]

14. AD 231

For the first time the location for the vota is specified as in Capitolio ante cellam Iunonis Reginae. The fragment tells us that the welfare of Julia Mammaea totiusque domus divinae eoru[m] was sought in addition to that of the emperor. The recipients of the sacrifices, performed in fulfilment, are the Capitoline Triad and Salus Publica P(opuli) R(omani), the victims being single and gilded.[33]

C. Sacrifices in Celebration of the 'Dies Imperii'[34]

1. AD 69, c. January 16 (Otho)

The record for this occasion is very fragmentary. Following the Capitoline Triad (restored), the list of recipients (promised single victims) includes Victoria, Salus (perhaps without epithet) and the Genius Ipsius (Otho).[35]

2. AD 69, May 1 (Vitellius)

This, much fuller, record tells us that Vitellius' dies imperii, though celebrated now, was actually April 19. Sacrifices were performed, in or in front of the Capitoline temple, for the members of the Capitoline Triad, Jupiter Victor, Salus (no epithets), Felicitas and the Genius Populi Romani, and in the Forum Augustum for Mars Ultor and the Genius Ipsius.[36]

3. AD 81, September 14 (Domitian)

Domitian's dies imperii is celebrated in Capitolio with single sacrifices to Jupiter O. M., Juno Regina, Minerva, Salus, Felicitas and Mars.[37]

D. 'Vota' for the Welfare of the New Emperor

1. AD 69, January 30 (Otho)

These are the first vota, for which the record survives, made after the accession of a new emperor and distinct from those of January 3 (Otho became emperor on January 15). Otho himself is magister of the college.

Celebratory sacrifices (not in fulfilment of vows) are performed, and the usual (appropriate to January 3), and single, victims are vowed, in or in front of the Capitoline temple, for the following January 3 (the emperor being safe up to that date, being the understood condition in the reported language of the record), to the Capitoline Triad, Salus P(ublica) P(opuli) R(omani), and the three divi (Augustus, Livia and Claudius).[38]

2. AD 81, October 1 (Domitian)

Similarly, sacrifices are now performed in Capitolio, ob votorum c[o]mmendandorum causa pro salute et incolumitate Caesaris: single victims to the members of the Capitoline Triad, Salus and the Genius Ipsius. The vota themselves, again in Capitolio, in annum proximum... pro salute imp(eratoris) (with no date given), promise the same victims to all but the Genius Ipsius; the same recipients are listed in turn pro salute of Domitia Augusta and Julia Augusta.[39]

E. Extraordinary Vows or Sacrifices for the Imperial Health or Safety

1. AD 50 - 54, June 28: Vows (only) for the Restoration to Health of Nero Caesar

In the Capitoline temple the Capitoline Triad and Salus are the recipients of vota promising a bos auratus to Jupiter O.M. and a bos aurata to each of the goddesses. Notably, despite her being invoked last, Salus as well as Jupiter, receives the vow in full:

> [Sa]lus Publica populi Romani Q[uiritium, te quaesumus precam]urque, uti tu Neronem Clau[dium, ... s]alvom incolumemque con[serves et in reliquom malae v]aletudinis primo quoque [tempore praestes expertem; quae si ita sunt e]runtve, astu ea ita facxsis, tum [nos bove aurata tibi vovemus esse futurum].

This is exceptional and is presumably because of the occasion.[40]

2. AD 59, April 5: 'Pro Salute Neronis'

Sacrifices only were performed as a result of a decree of the Senate for supplicationes ...pro salute Neronis, the occasion being Nero's 'deliverance' from the alleged plot of Agrippina. After the Capitoline Triad and Salus ('Publica' has to be restored), the recipients were Providentia[41] (a cow), the Genius of Nero (a bull) and the Divus Augustus (a male ox).[42] In contrast to the earlier vota for Nero's health, the Capitoline Triad receive their more usual victims: a male ox for Jupiter and cows for the goddesses.

3. AD 183 (after May) and 186 (date unknown): 'Pro Salute Imperatoris'

Fragments provide evidence of two, probably identical, occasions, in Capitolio, when sacrifices only were offered simply pro salute imp(eratoris), perhaps celebrating Commodus' salvation from conspiracies. Salus (without epithet) is attested for both occasions, receiving a bovem feminam in 183 and a cow in 186. In 183 Saluti follows the Capitoline Triad and precedes Providentia Deorum and a deity whose name is restored as that of the Genius of the Emperor on the basis of the survival of taurum as the last sacrifice offered in 186. Apart from this indication, together with [Sa]luti vaccam and the survival of bovem marem as the first victim, the deity and victim list for 186 has to be restored.[43]

F. **For Imperial Birthdays**

1. **AD 55, December 15: Nero**

On this occasion the Capitoline Triad, Salus and the Genius of Nero received sacrifices in Capitolio. This record was preserved in a manuscript which, for the last line of the entry, read Saluti eius b.m. Genio eius vaccam. This Henzen would not accept and, rightly, also objected to the inappropriate victims: thus he published Saluti Publicae vaccam Genio eius taurum.[44] S. Weinstock finds support for the idea of a Salus Eius (i.e. Salus Augusti) in the possibility of such a cult under Gaius: this may be indicated by the allegation in Cassius Dio that Gaius swore oaths by the tyche and soteria of his horse.[45]

For the story to have been plausible, there would have to have been a cult of the Salus of Gaius. Weinstock suggests that the implied re-establishment of the cult under Nero met with opposition which resulted in its replacement, in the acts of the Arvals on succeeding birthdays, by Salus Publica.

2. **AD 57, November 6: Agrippina Augusta**

On this occasion the magister collegi fratrum Arvalium nomine sacrificed in Capitolio, to the Capitoline Triad (Jupiter and Juno without epithets), Salus Publica and Concordia.[46]

3. **AD 58, November 6: 'Ob Natalem Agrippinae Aug(usti) Matris'**

The only notable change in this occasion is that Concordia is now qualified by ipsius.[47]

4. **AD 58, December 15: Nero**

This year Salus Publica[48] (following the Capitoline Triad) receives a cow. In addition, and following Salus, Concordia Honoris Agrippinae Aug(ustae) receives a cow. The Genius of Nero remains and receives a bull.[49]

5. **AD 59, December 15: Nero**

This year the sacrifices and venue (the Capitoline temple) are the same, but Felicitas[50] replaces Concordia Honoris Agrippinae Aug(ustae), Agrippina having been murdered in March.[51]

G. Sacrifices 'Ob Adoptionem Neronis': AD 59, February 25[52]

The sacrifices, made in Capitolio, were for the members of the Capitoline Triad and Salus Publica, all receiving single victims.[53] The adoption was that by Claudius, probably in AD 50.

H. The Election of the Emperor to the Tribunician Power

1. AD 69, February 28 (Otho)

Single victims are sacrificed in the Capitoline temple to the members of the Capitoline Triad, Salus (without epithets), Victoria, the Genius Populi Romani and the Genius Ipsius (Otho).[54]

2. AD 69, April 30 (Vitellius)

For Vitellius, the situation changes only in the omission of Victoria and the Genius of the Roman People from the list of recipients.[55]

I. For the Welfare and Return of the Emperor

1. AD 59, June 23: Sacrifices for the Return of Nero

Sacrifices were performed at three places pro salute et reditu of Nero. The members of the Capitoline Triad, Salus Publica, Felicitas[56] and another goddess whose name does not survive, all receive single victims, probably in Capitolio. In the new temple of Augustus, appropriate victims are offered to the divi (Augustus, Livia and Claudius), though some restoration of the record is necessary. In the Forum Augustum, Mars Ultor and the Genius of Nero both receive a bull.[57]

2. AD 59, September 11: Sacrifices for the Welfare and Return of Nero

In the Capitoline temple the usual, single, victims are offered to the members of the Capitoline Triad pro [salute et r]editu Neronis. Salus and the Genius Ipsius receive their sacrifices in the Forum Augustum, and the Dii Penates receive a cow in front of the Domus Domitiana.[58]

3. AD 69, March 14: Vows for the Welfare and Return of Otho

As befitted the occasion (Otho's departure to confront the forces of Vitellius[59]) vota were undertaken pro s[al]ute et reditu, promising single victims to the members of the Capitoline Triad, Salus P(ublica) P(opuli) R(omani) and the three divi. The location is not mentioned, perhaps because no sacrifices were performed. The name of Otho was shortly to be replaced by that of Vitellius which itself was to be partially erased.[60]

4. AD 89, January 29: Vows Fulfilled and Renewed for the Welfare and Return of Domitian

There is a startling contrast between the terseness[61] of the record of these acts, performed at the height of the war against the Marcomanni and Quadi, compared with the record of the vota of January 3, 87.[62] Even the emperor's titles are kept to a minimum. The recipients, in Capitolio ad vota solvenda et nuncupanda pro salute et re[ditu], are simply listed, all but one without epithets, and without even the performed or promised sacrifices being specified: Iovi, Iunoni, Minervae, Marti, Saluti, Fortunae, Victoriae Reduci, [Genio po]puli Romani; Salus being now moved to fifth place.[63]

J. For the Welfare and Arrival in Rome of the Emperor

1. AD 63 (date uncertain): Sacrifices for the Arrival of Nero

Three days before the ides of March, April or May of AD 63, Salus Publica probably received an offering (in the Capitoline temple) for the arrival back in Rome of Nero, Poppaea and Claudia: [...pu]blicae vaccam is extant after the names of the Capitoline Triad. According to the fragment, the list of recipients continued with another deity (whose name does not survive), Spes, the Genius of Nero, Poppaea Augusta and Claudia Augusta.[64]

2. AD 69 (date unknown): Sacrifices or Vows for the Welfare and Arrival of Vitellius

Presumably in about July, the Brothers either performed sacrifices or undertook vows [pro] salute et a[dventu] into Rome of Vitellius. Despite the fragmentary state of the record, the performances, actual or promised, seem identical to those performed on the dies imperii of Vitellius, apart from the omission, presumably in error, of the victims. Only the first three letters of Saluti survive and nothing of the names of the following two deities.[65]

3. AD 118 (two occasions on unknown dates): Sacrifices for the Arrival of Hadrian

Fragments indicate that on two occasions at unknown dates in 118 sacrifices were performed ob adventum of the emperor (perhaps from Syria and Moesia respectively). The two performances seem likely to have been identical, from what little remains: Salus is certainly honoured once, after the Capitoline Triad and before Mars Ultor and Victoria (all with single victims),[66] and may have been similarly honoured at the other, somewhat earlier, event which took place in Capitolio.[67]

K. For the Welfare, Return and Victory of the Emperor

1. AD 69, March 1: Sacrifices 'Ob Lauram Positam' (Otho)

The recipients of (single) sacrifices (performed in the Capitoline temple) in celebration of an unnamed victory (perhaps that against the Roxolani in Moesia) were: the members of the Capitoline Triad, Salus (no epithet), Mars, and the Genius Ipsius. Otho himself was now magister.[68]

2. AD 101, March 25: Vows for the Welfare, Return and Victory of Trajan

The occasion for the lengthiest surviving report is the opening of Trajan's first Dacian campaign, and vows only are undertaken (in Capitolio) pro salute et reditu et victoria of the emperor. The vow, promising a gilded ox to Jupiter Optimus Maximus, is an extended and modified version of the form of vow known to us from the January 3 vota of 91 and before.[69] After it come the individual, and almost identical (apart from the victims), invocations to the other deities, shortened by their reference to the invocation to Jupiter.

Salus, addressed, uniquely, as Salus Rei Pub(licae) P(opuli) R(omani) Quiritium, comes fifth after the Capitoline Triad and Jove Victor, and before Mars Pater, Mars Victor, Victoria, Fortuna Redux, Vesta Mater, Neptune Pater and Hercules Victor.[70]

3. AD 213, October 6: For the Welfare and German Victory of Caracalla and Julia Domna

A substantially extant record attests sacrifices in Capitolio ante cellam Iunonis Reg(inae) ob salute[m] victoriamque Germanicam of Caracalla and Julia (Domna) Augusta.[71] Salus Publica, following the Capitoline Triad, receives (as do all the goddesses) a b(ovem) f(eminam) a(uratam). She is followed by Mars Ultor, Jupiter Victor, Victoria, the Lares Militares (receiving a white bull),[72] Fortuna Redux, the Genius imp. Antonini Aug. n(ostri) (a white bull), and Juno Juliae Piae (with the rest of Domna's titles).

L. For The Entry of The Emperor (Caracalla) into Winter Quarters: 214 (late in the year, at Nicomedia, in the course of Caracalla's Parthian War)

This fragment attests a remarkable development. Sacrifices certainly, and perhaps vows, are performed [quod domi]nus n. imp. .. salv[us...]...felicissime ad [h]iberna Nicomediae ing[ressus sit].[73] After the Capitoline Triad, whose names have to be restored, comes Saluti imp. Antonini (who receives a b(ovem) f(eminam) a(uratam)) after whom come Fortuna Dux and a deity whose name is missing, then perhaps the [Lari V]iali[74] (a gilded bull), followed by the Genius Antonini Aug. (a gilded bull) and Juno Juliae Aug(ustae).

The only possible precedent in the Arval records for Salus Augusti or its equivalent is the doubtful Salus Eius, referring to Nero.[75] We may note, though, the record (of May 20, 213) of the ritual meal forming part of the annual festival of the Dea Dia. The record includes, in direct speech, the words of an otherwise unique (in the Arval records) acclamation of the emperor: <u>...te salvo et victore felicissime! o nos felices qui te imp. videmus!...te salvo salvi et securi sumus! ..., d(i) t(e) servant in perpetuo! (etc.).</u>[76]

Furthermore, in the record of a meeting on August 11, Caracalla is referred to as <u>dominus n(oster) imp. sanctissimus.</u>[77]

The personalized form of Salus Augusti appears only once on the central imperial coin issues, a few years later, as the SALUS ANTONINI AUG of the issues of Elagabalus.[78]

Concluding Remarks

The incidence of invocations to Salus seems broadly to correspond to the varying degree of survival of the Arval records as a whole. The records manifest no distinction in terms of cult-practice between Salus (and the other 'virtues') and deities such as Juno and Minerva. For the Arvals she is a divine force of great importance, invoked always with, and usually immediately after, the Capitoline Triad, and sometimes alone with the Triad. She is invoked on the most significant imperial occasions (indeed, of the 'virtues', she is the most frequently invoked). I have noted Henzen's explanation of the curious absence of cult-acts in Salus' own state temple.[79]

Usually she is 'Salus Publica' or one of the more expansive versions of the same idea; sometimes she is simply 'Salus'. Once, under Nero, she may be 'Salus Eius', and under Domitian she becomes 'Salus Augusta Publica Populi Romani Quiritium', the implications of which development I have discussed.[80] Under Caracalla she is once 'Salus Imperatoris Antonini', but in 231, in the latest record relating to Salus, she is Salus Publica.

The records convey the impression in their wide variations in the degree of enthusiasm and fullness shown that they may sometimes reflect the changing attitudes of the Brothers, and therefore perhaps of sections within the senatorial class, towards the reigning emperor. Conversely, and perhaps more significantly, there seems good reason to suppose that at other times the form of the records, and therefore perhaps that of the acts they represent, may reflect the prevailing ideology of the emperor's circle as expressed in public religious practice. This certainly seems to be strongly indicated by developments under Domitian.

NOTES

1a. Eg. Gordon, pl. 69a: photograph of squeeze of CIL, VI, 2074, tab. i, lines 34-52 (March 25, AD 101: below K.2).

1. H. Bloch, OCD^2, 447 ('Fratres Arvales'); Liebeschuetz, 62-63; Scullard, 30. At present it is uncertain how the worship of deities other than the Dea Dia came to be included in the rituals of the Arvals. There is an almost total dearth of evidence from the period before 21 BC; Olshausen, 822-823, 827-828.

2. AFA, p. 94.

3. Above, 9-10 ; cf. military practice attested in the Feriale Duranum, below, 56-58 and references.

4. Below, 110-111.

5. The antecedents of these vota were those made under the Republic for the welfare of the state on Jan. 1 on the Capitol by the incoming consuls; Schwarte, 226-228; Weinstock, 217.

6. AFA, XLI-XLII, 1-15. All the fragments attesting Salus are also published in A. Pasoli, Acta Fratrum Arvalium Quae post Annum MDCCCLXXIV Reperta Sunt, Bologna, 1950, 109-171, but reference is made to AFA with its preferable presentation; cf. also CIL, VI, 2028-2108, 32352, 32363.

7. AFA, LXVI-LXVII, 13-20.

8. Ibid., LXX-LXXI, 35-47.

9. Ibid., LXXVII, 23-30.

10. Ibid., XC, 7-16.

11. Ibid., C, 1-7.

12. Ibid., CI, 1-15.

13. Ibid., CVII, 35-55; reconstructed with reference to previous and succeeding vota; cf. ibid., p. 100.

14. Above, 38, nr. 1.

15. AFA, CXIII-CXIV, 1-25.

16. Cf. the vota of 38, above, 38, nr. 1.

17. AFA, CXVI, 1-17.

18. Ibid., CXVI, 18-21.

19. Above, nr. 10.

20. AFA, CXVI-CXVIII, 22-50; cf. above, nos 8 and 9.

21. See 'vota orbis terrarum' in nr. 10.

22. AFA, CXXIX-CXXX, 1-23.

23. Ibid., CXIV-CXV, 35-47; CXVIII, 70-CXIX, 12; CXXII, 26-30; CXXVI, 35-43.

24. Ibid., CXIV, 39-40.

25. Schwarte, 229-230.

26. Ibid., 231; above, nr. 10.

27. Schwarte; 229-238; above, 10.

28. Schwarte, 238-246; above, 24-25.

29. AFA., CLXXVIII-CLXXX, CLXXXIII.

30. Ibid., p. 103.

31. Ibid., CLXXXIX, 12.

32. Ibid., CLXXXV, 1-7 and note 1.

33. Ibid., CCXI, 1-7.

34. For the *dies imperii* and the oath of allegiance, especially as developed under Trajan, above, 10, and Schwarte, 232-238.

35. AFA, XCI, 35-39.

36. Ibid., XCIV, 84-88.

37. Ibid., CX, 27-32.

38. Ibid., XCII, 46-54; pp. 105-106.

39. Ibid., CX-CXI, 39-50; p. 105.

40. Ibid., LVII-LVIII, 1-29.

41. Ibid., LXXIV, 10-16. This is one of the two most likely occasions for the dedication of the Mainz Jupiter column, *pro salute Neronis*, by, or on behalf of, the inhabitants of the *canabae* at Moguntiacum, and perhaps depicting Salus among its reliefs (the other most likely occasion being that of the thanksgiving following the failure of the Pisonian conspiracy in AD 65); Instinsky, 1959, 131-139; below, 157 ff.

42. For Salus Publica and Providentia Aug., cf. the Corinth dedication, below, 109-110; for Salus Augusta and Providentia Augusti, cf. the Interamna dedication, below, 100-101.

43. AFA, CLXXXVIII, 14-18; CXCII, ii, 1-5; pp. 112-113; Fears, 930; above, note 42.

44. AFA, LXI-LXII, 6-14; cf. CIL, VI, 2057.

45. Weinstock, 172-173, 213; Cassius Dio, LIX.14.7.

46. AFA, LXIV, 6-13.

47. Ibid., LXX, 15-18.

48. AFA, LXX, 29-34. Cf. nr. F.1.

49. AFA, LXX, 29-34.

50. Cf., below, I.1 and note 56.

51. AFA, LXXVI, 8-14.

52. Ibid., LXXI, 57-62.

53. AFA., LXVII, 29 has Salus Publica receiving a sacrifice on this occasion in AD 58, but the reference to Salus actually has to be completely restored, cf. CIL, VI, 2040, 29.

54. AFA, XCII, 58-62.

55. Ibid., XCIV, 81-84; p. 73.

56. For Salus and Felicitas, cf. the equites singulares dedications, below, 63-67.

57. AFA, LXXIV-LXXV, 24-32.

58. Ibid., LXXV, 33-40.

59. Tacitus, Historiae, I.80.

60. AFA, XCIII, 76-80; p. 121.

61. Perhaps a sympton of growing senatorial resentment; cf. the fulsome invocations during Trajan's Dacian war, below, K.2.

62. Above, B.11.

63. AFA, CXXII, 40-45.

64. AFA, LXXIX, 1-15.

65. Ibid., XCIV, 1-5; p. 115.

66. Ibid., CLIV-CLV, 52-58.

67. Ibid., CLIII, 22-29.

68. Ibid., XCIII, 63-67.

69. Above, B.9-12.

70. AFA, CXL-CXLIII, 23-72; cf. the dedication of Splitska (Dalmatia), in honour of a victory of Caracalla, which honours a remarkably similar list of deities down to Fortuna Redux; below, 112.

71. AFA, CXCVII-CXCVIII, 22-29; p. 81.

72. For their association with Salus on the Apulum dedication, below, 73-74.

73. AFA, CC-CCI, B.1-9; cf. the comments of W.F. Snyder, FD, 151.

74. For another assocation with Salus, on the Apulum dedication, below, 73-74.

75. Above, F.1.

76. AFA, CXCVII, 16-19.

77. Ibid., CXCVII, 20.

78. Above, 26; cf. the SALUS POSTUMI AUG on issues of the Gallic empire, above, 28.

79. Above, 37.

80. Above, under B.11.

CHAPTER FOUR: THE EVIDENCE OF THE CALENDARS,
THE 'MENOLOGIA RUSTICA' AND THE 'FERIALE DURANUM'

A. The Calendars ('Fasti')

Six calendars note the festival of Salus on the nones of August. Four of these are among the forty-one surviving inscribed calendars (some of which are very fragmentary; forty from Italy, one from Sicily) and date variously from the later first century BC and from the first half of the first century AD. The painted Fasti Antiates Maiores is the oldest surviving calendar and the only one to pre-date Caesar's reform of 46 BC. The manuscript calendar of Filocalus dates from AD 354. Except for the Fasti Furii Filocali, the names of the individual fasti are those given by modern scholars.

The entries extracted are, in each case, those for August 5.

1. 'Fasti Antiates Maiores'

E[1] NON SALU[TI]

This fasti was found in 1915 in the Latin town of Antium, painted in red and black onto the white wall-plaster of a room of the so-called crypta Neroniana. It dates from the period 84 to 46 BC (thus, the month still has its republican name, Sextilis). Its nature and situation imply that its commission was due to private initiative, perhaps for a partly decorative purpose.[2]

2. 'Fasti Lateranensis'

A NO[N(AE)] SA[LUTI IN COLLE]

Three fragments of this calendar inscribed on 'Lunensian' marble were found in the course of excavations under a pavement in the Lateran Basilica, in Rome in 1933. The letters were originally picked out in colour. The sparse contents indicate a date in the second half of the first century BC. The fragments bear no indications as to the calendar's function - domestic, collegiate or public.[3]

3. 'Fasti Vallenses'

A NONAE SALUTI IN COLLE QUIRINALE SACRIFICIUM PUBLICUM

The surviving fragment of marble tablet was discovered in a private villa in Rome in the late fifteenth century, its exact provenance being unknown. Imperial festivals instituted after its original inscription, at some time after AD 7, had been added. There is a firm indication that it was the calendar of a collegium.[4]

4. 'Fasti Antiates Ministrorum Domus Augustae'

A NON(AE) NP[5] SALUTI IN COLLE

The three marble fragments were discovered in 1712 on the shore at Antium in what appears to have been a room in an imperial villa. The contents enable its inscription to be dated to the period AD 23 to 37, and the prefixed Fasti Magistrorum indicates that it was the calendar of a collegium of members of the imperial household.[6]

5. 'Fasti Amiternini'

A NON(AE) F(ASTUS)[7] SALUTI IN COLLE

The second half of this calendar, inscribed on marble tablets, was found before 1575 in the church at San Vittorino, the Sabine town of Amiternium. Its appearance and contents strongly suggest an official document on public display. Its inscription must have been later than AD 20 but was perhaps prior to 37. The relevant fragment is now lost.[8]

6. 'Fasti Furii Filocali'

(The Calendar of 354/'Fasti Philocaliani'/The Chronography of 354)[9]

D G A N(ATALIS) SALUTIS C(IRCENSES) M(ISSUS) XXIIII

This illustrated manuscript calendar with related elements, originally a codex, survives in nine, more or less partial, versions dating variously from the ninth to the seventeenth centuries.[10] The fasti and the illustrations relating to it represent one component of a much larger work comprising both religious (pagan and Christian) and secular elements. The calendar and related elements are essentially pagan with considerable astrological and astronomical elements.[11]

It is demonstrable from the fasti, and from the secular and Christian annexes, that the work was completed in or for the year 354. The dedication was to a certain Valentinus, and the work may have been presented to him on January 1, 354, perhaps as a present from its creator, Dionysius Furius Filocalus, a master calligrapher of Rome.[12] It has been suggested that copies may have been put on public sale.[13]

While it is assumed that Filocalus himself was a Christian, and certainly Valentinus is commended to the Christian god, the fasti itself contains no Christian elements.

The formulae expressing the cult observances differ from those of the earlier inscribed and painted calendars due to the now predominant place of ludi and circus-races in public religious expression.[14] It is thought that the calendar is an example of a genre common in Rome at this time.[15]

We already know from Cicero that August 5 was known in the first century BC as the foundation date of the Quirinal temple.[16]

Twenty-four is by far the commonest number (of circus-races) in the calendar for festivals celebrated in this way: twelve, thirty-six, thirty and forty-eight are the other specified numbers. Most of the feriae, and all of the great state ones, have ludi or circenses missus designated for them, or, where the festival lasts for several days, both.

At its most extreme, previous opinion has asserted that the festivals of the calendar were simple diversions bereft of religious significance, ceremonies neither pagan nor Christian, one could celebrate without performing sacrifices or going into temples.[17] In contrast, the analysis of H. Stern has sought to show that the calendar represents actual pagan practice at Rome under Constantius II, that the ceremonies associated with the named festivals were then being performed and that the calendar is testimony to the vigour of the traditional cults at Rome.[18] The circus-races and ludi, he argues, were the most official and solemn form a public festival could then take, and, on the basis of the evidence of Christian writers, he maintains that their religious elements, including the essential pompa from the Capitol to the Circus Maximus, were still important in 354.[19] Stern cites considerable epigraphic and literary evidence which suggests that the laws passed from 341 onwards intended to repress paganism were being ignored, at least at Rome. Indeed Constantius himself may have respected the pagan religion during his visit to the city of 357 when the privileges of the priesthoods were left intact. The situation is perhaps partly a reflection of a conciliatory attitude towards the pagan party following the defeat of Magnentius in 353.[20]

B. The 'Menologia Rustica'

> mensis August(us) ... sacrum Spei, Saluti, Deanae, Volcanalia
> (Menologium Colotianum)

(sic) mes(is) Aug(ustus) ... sacrum Spei, Saluti, Deanae, Volcano
(Menologium Vallense)

These two documents, called menologia by modern scholars, were found in Rome. The former (found near the Palatine in the seventeenth century) is inscribed on the four sides of a marble block (0.664 m in height). The latter was perhaps originally of the same form, but survived as a sixteenth century manuscript copy. They are almost identical in arrangement and in the information they provide. Their contents enable them to be dated to the period AD 36 to 121. They purport to be agricultural almanacks, but may have been primarily ornamental. All the major festivals of the official calendar of that period are alluded to and there is no indication here of any particularly agricultural function for Salus. Apart from Spes, Fors Fortuna is the only other of the 'virtues' featured.[21]

C. The 'Feriale Duranum'

The Feriale Duranum was found, among other archives of the cohors XX Palmyrenorum, in a room (W.13; serving as the unit's office) of the Temple of Azzanathkona, in the course of the 1931-1932 season of excavations at Dura-Europos.[22] The papyrus (23 cm in height and, perhaps originally, 120 cm in length) once bore four columns (of which much of the first two and a part of the third remain) comprising a list of festivals written in Latin in rustic capitals. It had been considerably worn in use and repaired.

The document's contents enable it to be dated with certainty to the reign of Severus Alexander and to be tentatively confined further to the years 225 to 227.[23] It is apparent, from the contents of the document and its find-circumstances, that it is an official military document, that it is a copy of the feriale applicable to all the armies of the empire and that it is based upon the traditional Roman calendar of religious observances. It is possible that the original decision to provide such a list for the army was taken during the reign of Augustus.[24]

The list chiefly comprises festivals from the official civil calendar. Cults not of Roman origin, even if accepted into the official pantheon, are excluded. The past achievements of Roman armies are celebrated. An important category of observances concerns the anniversaries of the present ruling house and the cult of the divi and divae. Another concerns the deities upon which the survival of the state depended - Salus, Vesta and Urbs Roma. There are festivals, such as the Quinquatrus and the Saturnalia, thought to be included chiefly because they were important periods of merrymaking in civilian life.

The last category perhaps indicates one of the chief purposes for the military feriale: the need to provide an official list of days when, the contigencies of military life permitting, soldiers could enjoy relaxation and abstention from normal activities.[25]

The evidence of the document itself and awareness of the general religious and civil policy of Augustus prompts the conclusion that it was Augustus, as commander-in-chief of the army, who issued the first directive providing the military feriale which, essentially, remained the basis of that in use in the third century. (This is not to assume that the original reasons for its institution were the same as those for its retention until the third century.) Apart from a few additions the only regular changes necessary would be those relating to imperial anniversaries and to the observances connected with the divi and divae. However, these regular changes would have meant regular review of the document, which in turn implies that, far from being purely a survival in army practice maintained for tradition's sake, there was a constantly reaffirmed policy decision to keep the feriale in the form essentially as established, probably, by Augustus.[26]

The most problematic aspect of the document concerns its possible function as a medium of Romanization,[27] especially as regards the army itself. It seems unlikely that there would have been any obligation upon the ordinary soldier to involve himself in the actual observances. Rather, it may have been the case, that, apart from providing him with holidays, the <u>feriae</u> listed in the <u>Feriale</u> (selected as appropriate for the army) gave him the opportunity to participate in the festivals as any Roman citizen would have had in civilian life, but this would have been as a private, even if corporate, cult-observance: for it seems unlikely that there was any <u>religious</u> necessity for the army to duplicate the cult-observances of the official state calendar which took place at Rome.[28]

Once it had been decided to regularize, by a permanent directive for the whole army, that which during the Republic must have been provided for <u>ad hoc</u> by commanders, then certain other purposes of central government could be served: the encouragement of an understanding and acceptance of Roman culture and attitudes and the upholding and inculcation of traditional Roman religion.[29]

Column I, lines 7-9:-

[VII ·idus] Ianu[arias quod detur emeritis honesta missio cum privi]legio[rum] vel nume[re]n[t]ur [militibus stipendia I(ovi) O(ptimo) M(aximo), b(ovem) m(arem), Iunoni b(ovem) f(eminam), Minervae] b(ovem) f(eminam), [Salu]ti b(ovem) f(eminam), Marti Patri t[aurum ---- ---- ----

The reading and restoration, though plausible, are uncertain.[30] The entry must have been an important one, as it was one of the three longest in the <u>Feriale</u>. It is apparent from the <u>diplomata</u> and other evidence that January 7 (or 6) is a likely date for the granting of the honourable discharge to time-expired soldiers. It also seems likely that, even before the occurrence of the <u>honesta missio</u> became regularized on January 7, perhaps under Septimius Severus, the date already had significance for the soldiers in that the first of the four yearly payments, <u>stipendia</u>, was made to them and, for those not eligible for discharge, in that the occasion marked the recording of another year's service. January 7 was, in any case, also the anniversary of Augustus' assumption of the <u>imperium</u> and, whether for this or for other reasons, the evidence suggests that this date held a further particular significance for the army.[31]

Salus' position here, following the Capitoline Triad, is exactly analogous to her almost invariable position in the acts of the Arvals with Mars, where he is included, usually following. The sacrifice too is a usual one. The Arval evidence and Salus' commemoration in the <u>Feriale</u> on August 5 (below) leaves no doubt that Salus Publica was intended here.[32]

There are sufficient gaps in the entries for January 3, on the occasion of the <u>vota</u> "for the welfare of the emperor and the eternity of the empire of the Roman people", and for March 13, Alexander's <u>dies imperii</u>, to allow the restoration of Salus' name on these occasions.[33]

Column II, line 25:-

> [nonis Augustis] o[b circenses Sa]lutares Salut[i b(ovem)] f(eminam)

To support the restoration, there is, in II.9, <u>ob circenses Ma[rtiales]</u>. The date, the anniversary of the foundation of the Quirinal temple,[34] as well as the character of the <u>Feriale</u> generally, strongly indicate that Salus Publica is intended here.[35]

It is unlikely that the circus-races would have taken place at Dura, but rather the entry refers to races held at Rome in the Circus Maximus. Thus, <u>circenses Salutares</u> may have come to indicate the festival itself and not, except in Rome, primarily, the mode of its celebration. The races in honour of Salus are otherwise only mentioned in the calendar of Filocalus. The word <u>circenses</u> may have come to be used, rather than <u>ludi,</u> in order to indicate the importance of the celebration, <u>ludi circenses</u> having by now come to be regarded as much greater occasions than the more numerous <u>ludi scaenici</u>.[36]

The appearance of Salus (Publica) is consistent with the impression, gained from the rest of the extant <u>Feriale,</u> of a restrained and restraining attitude on behalf of the central authority towards the imperial cult as practised by the army. The tone is that of the Principate and of Augustus' supposed original directive with the emphasis still upon the eternity of the empire, and away from the person of the emperor.[37]

D. Conclusion

The <u>fasti</u> and the <u>Feriale Duranum</u> confirm the testimony of Cicero that August 5 was the foundation date of the Quirinal temple. The five early <u>fasti</u>, and particularly the <u>Fasti Vallenses</u> (with the <u>menologia rustica</u> providing less specific, but possibly later, confirmation), tell us that, certainly at some time previously, and perhaps contemporaneously with the calendars, annual public sacrifices took place in Salus' temple on the Quirinal Hill (assuming, for the period after Claudius, that the temple, burnt down in this reign, had been rebuilt[38]). Only the <u>Fasti Amiternini</u> (with the relevant fragment now missing) seems to have been an official public calendar: the others being calendars for, respectively, collegiate and private use. The records of the Arvals and the <u>Feriale Duranum</u>, however, provide confirmation of the importance of the state cult of Salus, the latter specifically for the festival on August 5. From the former we know that sacrifices to Salus Publica were still taking place in 231 (on January 3), whilst the <u>Feriale</u>, dating from exactly this time (though probably based upon an Augustan original), shows that for the army too, Salus Publica was important - she being honoured, after the Capitoline Triad, on the significant date of January 7. The <u>Feriale</u> also shows that the festival of the <u>natalis</u> of Salus was by now, and perhaps that it had been for some time (as is perhaps indicated by the fact of the <u>circenses Salutares</u> apparently having become synonymous with the festival itself), celebrated by <u>ludi circenses</u>. The <u>Feriale</u> also confirms the impression, conveyed by the Arval records, that Salus was honoured in exactly the same way as the other state deities: in the

Feriale she receives a bovem feminam,[39] as do Juno and Minerva, and, like Mars Pater Ultor, ludi circenses are held in her honour (at Rome).

The question of a Romanizing function for the Feriale, which might include the inculcation of an awareness of the religious requirements for the state's survival, has been the subject of much debate.[40]

The fasti of Filocalus, though not itself an official publication, may indicate the continued observance, in some form, of the cult of Salus to the middle of the fourth century, at least at Rome. However, the legislation of Constantius II intended to suppress pagan rites must make the reality behind the calendar of 354 uncertain. However, even if the circus-races were taking place at that time, it is uncertain that their former religious aspects would have been retained. On the other hand, the arguments of H. Stern and the circumstantial evidence he cites to the contrary are compelling.

NOTES

1. The <u>nundinal</u> letter (referring to the Roman eight day week and of uncertain significance) is <u>A</u> on the other five <u>fasti</u>.

2. <u>II</u>, XIII, ii, pp. 1-28 and <u>tab</u>. I-III; Michels, ix and 23-26.

3. <u>II</u>, XIII, ii, p. 101 and <u>tab</u>. XXX.

4. <u>Ibid</u>., pp. 146-152 and <u>tab</u>. L-LI.

5. The <u>Fasti Amiternini</u> and <u>Fasti Maffeiani</u> give the religious character as <u>F</u>. Tiberius may have changed the character of the day: on the other hand the negligent execution of this calendar suggests a stone-cutter's mistake; <u>ibid</u>., pp. 211, 492; Michels, 177-178.

6. <u>II</u>, XIII, ii, pp. 201-212 and <u>tab</u>. LXIV-LXVI.

7. Above, note 5.

8. <u>II</u>, XIII, ii, pp. 185-200, 492 and <u>tab</u>. LXI-LXIII.

9. Stern, <u>passim</u>; <u>II</u>, XIII, ii, pp. 237-262.

10. Stern, 14-41.

11. <u>II</u>, XIII, ii, p. 237; Stern, 356-357. The three columns of letters to the left of the list of days refer, from right to left, to the <u>nundinae</u>, the planetary week and the lunary cycle; Stern, 55-57; Michels, 89 167, 192.

12. <u>II</u>, XIII, ii, p. 237; Stern, 357.

13. A.S. Hoey, <u>FD</u>, 36.

14. Stern, 91; for a stage in the process by which this came about, cf. the <u>Feriale Duranum</u>, below, and A.S. Hoey, <u>FD</u>, 201.

15. <u>II</u>, XIII, ii, p. 237.

16. Above, 3.

17. Cited by Stern, 8, 94-96.

18. Stern, 10, 91, 96, 98, 106-107, 109, 355: "<u>les fastes du calendrier ne sont ni un pieux souvenir ni un document révisé sur l'ordre des empereurs chrétiens. Ils mentionnent bien des fêtes réelles et représentent l'actualité du culte païen romain au milieu du ive siècle</u>" (109); cf. <u>II</u>, XIII, ii, p. 237.

19. Stern, 90-92.

20. Ibid., 103-104, 111-113; cf. Liebeschuetz, 299-301: "continuous and systematic government-supported suppression of paganism only came in the last decade of the fourth century. Until then, the imperial administration was, most of the time, over most of the empire, neutral between the old and new religion" (300).

21. II, ii, pp. 284-298 and tab. LXXXI-LXXXVI.

22. Dura V, (P. Dura, 54), 191; R.O. Fink, FD, 11 and plates I and II; R.O. Fink, Roman Military Records on Papyrus, Philological Monographs of the American Philological Association, 26, Case Western Reserve University, 1971, 422-429, nr. 117.

23. Dura V, 191.

24. Ibid., 192-196.

25. Ibid., 193-197.

26. Ibid., 194-195.

27. For a summary of views with references, ibid., 193-197.

28. Ibid., 193, 195-196.

29. Ibid., 195-197.

30. Ibid., 197-199, 202-205; R.O. Fink, FD., 40-41, 66-73.

31. Dura V, 203-205.

32. Chap. 3, passim, especially 46-47.

33. Dura V., 197, 202, 207; cf. R.O. Fink, FD, 56, 58-59.

34. Above, 3, 53-54.

35. Dura V, 210; W.F. Snyder, FD, 150-152; the Arvals sacrificed to S. Publica in 231; above, 42.

36. Dura V, 208; A.S. Hoey, FD, 127; W.F. Snyder, FD, 150, note 678; above, 55.

37. Dura V, 210; A.S. Hoey, FD, 177-179; the one item in contrast to this general tone is dominus noster in II.16.

38. Above, 3, 37.

39. In accordance with her sex; in the Arval acts she receives this (sometimes gilded or white) or a vaccam (cf. Arnobius, Adversus Nationes, VII.19); Chap. 3, passim; and cf. the dedication of Pinquentum, below, 106; for the rite, above, 40.

40. See note 27.

CHAPTER FIVE: THE MILITARY DEDICATIONS,
I: THE DEDICATIONS OF THE 'EQUITES SINGULARES AUGUSTI'

A.   Introduction

A distinctive group of military dedications was erected by members of a distinctive unit within the army and calls for a collective treatment. The equites singulares Augusti, the imperial mounted bodyguard, was probably formed in the last years of Domitian. In peace time it was stationed in a permanent barracks within the city. Its members, most of them originating from the Danubian and Rhineland provinces, were mostly selected from the alae, and included both those already possessing citizenship and those who were to gain it on discharge.[1]

Salus is among the twenty deities honoured regularly in the dedications of these men found, for the most part, on or near the site of their pre-Severan barracks on the Caelian Hill. Within this remarkable body of dedications, dating overall from the period AD 118 to 250,[2] there is a strikingly formalized group, essentially numbering fourteen, dating from the years AD 118 to 143,[3] all of which are altars celebrating the receipt of the honourable discharge and, apart from three of a distinctive type,[4] represent the fulfilment of vows. Of these altars all except one[5] are corporate dedications by several or many men, and all but the distinctive three are dedicated to not less than nine specifically named deities (whether singular or plural names); Salus is honoured on all of this group of (eleven) multiple dedications.[6]

Salus is also included in two other dedications, on marble cippi, which share some of the essential characteristics of the eleven: however, they represent the fulfilment of vows of individuals and do not celebrate the honourable discharge.[7]

All the Salus dedications were found, with others, in the years 1885 to 1892 in the course of extensive rebuilding on the Caelian Hill.[8]

They and others can be assigned, with varying degrees of certainty, to the camp of the equites singulares, which was itself partially uncovered near St John's in Lateran, though its identity was not at first apparent. This was the unit's first and pre-Severan camp.[9] The remains of the barracks consisted principally of a large rectangular court in the walls of which were niches and, in front of these, inscribed pedestals. According to A.E. Gordon four of the dedications including Salus were found in situ in the ruins of the barracks.[10] Thus, it seems quite possible that the whole series was originally erected within the barracks.

B. The 'Honesta Missio' Altars

All of the honesta missio altars which include Salus bear consular dates, and those of AD 128, 137, 138 and 141 also bear a calendar date which is January 6 except that of 141 which is January 5. The dedications are all of different years and, with the exception of the first, are closely grouped together in time: 31128,[11] AD 118; 31139, AD 128; 31140, AD 132; 31141, AD 133; 31142, AD 134; 31143, AD 135; 31144, AD 136; 31145, AD 137; 31146, AD 138; 31148, AD 140; and 31149, AD 141.

All but one (31139) of these are corporate dedications, and all but the first name the men.

The inscriptions borne by these marble altars are either finely or very finely executed and, in most cases, symmetrically arranged: the altars' heights range from 70 to 112 centimetres; their widths (as known) from 32 to 55 centimetres; and their depths (as known) from 24 to 45 centimetres.[12]

1. CIL, VI, 31139

On the front:-

        voto suscepto sacr. Iovi Optimo Max. Soli Divino Marti
        Mercur. Herculi Apollin. Silvan. et dis omnibus et
        Genio imp. Hadriani Aug. et Genio singularium M.
(sic)   Ulpius Tertius cives Tribocus Cl. Ara missus honest.
(Jan. 6) mission. ex numer. eq. sing. Aug. VIII id. Ianuar.
(AD 128) Asprenate II et Libone cos. vot. solvit libens merito

On the front are carved a ewer, a bucranium and a patera.

On the back:-

      voto suscepto sacr. Iun. Victoriae Fortun. Felicitati
      Minervae Campestrib. Fatis Salut. et omnibus deabus et
      Genio imp. Hadriani Aug. et Genio singular. M. Ulpius
(sic) Tertius cives Tribocus Cl. Ara missus honest. mission.
      ex numero eq. sing. Aug. VIII id. Ian. Asprenate II et
      Libone cos. votum solvit libens mer.

On the left side of the altar is carved a figure of Jupiter holding a spear and thunderbolt: on the right is carved a figure of Mars armed with a spear and round shield. Both texts state the man's citizenship of the Tribocii of Germania Superior, whereas his origo is the Colonia Claudia Ara Augusta Agrippinensium (Cologne), perhaps indicating his Roman citizenship prior to enlistment. It is possible that January 6 or 7 was already the established date for the discharge of men from the unit.[13]

This dedication, the only one of the eleven by an individual, is exceptional in arrangement and composition. Notably, it is divided into two partly complementary, partly parallel, halves, for the purpose of listing the male and female deities separately. However, both lists are completed by the Genius of the emperor and that of the unit. The inclusion of the former is unique among the dedications in question.[14]

Among the highly formalized <u>honesta missio</u> dedications, Sol Divinus only occurs here.[15] The exceptional position of the Campestres, before, instead of after, the Fata and Salus, may reflect the known importance of these deities to men of the unit.[16]

2. <u>CIL</u>, VI, 31138

(AD 118)
<u>Iovi Optimo Maximo Iunoni Minervae Herculi Fortunae Felicitati Saluti Fatis Genio sing. Aug. emeriti ex numero eod. HOMC missi honesta missione ab imp. Traiano Hadriano Aug. ipso II cos. l. l. m. v. s.</u>

Above the dedication are carved a <u>secespita</u> and a <u>lituus</u>. On the left side of the altar is carved a ewer: on the right a <u>patera</u>. In my third line, <u>HO</u> replaces an erasure, presumably as a correction. H. Dessau thought that <u>HOMC</u> replaced <u>em</u>, which would complete <u>eodem</u> which is never abbreviated in the rest of the series.[17] C. Hülsen (<u>CIL</u>) accepts only <u>HO</u> as being in the <u>litura</u> and expands <u>HOMC</u> as <u>hom(ines) c(entum)</u>; M.P. Speidel, by implication, accepts this.[18]

3. <u>CIL</u>, VI, 31140-31146, 31148, 31149

The nine dedications, though not uniform in content or arrangement, are so similar as to be treatable collectively. They bear consecutive dates from AD 132 to 141 with the exception of AD 139. 31146 has all the possible components, so it is useful to take this as a model with which to compare the others:-

(sic)

(AD 138)
(AD 111)
<u>I. O. M. Iunoni Minervae Marti Victoriae Herculi Fortunae Mercurio Felicitati Fatis Saluti Campestribus Silvano Apollini Dianae Ephonae Matribus Sulevis et Genio singularium Augusti ceterisque dis immortalibus veterani missi honesta missione ex eodem numero ab imp. Traiano Hadriano Aug. p. p. Camerino et Nigro cos. idus Ianuarias qui militare coeperunt Pisone et Bolano cos. l. l. m. v. s.</u>

On the right side of the altar are inscribed the names of six veterans, four of which are accompanied by a rank, and all of which are accompanied by one of two <u>origines</u>: two are from Colonia Ulpia Oescus (Lower Moesia), and four are from Colonia Flavia Sirmium (Lower Pannonia).

Though the nineteen deities or deity-groups do not include all those honoured by the unit, these are all those named on the <u>honesta missione</u> monuments under discussion. Four others have the full complement, the four that do not being those of the years AD 133-136, respectively.[19] From these Hercules and Fortuna are missing, whilst the last two are also without the Matres and Suleviae. Hercules, though, was clearly popular with the unit, but perhaps especially from the late second century.[20] M.P. Speidel regards him here as one of the Roman state deities represented in these dedications,[21] along with the Capitoline Triad, Mars, Victoria, Fortuna, Felicitas, Salus, and, probably, Mercury and the Fata.[22]

The order of the deities is flexible only to a very limited extent. Mars always follows the Capitoline Triad, and Victoria always follows Mars. Hercules, when present, always follows Victoria, Fortuna is always present with Hercules and follows him.[23] Mercury,[24] always present, follows Victoria except on the four occasions when Hercules and Fortuna intervene. After Mercury there always comes the inseparable triad Felicitas, Salus[25] and the Fata: in this order, apart from the two occasions when the Fata precede Salus.

The identity of the Fata is problematic here. They are either the last of Roman state deities or they mark, as Speidel suggests, the watershed between these and the rest - both those special to the unit and those deriving from the recruiting areas. It is possible that the Fata too owe their presence to a recruiting area influence, their veneration being attested in the Rhineland.[26]

In all nine dedications Felicitas, Salus and the Fata are followed by the Campestres, Silvanus, Apollo, Diana and Epona, always in this order, and, except for in 31143 and 31144 (AD 135, 136), these are followed by the Matres and the Suleviae. Epona and the Campestres, Celtic in origin, now "naturalised" Roman deities, had a special significance for the <u>equites singulares</u> as mounted troops. Of the nearly forty dedications honouring the Campestres (who presided over the <u>campus</u>), eighteen were erected by members of this unit.[27] Epona presided over the welfare of horses and was adopted widely by horsemen and others in the army, from Britain and Spain to the Danube and Dacia.[28]

A. von Domaszewski's identification of Silvanus, Apolla and Diana as native deities of the unit's recruiting areas in Roman guise is accepted by Speidel, with Silvanus representing the native deity of Illyricum, and Apollo and Diana as deities of the west Thracians and the neighbouring people of Moesia and Dacia.[29]

The Matres and Suleviae are now taken here to represent distinct deity-groups, both Celtic and both common in the unit's Rhineland recruiting area: the Matres (or Matronae), often with distinguishing epithets, were worshipped in Lower Germany and Britain,[30] whilst the Suleviae occur, again with a variety of forms of address, in Britain, Switzerland, and both Germanies.[31]

The list of named deities in all nine dedications closes with the <u>Genius singularium Augusti</u>, in, according to M. Durry, the place of honour.[32] A development in the last four (of AD 137, 138, 140 and 141)[33] is the final addition of <u>ceterisque dis immortalibus</u>, echoing perhaps the <u>et dis omnibus...et omnibus deabus</u> of Ulpius Tertius' dedication of 128.[34]

In all the dedications there occurs after the deity-list <u>veterani missi honesta missione ex eodem numero</u>, which is followed by <u>ab</u> and the name of the emperor, that either of Hadrian or of Antoninus Pius. All the altars except one bear a list of names of the <u>missi</u> on one or both sides: 31148 has only three names included in the text. <u>Origines</u> rarely accompany the names,[35] but there are indications of rank (all below that of decurion) accompanying some of the names on the altars from 31141 (AD 133) onwards.

All the dedications except one employ the abbreviated formula <u>l(aeti) l(ibentes) m(erito) v(ota) s(olverunt)</u>, either before or after the date of discharge: 31148 has instead <u>voto solverunt animo libenti</u>.

All provide the date of discharge whilst four give a calendar date for this also.[36] The date or dates designating the groups of <u>missi</u> by their year of enlistment are given either in the texts or with the lists of names.

From AD 135 (31143) the formula <u>qui militare coeperunt</u> is always used, and after this year there is only one discharge-group annually, whereas there had been two in AD 132, 133, and 135.[37]

C. <u>The Dedications of M. Ulpius Festus and P. Aelius Lucius</u>

These two dedications, inscribed on marble <u>cippi</u>, are in several respects similar to the eleven already discussed, but they do not celebrate the <u>honesta missio</u>. Both are by senior officers and fulfil vows of an unspecified nature.

1. <u>CIL</u> VI, 31174

(<u>sic</u>)
<u>I. O. M. Iunoni Minervae Marti Victoriae Hercul.</u>
<u>Mercurio Felicitati Saluti Fatis Campestribus Silvano</u>
<u>Apollini Deanae Eponae Matribus Sulevis et Genio sing.</u>
<u>Aug. M. Ulpius Festus s. dec. prin. eq. sing. Aug.</u>
<u>v. s. l. m.</u>

A ewer is carved on one side of the altar and a <u>patera</u> on the other. In contrast to the situation with regard to the previous group of dedications, Fortuna is missing but Hercules is not. Otherwise the deity-list is identical to that of the previous group prior to the introduction of <u>ceterisque dis immortalibus</u> in AD 137 (31145). M. Ulpius Festus, <u>dec(urio) prin(ceps)</u>, has been tentatively identified with Ulpius Festus, one of the eight decurions of the <u>equites singulares Augusti</u> who erected an inscription at Gerasa, probably in the winter of either 132 or 133.[38] The analogy of Aelius Lucius' dedication perhaps indicates that here too a vow is being fulfilled on receipt of promotion.

2. CIL, VI, 31175

(sic) I. O. M. Iunoni Minervae Marti Victoriae Herculi Fortunae Mercurio Felicitati Salutis Fatis Campestribus Silvano Apollini Dianae Eponae Matribus Sulevis ceterisque dis immortalibus Genio numeri eq. sing. Aug. P. Aelius Lucius (centurio) leg. VII Geminae v. s. l. l. m.

The s ending Salutis has been erased. The deity-list includes all those represented in the group of nine, in the established order, except that ceterisque dis immortalibus now precedes the Genius of the unit who here, uniquely, has numeri in his title. P. Aelius Lucius is presumably celebrating his promotion to the centurionate of legio VII Gemina.[39] The dedication is presumably of a similar date to that of the nine.

D. Conclusion

The deities honoured in the dedications, discussed above, erected by members of this unique unit of the army can be usefully divided, on the suggestion of Speidel, into three categories:[40] Roman state deities, deities special to the unit as mounted men and native deities deriving - some in Roman guise - from the recruitment areas of the unit. Salus, as manifestly belonging to the first category, is, as has been observed, here to be interpreted as Salus Publica.[41]

Salus and the other state deities are readily understandable here as a manifestation of loyalty and perhaps also of a desire, otherwise widely attested on the part of soldiers, to placate the chief deities of the locality. The effect of a process of Romanization may also be indicated.[42]

Three of the dedications are by individuals, one highly idiosyncratic, celebrating the honesta missio, the other two perhaps celebrating promotions. The remaining ten are the result of vows fulfilled by men on the point of discharge from the unit. Their votive character, the fact of their not being on behalf of the unit as a body, the absence of any involvement by commanding officers, the selection of deities involved and the ambivalence of the provenance (the barracks) all indicate personal, even if corporate, acts of piety. However, the notably formalized nature of the dedications, their increasing sophistication, size, fineness of execution and the regularity (after AD 132) of their erection (all giving the impression of a developing institution) combine with their probable siting inside the barracks, to imply a measure of official cognizance and acceptance.

NOTES

1. Speidel, 1965, 16-21, 64-67, 88-89, 91.

2. Speidel, 1965, 98-105.

3. CIL, VI, 31138-31151.

4. Ibid., 31147, 31150, 31151; Speidel, 1965, 10-11, 78.

5. CIL, VI, 31139.

6. Thus: CIL, VI, 31138-31146, 31148, 31149. See, for example, Gordon, pl. 83b: photograph of squeeze of CIL, VI, 31140.

7. Ibid., 31174, 31175.

8. Ibid., 31178-31187; in and between the Via Tasso and the Via Emanuele Filiberto, just north-west of the Scala Santa; Platner-Ashby, 406; C. Hülsen, CIL, VI, p. 3057 (1902); R. Lanciani, The Ruins and Excavations of Ancient Rome, London 1897, 338.

9. For the Severan castra nova, Speidel, 1965, 14-15, 88-89, Lanciani, op. cit., 338.

10. Gordon, 188-190, 192.

11. Henceforth, the unaccompanied numbers refer to CIL, VI.

12. CIL, VI, 31138-31146, 31148, 31149; Gordon, 188-190, 192.

13. Above, 57; Dura V, 203-205.

14. Cf. the probably official honesta missio dedications, CIL, VI, 31147, 31150, 31151; Speidel, 10-11, 78.

15. Otherwise: CIL, VI, 31171 (Sol); 715; 31181 (Sol Invictus).

16. Below, 65.

17. ILS, 2180.

18. Speidel, 1965, 7.

19. CIL, VI, 31141-31146.

20. Birley, 1953, 98; CIL, VI, 224, 226, 227, 273, 31150, 31158, 31162, 31171.

21. Domaszewski, 46-50, identified Hercules with the Germanic Donar and regarded him as the special deity of the unit, his absence with that of Fortuna, and twice with her and the definitely Germanic Suleviae, being, he thought, significant; cf. Speidel, 1965, 70, note. 422; Birley, 1978, 1527-1528.

22. For the inclusion here of Mars, Victoria, Hercules, Fortuna and Salus, purely as state deities, Speidel makes a telling comparison with the deities honoured by the Arvals and those included in the Feriale Duranum; Speidel, 1965, 69-70; above, 47; Dura V, 197-201; cf. the Splitska dedication, below, 112.

23. See note 21.

24. Mercury is not now thought likely to be the Germanic Wodan as suggested by Domaszewski, 47; Speidel, 1965, 70, note 423; Birley, 1978, 1527-1528.

25. For Salus with Felicitas in the Arval acts, above, 42, 44-45.

26. Speidel, 1965, 71; on the Fata, Fatae and Parcae, Palmer, 90-91, 108-114, 164-165, 168-169, 171.

27. Birley, 1978, 1529; Speidel, 1965, 55-57, 72.

28. Speidel, 1965, 73-74.

29. Domaszewski, 53; Speidel, 72-73; Birley, 1978, 1527-1528; but, for Silvanus, cf. Mócsy, 250-2, who disagrees.

30. Speidel, 1965, 72; Birley, 1978, 1526-1527; Birley, Deities, 49-51.

31. Speidel, 1965, 71-72; Birley, 1978, 1528; Birley, Deities, 53; cf. Domaszewski, 47-48.

32. M. Durry, Les cohortes prétoriennes, Paris, 1938, 30.

33. CIL, VI, 31145, 31146, 31148, 31149.

34. Ibid., 31139, where it precedes the genius.

35. Apart from those of CIL, VI, 31139 and 31146, above, 63-64, 31140 has the names of four from the territory of the Colonia Traiana Baetasiorum in Lower Germany and one from Col. Flavia Sirmium in Lower Pannonia; 3144 has M. Ulpius Saturninus 'Raetus'; whilst among indications in the cognomina P. Aelius Vangio of 31149 indicates the Vangiones of Upper Germany. For the unit as a whole, Speidel, 1965, 16-21.

36. CIL, VI, 31139, 31145, 31146, 31149; above, 63-64.

37. CIL, VI, 31140, 31141, 31143; Speidel, 1965, 7.

38. G.L. Cheesman, JRS, IV (1914), 15-16; Speidel, 1965, 36, 102.

39. For similar promotions, Speidel, 1965, 48; Birley, 1978, 1513, note 24; 1530.

40. Speidel, 1965, 75.

41. Speidel, 1965, 69; A.S. Hoey, FD, 151-152; cf. Domaszewski, 43, 47, who suggested, on the basis of these dedications, that Salus and Felicitas were exclusively worshipped in the army by the peregrine troops of the auxilia, for whom they took the place of Honos and Virtus as worshipped by the citizen-troops of the legions. Some of the equites were Roman citizens before enrolment; Speidel, 1965, 64-67.

42. Perhaps, in particular, as a result of the observances listed in the military feriale; Dura V, 193-197; above, 56-57.

CHAPTER SIX: THE MILITARY DEDICATIONS,
II: DEDICATIONS OTHER THAN THOSE OF THE 'EQUITES SINGULARES AUGUSTI'

A. Introduction

In this and the next chapter the details provided concerning the find-circumstances, form, dimensions and state of preservation of each inscription will not be entirely uniform. Beyond certain basic information (where known), this will chiefly reflect a selection of what appears to be, or potentially to be, significant. Sometimes, though, this will reflect inadequate information concerning the inscriptions due either to its complete unavailability or, in a few cases, because either the original or a definitive publication has not been obtainable (this will be obvious from the references). With regard to the discussion of content, this will, necessarily, reflect a considerable degree of selection with regard to the issues and associations involved.

Unless it is stated otherwise, inscriptions may be assumed not to have been found, or known to have been found, in situ.

Though not direct evidence for cult-practice, the evidence for the ship or ships called 'Salus' in the imperial navy is included here (Section H). The dedication of the temple of Aesculapius and Salus at Lambaesis, built by legio III Augusta, is included in Chapter Seven.

B. Salus as Equivalent to Hygieia

Salus-Hygieia is implied in these dedications by virtue of, among other indications, her association with Aesculapius.[1]

I. Dedications by 'Medici'

1. Obernburg, West Germany; NEMANINGA, GERMANIA SUPERIOR

I. O. M.	Apollini et Aes	culapio Saluti	Fortunae
sacr.	pro salute L. Pe	troni Florentini	praef. coh.
IIII	Aq. eq. c. R. M. Ru	brius Zosimus	medicus
coh(ortis) s(upra) s(cripta)		domu Ostia	
v. s. l. l. m.			

An imposing, though now damaged, sandstone altar with carefully executed lettering was found in or before 1776 near the fort. In the first line I. O. M. is half-sized and thought to be a later addition. On the right side of the altar is a relief of Neptune: on the left side is, among other things, a bust thought to represent Fortuna. The

71

circumstantial evidence of the known history of the fort and of the cohort provides only a broad indication of date, c. AD 85 to c. 250 (though the cohort is securely attested there in AD 162).[2] (See below.)

2. Rome

Asclepio et	Saluti	commilitonum	Sex. Titus
(sic) Alexander	medicus cho. V Pr(aetoria)	donum dedit
[imp. Domitiano]	Aug. VIII	T. Flavius Sabino cos.
(AD 82)

The purpose of this private dedication, of unrecorded form, by the medical officer (see below) of cohors V Praetoria is perhaps implicit in Salus' unique title, 'of fellow soldiers'. The spelling of Asclepio reinforces the impression that the dedicant is a Greek.[3] We know also of M. Naevius Harmodius, medicus of cohors X Praetoria and of an Artemidorus, doctor of the third Praetorian cohort, both, ultimately at least, of Greek origin.[4] (See below.)

3. Binchester, England; VINOVIA, BRITANNIA

[Aesc]ulapio	[et] Saluti
[pro salu]te alae Vet	[tonum]
c(ivium) R(omanorum) M. Aure	[lius
...]ocomas me	[dicus v. s.] l. m.

A sandstone dedication-slab, now damaged, bears a relief depicting Salus and Aesculapius standing joining hands, the latter holding a snake-wreathed staff. It represents the fulfilment of a vow for the salus of the unit, which was probably the garrison of the fort in the late second or early third century.[5]

'Medici'

It seems certain that M. Rubrius Zosimus, Sex. Titius Alexander and M. Aurelius [...]ocomas were the senior medical officers of their respective units in charge of medical staff and orderlies.[6] Zosimus and Alexander are, despite the former's home at Ostia, probably Greeks, and certainly of Greek origin. The evidence for the medici cohortium suggests that they were fully-trained doctors before enlistment, usually Greeks, and that they joined the army for short-service commissions attracted by the privileges they enjoyed, officer status (perhaps that of an equestrian officer) and the unparalleled experience to be gained. They would return to important positions in civilian life. They were probably granted Roman citizenship on enlistment, if they did not already possess it.[7]

All three dedications respresent private acts, Obernburg and Binchester being in fulfilment of vows, and the former being presumably erected following the recovery from illness of the cohort commander.[8] Its original recipient deities including, at least, the whole "divine ministry of health"[9] (Apollo, Aesculapius and Salus-Hygieia) as well as Fortuna.

Among comparable dedications is that of Ulpius Julianus, medicus of cohors III Aquitanorum, for the salus of that unit, at Osterburken (AD 198).[10] Martius Marcellus at Aquincum, medicus, perhaps of legio II Adiutrix, made a dedication to Aesculapius and Hygieia.[11] M. Ulpius Honoratus, a decurion of the equites singulares Augusti, fulfilled a vow by setting up an altar "to Aesculapius and Hygieia for the salus of himself, his family, and of L. Julius Helix, medicus, who has ... looked after me".[12] A metrical Greek dedication of the late second century from the legionary praetorium at Chester by Antiochus, a doctor, perhaps attached to legio XX, and obviously well-educated, honoured "the saviours of men, pre-eminent among the immortals, Asclepios of healing hand, Hygieia, Panaceia".[13]

II. The Ammān and Apulum Dedications

1. Ammān, Jordan; PHILADELPHEIA (RABBATAMANA, etc), ARABIA

[Salu]ti et Aescul	[api]o sanctissimis	[d]eis
Terentius	Heraclitus b(eneficiarius)	Claudi
Capito	lini pro inco	lumitate do	m[us] divinae
R[...	...] S[...]SSOI[...	...]SOQVEB[...	...]
votum sol	vit.

Parts of the dedication are borne on both the capital and base as well as on the die of this limestone altar found in 1904 south of the baths.[14]

The restoration of [Salu]ti cannot be entirely certain, but it is perhaps preferable to that of [Caeles]ti. The dedication would be unique in two respects: in the epithet sanctissima dea and in the precedence of Salus over Aesculapius.[15] An f may be conflated with b in the fourth line.

Claudius Capitolinus has now been identified as legatus Augusti pro praetore of Arabia in AD 245-246.[16] Terentius Heraclitus, who as one of his beneficiarii would have been a legionary principalis on secondment to his staff, is fulfilling a vow for the imperial incolumitas.

2. Cetate, Romania; APULUM, DACIA APULENSIS

	Dis Penatibus Lari	bus Militaribus Lari	Viali
(sic)	Neptuno Sa[lu]ti	Fortunae Reduci	Esculapio
	Dianae	Apollini Herculi	Spei Fa(v)ori
	P. Catius	Sabinus trib. mil.	leg. XIII G.
	v. l. s.

An alternative restoration would provide an epithet, Sa[nc]to for Neptune.[17] The remarkable selection of deities contained in this dedication set up by a legionary tribunus laticlavius (see below) in fulfilment of a vow strongly suggests that a journey has been safely completed. Aesculapius' presence suggests Salus-Hygieia, but only in the also restored Ammãn dedication does Salus, as the companion of Aesculapius, otherwise precede him.[18] In another multiple dedication from Dacia, that by the procurator at Sarmizegetusa (c. AD 250), Salus again occurs preceding Aesculapius (and next to Fortuna Redux) but certainly there not as Hygieia who occurs as such immediately after Aesculapius.[19]

If P. Catius Sabinus is correctly identified as the man who was consul for the second time in AD 216, then he should have held the military tribunate not long prior to 200 when legio XIII Gemina was stationed at Apulum.[20]

The Lares Militares and Fortuna Redux are associated with Salus in the Arval sacrifices celebrating the victory of Caracalla in AD 213, and the Lar Vialis and Fortuna Redux are combined with Salus in those of the following year marking the arrival of Caracalla and the army at Nicomedia.[21]

There are a notable number of coincidences, also, with the description by Martianus Capella of the first region of the heavens, where, among others, reside Salus, the Penates, and Lares and the Favores opertanei Nocturnasque.[22]

C. Salus Regina

Caerleon, Wales; ISCA SILURUM, BRITANNIA

Saluti Re|ginae P. Sal|lienus P. f. | Maecia
(tribu) Tha[la]|mus Had[ria]| pr(a)ef(ectus)
leg(ionis) II A[ug(ustae)]| cum fili(i)s suis
Ampeiano et Lu|ciliano d(ono) d(edit)

The now damaged oolite altar was found in 1845 in the principia of the legionary fortress: however, the phrase dono dedit and the mentioning of the prefect's sons imply an unofficial act.[23] The altar's restoration and date, c. AD 198 to 209, are established by reference to another dedication by the same officer, from outside the fortress.[24]

The dedication is especially interesting in the light of the medici dedications, because of the duties attaching to the post of praefectus legionis. The title praefectus legionis (originally a shortened form of praefectus castrorum legionis) had, by the time of Septimius Severus, replaced that of praefectus castrorum as the title of the third in command and senior professional officer of the legion, who, according to Vegetius, "was responsible for the sick soldiers and the medici, by whom they were looked after and also the expenses involved".[25]

The title Regina is unique in dedications to Salus and is more usually a title of Juno and Diana. It had great significance in Juno's cult: perhaps here it is simply an indication of Thalamus' esteem for the deity.[26] Thalamus is from the north-eastern Italian town of Hadria.

D. Salus Augusti

Bonn - Beuel, West Germany; BONNA, GERMANIA INFERIOR

```
              [I]ov[i] | Propugnatori | [Victo]riae Saluti imp.|
              [Seve]ri Alexandri Aug. et |[Iul. M]ameae Aug.
   (sic)      matri eius |[et e]xercitus M. Aureli Se|[ver]i
              Alexandri Pii Felicis |[inv]icti Augusti totiu[s]|
              [que] domus divin(a)e eius |[le]g. I M[(inervia)
              p.] f. Severiana Ale|[xa]nd[ria]na cum auxilii[s]|
              |[si]gna rebus peractis |[c]umq[ue] Titio Rufin[o]|
              [c.]v. leg. [l]egionis eiu[s] |[de]m ag[en]te sub
              Flav[io] | [Tit]ian[o legato Augusti pro praetore
              c]o(n)s(ulari) n(ostro) po|[n]enda [cur]avit VI
  (AD 231)    kal|[... Pompeia]no et Pa[e]|[ligniano] cos.
```
[27]

Fragments of this volcanic stone monument, now badly damaged, in the form of a pillar surmounted by an ornate capital, were found during building operations in 1898 on the east bank of the Rhine, opposite the legionary fortress, the site previously forming an island. Though then in an overturned state, it was thought to have been *in situ* and not enclosed in a shrine or building.

The restoration of the first line depends upon the location there of a separate fragment. In the twelfth line [pu]gna is an alternative restoration which makes use of another fragment to provide the final m for ponendam which the sense would require. Of the two possible consular dates, that provided is the one now preferred to that for AD 229.[28]

The calendar date is one six days before the kalends of a month whose name does not survive: among others June 26, the anniversary of Alexander's assumption of the *toga virilis* (and perhaps of his designation as Caesar) and April 26, the birthday of Marcus Aurelius, have been suggested.[29]

The monument, apparently commemorating a victory on the part of the army of Lower Germany, manifestly represents an official act; the legionary legate is acting under the authority of the governor of the province in the name of *legio I Minervia* and its associated auxiliary regiments. After Jupiter Propugnator (or, alternatively, I.O.M. and Mars Propugnator) and Victoria comes, essentially, Salus Augusti, ponderously expressed as "Salus of the emperor, his mother, the army of the invincible emperor and of all his *domus divina*". The usage would seem to be inconsistent with both military and civil official religious practice as attested for Alexander's reign in the *Feriale Duranum* and in the Arval records, with Salus Publica implicit in the former and specified in the latter.[30]

75

E. Salus Combined with Jupiter Dolichenus

1. Rusovce (/Oroszvar/Karlburg), Czechoslovakia;
GERULATA (?), PANNONIA SUPERIOR

> [I. O.]M. Dol[icheno]| Sal(uti) Aug.|
> ...] alae (I) Ca[nnanef(atium)]|...]
> dec(urii) dupli[carii ...

The fragment, broken on all sides, was found in situ but re-used, in the course of excavations in 1967 on or near the supposed site of the fort. It is by inference from it that the altar found in the same place, and thought to be dedicated to the same two deities by two freedmen, is restored.[31]

The known and probable movements of the ala I Cannanefatium and the history of the cult of Jupiter Dolichenus in Pannonia combine to suggest a date during the later second century or in the first third of the third century.[32]

The restoration in favour of Salus has to be uncertain as the name is otherwise very rarely abbreviated and only once in this way.[33] The civilian dedication is even less certain in respect of the dedication to Salus, though certainly that dedication is that of an aedes to Dolichenus for the salus of a third person.[34]

The previously suggested interpretation, dec(urio) dupli[carius] is problematic as these words are more likely to refer to more than one officer; a more likely interpretation might involve one or more decuriones and duplicarii perhaps combining to make a dedication.[35]

2. Corbridge, England; CORSTOPITUM, BRITANNIA

> Iovi Aeterno | Dolicheno | et Caelesti|
> Brigantiae | et Saluti | C. Iulius Ap|olinaris|
> (centurio) leg(ionis) VI iuss(u) dei

The last three lines are within a previous erasure. The left side of the altar bears the relief of a genius wearing a mural crown and pouring a libation: the right side has a cupid holding a bunch of grapes and a sickle. The altar, of buff sandstone, was found re-used in a road surface inside the base.[36]

The several factors bearing upon the date of the altar combine to indicate a date in the early third century.[37]

N. Jolliffe has suggested that an officially Romanized cult of Brigantia is to be connected with the reorganisation of the province, and in particular of the Brigantian region, during the reign of Septimius Severus and his sons and after AD 197.[38] It has further been suggested that there was a "deliberate identification of Brigantia with the person of the empress", Julia Domna, as Caelestis.[39] If Brigantia had been adopted as the guardian deity of the new colony at York, then this would have been a likely place for a centurion of legio VI to have encountered her cult: hence, perhaps, the mural crown worn by the genius.

The view that the assimilation of Caelestis-Brigantia into the Dolichene cult may have been a calculated attempt by the priests to attract men of legio VI has now been challenged by M.P. Speidel.[40]

Caelestis may represent Juno Caelestis, the Roman interpretation of the tutelary deity of Carthage (whose Punic or Libyan identity is uncertain),[41] or she may be the Dea Syria Caelestis (Atargatis) who was also equatable with Juno Regina Dolichena, the consort of Jupiter Dolichenus.[41a]

I.A. Richmond suggested that an affinity between Juno Caelestis, equatable with the Dea Syria and with Julia Domna, and Brigantia was encouraged "in loyal compliment to the Afro-Syrian dynasty of Severus and in particular to Julia Domna".[42]

Though Domna was identified with Caelestis in dedications, the idea of imperial patronage of the cults of Jupiter Dolichenus and Caelestis (before Elagabalus) has now been firmly challenged.[43]

Apolinaris' cognomen, though it may indicate his membership of the Dolichene priesthood, does not need to indicate a Graeko-oriental origin (as has been supposed), as it is a genuine Latin form.[44]

Apolinaris' perception of Salus is problematic. The Dolichene formula iussu dei may indicate an incubatio which may imply that Dolichenus was being invoked here as a healing deity.[45] In which case it is relevant to note a function of Brigantia as a water-goddess and therefore as a goddess of healing.[46] We shall notice below a similar association of Salus with water in several places in the empire,[47] and notably in parts of Spain. Perhaps Julius Apolinaris' dedication is addressed primarily to the healing aspects of these deities.[48]

F. Salus Associated with a Bath-House

Bu-Ngem (Tripolitania), Libya; GHOLAIA, AFRICA PROCONSULARIS

<table>
<tr><td></td><td>Quaesii multum quot memoriae tradere</td><td></td><td>Inveni tandem nomen et numen deae</td></tr>
<tr><td></td><td>Agens prae cunctos in has castra milites</td><td></td><td>Votis perennem quem dicare in hoc loco</td></tr>
<tr><td>5</td><td>Votum communem pro que reditu exercitus</td><td>15</td><td>Salutis igitur quan dium cultores sient</td></tr>
<tr><td></td><td>Inter priores et fu turos reddere</td><td></td><td>Qua potui sanxi nomen et cunctis dedi</td></tr>
<tr><td></td><td>Dum quaero mecum dig na divom nomina</td><td>20</td><td>Veras Salutis lymphas tantis ignibus</td></tr>
</table>

<u>In istis semper ha
renacis collibus</u>   30   <u>Aestuantis animae
                                    fucilari spiritum</u>

<u>Nutantis Austri solis
flammas fervidas</u>   <u>Noli pigere laudem
                                    voce reddere</u>

25 <u>Tranquille ut nando
delenirent corpora</u>   <u>Veram qui voluit
                                    esse te sanum tib[i]</u>

<u>Ita tu qui sentis mag</u> 35   <u>Set protestare vel
nam facti gratiam</u>   <u>Salutis gratia</u>

A stele "of hard grey limestone of marble-like quality" was found by soldiers in 1927 in the baths in the fort, with the inscription set within a moulded panel.[49] The third century lapidary capitals are consistent with the period from the date of the fort's establishment in AD 201[50] to that of the erasure in 238 of the name of <u>legio III Augusta</u> from the inscription borne by the matching stele found in the same place: <u>centurio [leg. III Aug.] faciendum curavit</u>.[51]

The poem seems to be commemorating the establishment of a shrine of Salus related to the baths. The acrostic utilizing the initial letters of the odd-numbered lines provides the name of the dedicant Q. Avidius Quintianus, who is presumably the centurion of the other stele, as is confirmed by the first four lines of the poem.

The first six lines refer to Quintianus' official religious activities "in this camp". Lines eleven to twenty-one describe the establishment of a cult of Salus who is said to be a deity worthy to be addressed in <u>vota</u> and to be called eternal (<u>perennem</u>). The place is described as "of Salus" (lines 14 to 15), which is perhaps a reference to the vital presence of a water-supply. How he "made the name sacred" is unspecified (line 17). The "<u>veras Salutis lymphas</u>" which Quintianus "gave to so many" presumably refers to the bath-house or to its water-supply. Lines twenty-one to twenty-six refer to the relief to be anticipated in the bath-house[52] from the rigours of the desert. From line twenty-seven onwards the address is to the user of the baths. The confused message seems to be that the beneficiaries are urged to proclaim their gratitude to Salus.

The poor Latin, many mistakes and tortured style render several lines intractable (especially: 7, 8, 29, 30). The implication is clearly that of Salus as a health-goddess. Equally clear is the association, attested elsewhere, of Salus with water-sources.[53]

G. <u>Salus and a Genius (?)</u>

<u>Theilenhofen, Bavaria, West Germany; ICINIACUM (?), RAETIA</u>

<u>Sa[luti ...</u> | <u>et Ge[nio ...</u> | <u>sig[...]</u>
<u>pr[...</u> | <u>s[...</u>

Two fragments of a limestone base or altar were found in 1893 in

the course of excavations in the south wing of the fort's principia
(and thus near the aedes principiorum).[54] For the first line
sa[ncto] or sa[crum] are alternative restorations. The third line
could contain sig[(norum)]. At present the period from Hadrian to c.
AD 260 has to be allowed for the fort's occupation.[55]

H. Epitaphs of Sailors of the Misene Fleet

Five epitaphs of sailors of the classis Misenensis attest a ship,
or successive ships, called 'Salus'. One example will suffice:-[56]

D. M.	L. Terentio Sabin[o]	III Salute
mil(es) cl(assis)	praet(oriae) Misen(ensis)	
nat(ione)	Pannonio Aelius	Romanus h(eres)
b(ene) m(erenti) f(ecit)		

III Salute stands for triere Salute, thus: "belonging to the
trireme 'Salus'". In this case the gentilicium, Aelius, may indicate a
date during or after the reign of Hadrian. Otherwise the stones bear
no intrinsic indication of date, though all must post-date the
formation of the Misene fleet by Augustus shortly after 27 BC.[57] It
seems likely, though, that ships' names would be perpetuated as
individual ships went out of service. Of the eighty-five, at least,
attested ships' names, in Latin (of both praetorian fleets), about half
are those of deities, including most of the great state deities. The
deified 'virtues' are well represented.[58]

The deity after which a ship was named might or might not be the
same as the ship's tutelary deity, whose image was displayed on the
poop-deck.[59]

I. Conclusion

As the associate of Aesculapius, Salus is a deity of health,
certainly in the dedications of the medical officers (see discussion
above) and perhaps in both that of the beneficiarius at Amman and the
remarkable multiple dedication of the legionary tribune at Apulum.[60]
She is a deity associated with health and water in the centurion's poem
at Bu-Ngem, and there is the possibility of a connection with health at
both Caerleon and Corbridge.

Salus Augusti is honoured on the official victory monument set up
by the army of Lower Germany in AD 231. Salus Aug., in association
with Jupiter Dolichenus, may be the object of the Rusovce dedication.
The provenance of the uncertain Theilenhofen dedication may indicate an
official nature.

The Caerleon stone too is from a military principia but inherently
represents an unofficial act. Both this stone and the Rome dedication
bear the "he gave this gift" formula. The Obernburg, Binchester, Amman
and Apulum dedications are in fulfilment of vows. The Corbridge altar
is "by command of the god" (Dolichenus).

The motive for the Ammān altar is the <u>incolumitas</u> of the imperial household, whereas the stated or implicit motives for the other unofficial dedications are more parochial: the health or welfare of the dedicant (Apulum and Corbridge), that of his family (Caerleon), of his unit (Binchester, Rome), and of his commanding-officer (Obernburg). The dedicants of these are all officers or N.C.O.'s, the lowest ranking being the <u>beneficiarius</u> at Ammān and the <u>duplicarii</u> (?) at Rusovce.

The dates, where usefully known (in nine cases) and apart from that of the Rome dedication (AD 82), are of either the late second or the first half of the third century.

Along with most of the great state deities, Salus had at least one ship of the imperial fleet named after her.

NOTES

1. Above, 13-14.

2. CIL, XIII, 6621; ILS, 2602; AE, 1903, 382; A.D. Conrady, ORLR, Abteil. B, III, Heidelberg, 1914, nr. 35, 24, 27 and Taf. IV, Fig. 8a-c; J. von Elbe, Roman Germany, A Guide to the Sites and Museums, Mainz, 1977, 24, 297-298; E. Espérandieu, Recueil général des bas-reliefs statues et bustes de la Germanie romaine, Paris and Brussels, 1931, 200, nr. 323; L. Hefner, in Führer zu vor- und frühgeschichtlichen Denkmälern, VIII, Mainz, 1967, 149-155; Speidel, 1978, 42, note 134; Davies, 1969, 86; Davies, 1972, 3.

3. CIL, VI, 20; ILS, 2092; Davies, 1969, 85-86.

4. Davies, 1972, 2.

5. RIB, 1028; Davies, 1969, 86; Davies, 1970, 102; P.A. Holder, The Roman Army in Britain, London, 1982, 110.

6. Below, 74, for the responsibilities of the praefectus castrorum.

7. Davies, 1969, 85-87, 91, 93; Davies, 1970, 87-88, 102; Davies, 1972, 2-7, 9-10.

8. Birley, 1953, 99; Elbe, op. cit. (note 2), 298; Davies, 1969, 86; Davies, 1972, 3.

9. Above, 13.

10. CIL, XIII, 11767.

11. CIL, XIII, 3413.

12. CIL, VI, 19.

13. JRS, LIX (1969), 235, nr. 3 (cf. RIB, 461 from the same place); Davies, 1972, 2-4; Davies suggests that medici of the kind under discussion may have had quarters in the praetorium of the fort or fortress, where they may have been permitted to set up such unofficial dedications. M. Henig has suggested that the engraved Hellenistic signet gem (of mottled chalcedony set in a bronze ring) found at Chester and depicting Hygieia (enthroned and holding her snake) may have belonged to a medicus; M. Henig, A Corpus of Roman Engraved Gemstones from British Sites, Brit. Arch. Reports, 8, Oxford, 1974, i. 91, and ii. 42, nr. 285.

14. R. Sauvignac, Revue biblique internationale, nouvelle série, II (1905), 93 (with fig.); AE, 1905, 211; ILS, 9258.

15. Though cf. Apulum, below, where the two are separated.

16. PIR², II, pp. 188-189: C.286; H.G. Pflaum, Syria, XXXIV (1957), 140.

17. AE, 1956, 204; I.I. Russu in RR, 61.

18. Above, 73.

19. Below, 112-113. Apollo is explicable enough in conjunction with Aesculapius, but, as in the dedications of the equites singulares Aug., Apollo and Diana may represent native deities of west Thrace and parts of Moesia and Dacia. Domaszewski thought this especially likely in cases where Diana preceded Apollo; above, 65; Domaszewski, 52-53; Birley, 1978, 1527, 1535, nos. 48 and 49 (by another legionary tribune).

20. PIR², II, pp. 130-131: C. 571.

21. Above, 47.

22. Above, 15.

23. RIB, 324; G.C. Boon, Isca, The Legionary Fortress at Caerleon, Monmouthshire, Cardiff, 1972, 49.

24. RIB, 326; Boon, op. cit., 49.

25. Vegetius, Epitoma Rei Militaris, II, 10; Webster, 117, 251; Davies, 1969, 8; Davies, 1972, 5-6; Davies, 1970, 86; B. Dobson, 'The Significance of the Centurion and the Primipilaris in the Roman Army and Administration', ANRW, II.1 (1974), 413-414; B. Dobson, Die Primipilares, Beihefte der bonner Jahrbücher, 37, Köln, 1978, 31, 32, 68-71.

26. Palmer, 21-29 (Juno); RIB, 1126; Birley, 1978, 1527, nr. 33.

27. CIL, XIII, 8017; AE, 1899, 7; H. Nissen, Bonner Jahrbücher, 103 (1898), 110-114; P. Hertz, Untersuchungen zum Festkalender der römischen Kaiserzeit nach datierten Weih- und Ehreninschriften, (Dissertation) Mainz, 1975, 232. My text is essentially that of CIL as modified by W.F. Snyder, FD, 141, note 618, and Hertz (as cited); cf. also G. Alföldy, ES, III, Köln, 1967, 56-57, nr. 72.

28. Hertz, op. cit. (note 27), 232; Alföldy, op. cit. (note 27), 56-57.

29. Hertz, op. cit. (note 27), 232; Snyder, op. cit. (note 27), 141, note 618.

30. Above, 57-58, 42.

31. R. Hošek, Acta of the Fifth International Congress of Greek and Latin Epigraphy, Cambridge, 1967, Oxford, 1971, 308-309 and pl. 31; AE, 1972, 446; below, 108.

32. J. Fitz, KP, II (1967), 775 ('Gerulata'); J. Fitz, RE, Suppl. IX (1962), 73 ('Gerulata'); CIL, III, 4391; AE, 1972, 442-444; A. Lengyel, G.T.B. Radan (ed.), The Archaeology of Roman Pannonia, Lexington (Kentucky) and Budapest, 1980, 221-222; Mócsy, 255-259; Speidel, 1978, 10.

33. At Marchena, Hisp. Baetica; below, 117.

34. Below, 108.

35. P.A. Holder, Studies in the Auxilia of the Roman Army from Augustus to Trajan, Brit. Arch. Reports, International Ser., 70, Oxford, 1980, 91-93, 105 and inscriptions listed in table 7.4.

36. RIB, 1131; Jolliffe, 42-43 and pl. II, facing 37; Merlat, 266-267; Richmond, 194-197; Harris, 56-57; Birley, Deities, 82 and note 426; Speidel, 1978, 35-36; Marwood, 316-328; Phillips, 17-18, nr. 51.

37. For full discussion, Marwood, 318-323, 325-327.

38. Jolliffe, 39-41, 60-61; also A.F. Norman, in R.M. Butler (ed.), Soldier and Civilian in Roman Yorkshire, Leicester, 1971, 146-147; Henig, 83, 120, 135, 210, 213, 253; cf. Phillips, 18.

39. Norman, op. cit. (note 38), 146; see also Henig, 79, 120, 210, 213; cf. Phillips, 18.

40. Speidel, 1978, 35-36; also Phillips, 18; cf. Richmond, 195 and Merlat, 266-267.

41. Summoned to Rome in 146 BC; Palmer, 28, 46-49; Marwood, 321, 324-326; cf. Phillips, 17.

41a. Marwood, 325-326.

42. Richmond, 194-195; also Henig, 210; cf. Phillips, 18.

43. Speidel, 1978, 10, 64-71; Mundle, 228-237; cf. though Henig, 79, 120, 210.

44. Speidel, 1978, 22, 46-54; Kajanto, 20, 53-55, 107; Marwood, 322 and note 22.

45. Jolliffe, 48-49.

46. Ibid., 58-59; Marwood, 328.

47. Eg. at Bu-Ngem and Brigetio; below, 77-78 and 95-96.

48. Marwood, 322, 328.

49. J.M. Reynolds, J.B. Ward Perkins (ed.), <u>The Inscriptions of Roman Tripolitania</u>, London and Rome, 1952, nr. 918; R.G. Goodchild, <u>Libyan Studies, Select Papers of the Late R.G. Goodchild</u> (ed. J.M. Reynolds), London, 1976, 48. I am most grateful to Dr. J.P. Wild for his help in translating this poem.

50. Reynolds and Ward Perkins, <u>op. cit</u>. (note 49), p. 225 and nos. 913-916.

51. <u>Ibid</u>., nr. 919.

52. <u>Ibid</u>., nr. 913, found in the baths, records their erection in 201-202 by a vexillation of <u>legio III Augusta</u>.

53. Above, 13-14 and note 91.

54. <u>CIL</u>, III, 13545; Dr. Eidam, <u>ORLR</u>, <u>Abteil</u>.B, VII, Heidelberg, 1914, nr. 71a, 15, with photograph.

55. <u>Ibid</u>., 11-12; H.J. Kellner, <u>Die Römer in Bayern</u>, München, 1971, 51; H. Schönberger, <u>JRS</u>, LIX (1969), 170, 176-177.

56. <u>CIL</u>, X, 3639; the others, all referring to triremes, are: <u>CIL</u>, X, 3402, 8119; <u>CIL</u>, VI, 3134, 3147.

57. C.G. Starr, <u>The Roman Imperial Navy, 31 BC to AD 324</u> (Cornell Studies in Classical Philology, XXVI), New York, 1941.

58. F. Miltner, <u>RE</u>, <u>Suppl. V</u> (1931), 952-956 ('Seewesen').

59. Starr, <u>op. cit</u>. (note 57), 54, 59, 86.

60. See the Lambaesis dedication, below 93, which could also be considered as a military dedication; also, potentially, that from Timacum Minus; below, 99.

CHAPTER SEVEN: THE EPIGRAPHIC EVIDENCE FOR THE CIVILIAN CULT
EXCLUDING THAT OF THE ARVAL BROTHERS AND THAT OF THE CALENDARS

A.   Introduction

The general remarks in the introduction to the previous chapter, regarding the discussion of individual items and the inclusion of details of the form and find-circumstances of inscriptions, also apply here.

The material here includes all the known epigraphic evidence not covered in the preceding chapters, including both that of a definitely civilian nature and that concerning which there is either uncertainty or ambiguity.

The geographical information contained in the headings indicates (where it is thought useful and where it is known), firstly the modern name of the town or village in or near which the inscription was found, followed by, in most cases, the present name of the country. After the semi-colon, and in higher-case, there is given the ancient name by which the site is usually known (where one is known), followed by the provincial name, which is either, that by which the area was known for most of the Roman period, or that obtaining at the date of the inscription where this is known.

Where thought useful, regional names, both modern and ancient, are added. In particular, in Spain and Portugal, where a relatively large number of dedications is involved, it was thought useful to indicate the conventus.

As regards the establishment and presentation of the texts, the extent of discussion of doubtful readings and alternative interpretations and restorations is determined by, on the one hand its relevance to the cult of Salus, and, on the other hand, its usefulness. Abbreviations are only sparingly and selectively expanded, either to remove ambiguity or to indicate my assumption of their likely meaning (or, where appropriate, my preferred alternative).

The eighty-four items are arranged under the following headings:-

B   The Earliest Italian Evidence

C   Salus Semonia

D   Salus as the Equivalent of Hygieia

E   Salus as Qualified by the Imperial Epithet

F Salus Publica or her Equivalent

G The 'Augurium Salutis'

H The Private Cults of Salus

I Inscriptions Attesting Cults of an Uncertain Nature

J Seals and a Graffito (or Stamp)

B. The Earliest Italian Evidence

In the absence of a firm indication of date, the Tarracina and Herculaneum altars are included here because of their similarity in wording to the Pompeii dedication and, in the light of this, because of the geographical proximity of the three towns. No useful dates have been assigned to the altars or to the Pompeii diptinti, though K. Latte regarded the Pompeii dedication (2B, below) as comparable in date to the Praeneste statue base[1] (of the mid-second century BC or earlier), though for no specified reason.

On the grounds of general probability the altars of Herculaneum and Tarracina can perhaps be tentatively regarded as of late republican or early imperial date (no later, of course, than AD 79 for the Herculaneum stone).

1. Ercolano; HERCULANEUM, CAMPANIA

Saluti | sacrum

The small marble altar was found in 1872 in the course of excavations.[2]

2. POMPEII, CAMPANIA

A. Salutis B. Salutei | sacrum

The dipinti were discovered in the course of the excavations of 1886 to 1888 on the wall of a passage-way next to Building 8 of Insula 7 in Regio IX. The first was written "negligently and almost in cursive script" in violet ink on white plaster. It was below the depiction of a wreath and above that of two cornucopiae. All were situated in a niche, which also contained, below the paintings, an altar partly embedded in the wall.

The successive layers of plaster indicate at least that the wreath and dipinto do not belong to the final period of Pompeii. The second dipinto, in violet ink and with fine letters of small but irregular size, was at the upper edge of the painted wreath but on an older plaster surface.[3]

The evidence here perhaps indicates a street shrine dedicated to Salus. We may note the archaic form of the dative in Salutei and the recurrence of the painted wreath on the Horta patera (below). We may also note the cornucopiae in the light of K. Latte's suggestion that the cult of Salus, in the form of Salus Semonia (see below), had originally been connected with a cult of crop-fertility.[4]

3. Terracina; TARRACINA, LATIUM

Saluti sacr(um)

The altar, first recorded in the eighteenth century, was found "between the inner and outer Roman Gate". It bears relief carvings of a patera, an urceus and a lituus.[5]

4. Pesaro; PISAURUM, UMBRIA

Salute

The limestone cippus, in the form of a pyramid truncated at the top, was first recorded in 1738 with twelve other similar dedications in a grove just outside the town.[6]

The cippus is one of fourteen similar cippi, thirteen of which were found close together in the grove outside Pisaurum.[7] A further seven of these similarly bear only the name of a deity using an archaic form of the dative, Salute being the equivalent here of Salutei. All of the dedications display a greater or lesser number of archaic characteristics in their orthography and letter-forms. The selection of deities honoured also suggests an early date; all are Italic deities except for Apollo, the earliest of the Greek deities introduced at Rome. The list includes Mater Matuta, Feronia, Dea Marica and the Dii Novemsedes. Furthermore, the fact that none of the minimum of four female dedicants has a praenomen, is taken by T. Mommsen to indicate an early date.[8] Given the archaic characteristics, an obvious possible date for the establishment of the sacred area would be at, or just after, the foundation of the Roman citizen colony at Pisaurum in 184 BC.[9] However, those cippi bearing the names of the deities alone, which are regarded as being the products of the same stone-cutter, are thought to display somewhat earlier characteristics than the other six.

Moreover, it has been suggested that there may have been an earlier settlement, a conciliabulum civium Romanorum, at Pisaurum, prior to 184 BC and subsequent to the subjugation of the Senones in 283 BC (perhaps in the period 232 to 184 BC).[10]

Thus, a date around the time of, or previous to, the Hannibalic war has been suggested for the earlier group of dedications.[11] The archaic letter-forms were in use over a long period and so are not, in themselves, indicative of an exact date.

Two of the dedications were by individual matronae, one being named, the other calling herself matrona Pisaure(n)se(s) (though alternatively restorable as matronae Pisaure(n)se(s)).[12] This fact and both the fact that the female deities honoured greatly outnumber the male and, likewise, that the certainly female dedicants predominate over the maximum (depending on the restorations) of two male dedicants, prompted Mommsen to suggest that here had been the sacrarium matronarum Pisaurensium: an idea not endorsed by A. Degrassi.[13]

5. Orte; HORTA, ETRURIA

Salutes pocolom

The words, within three concentric circles and an olive-wreath border, are painted, along with the figure of a cupid, in the style of 'Gnathia Ware' on a bowl or patera of black glazed fabric of fair quality.[14]

Both the letter-forms and the spelling of the words display archaic characteristics, in particular the forms of the letters A, L and P. Salutes is an archaic form of the genetive Salutis.[15] Moreover, the fabric of the pottery and the style of its decoration combine to indicate a date in the third century BC, which is variously estimated as early, middle and late. The more recent assessments favour an early date. However, for another patera of the same type A. Degrassi allows the possibility of a fourth century date.[16]

The fabric and decoration of the patera as well as its inscription place it within a ceramic group of bowls and other vessels (twenty-one vessels in all) of a similar or identical fabric and decoration, of which sixteen bear a painted inscription comprising the name of a deity in the genetive (with one exception) followed by pocolo(m).[17]

The find-locations of these sixteen, where known (all except two), are, with one exception, in central Italy with eleven in Etruria. Another two, including that from Rome, are from Latium. Three are from Horta. Our specimen is most closely paralleled in decoration by the Rome patera dedicated either Me[nervai] or Me[rcuri].[18]

The similarity in the fabric of the group and the uniform nature of the inscriptions are taken to indicate a single centre of production: Etruria, Latium, Campania, Tarentum and Rome have all been suggested as possible centres.[19] 'Gnathia Ware', to which, in both fabric and ornament, the group is related, whilst originally a product of Apulia, had production centres in many parts of Italy by the middle of the third century.[20] The inspiration for the pocula may well have been provided by Greek antecedants, in the same ware and inscribed with the names of Greek deities, which were manufactured in southern Italy and were probably familiar to the potters of central Italy.[21] The Latin inscriptions and the selection of deities honoured have been taken to indicate manufacture in Rome, and circumstantial and other indirect evidence would favour a Roman pottery at least as convincingly as a centre elsewhere. J.D. Beazley considers them to be definitely of Latin manufacture, "but quite possibly by Tarentine settlers".[22]

The other names inscribed on the vessels are: Coera and Lavernai, at Horta; Aecetiai, Junonenes and Keri, at Vulci; Menervai, Veneres and Volcani, at Tarquinii; Aisclapi, at Clusium; Vestai, at Lanuvium; Venere[s], at Caere; Fortunai, at somewhere in Calabria; and Belolai and Saeturni, at unknown provenances.[23] After making allowances for the idiosyncratic and archaic spellings, only three of these deities are not known in Roman religion of the third century: 'Coera' (perhaps to be construed as Cura), 'Aecetia' (perhaps as Aequitia or Aequitas) and 'Kerus' (perhaps as Cerus).[24] Although seven of the sixteen vessels are recorded as having the depiction of a figure as part of their decoration, this is usually Cupid, and on none of them is the figure thought to represent the deity concerned in the inscription.[25]

The intended purpose of the pocula is not certain, both a funereal purpose and one relating to shrines (the Lanuvium example was found near a temple) have been suggested. G.C. Picard has suggested a use at banquets where the named deities would have been those invoked.[26]

6. Palestrina, Italy; PRAENESTE, LATIUM

L. Gemenio(s) L. f. Pelt[.] | Hercole dono | dat
lub(ens) mer(i)to | pro sed sue(is)q(ue) e(is)de(m)
leigibus | ara(e) Salutus

The dedication is one of three tufa cippi found in 1882 "under Praeneste, on the Roman side, between the Via Praenestina and the turning to Labici".

The cippus is in the form of a truncated and elongated pyramid with the inscription confined to the uppermost third of one of the sides; the upper surface indicates that it once bore a statue.[27]

In the fourth line idem has been alternatively construed for ede, and in the fifth line on the one hand ara Salutus, and on the other hand (dedicata est/dedit) ara(m) Salutus, are alternative interpretations. Idem would refer to Gemenios and, with this construction, would require dedit or a similar verb to govern ara(m), but, as R.E.A. Palmer has noted, this would imply an unexpectedly close association between Salus and Hercules.[28] The genitive ara(e) would be consistent with leigibus, but if the ablative, ara, is preferred then it could be dependent on e(is)de(m), thus meaning "with the same rules as at the altar of Salus" instead of "with the same rules as of the altar of Salus". Palmer rejects the interpretation meaning that the "same person" gave, or dedicated, an altar merely "according to the rules". There are parallels for the genitival form in -us as in Salutus.[29]

Although some of the forms in the dedication may represent dialectical traits or reflect the influence of spoken Latin, some are genuinely archaic.[30] E. Pulgram refers to the stone as of mid-second century BC date, while A. Degrassi has assigned it to the third century.[31]

The text attests a body of sacral law which governed the practice of a cult of Salus at an unspecified place. Furthermore, the cult was thus well-enough known and respected for its canon to be adopted for the cults of other and unrelated deities, moreover without even a designation as to place. It had been assumed that a local cult and altar of Salus were implied: however, Palmer has suggested that the altar referred to may have been that of the Quirinal temple of Salus at Rome.[32]

The canon of Salus mentioned in the dedication would, despite the uncertainties as to its precise date, be the earliest attested such canon with the possible exception of the 'Alban lex' adopted for a cult at Bovillae.[33]

C. *Salus Semonia*

Rome

(AD 1)

> Mercurio | Aeterno deo I[ovi] | [I]unoni Regin(ae) Min[ervae] | [So]li Lunae Apol[lini] | [Dia]nae Fortuna[e Matri?] | [Mag?]nae Opi Isi Pi[etati?] | [Mart?]i Fatiis D[ivinis?] | [quod bo]num [faustum] | [feli]xque [siet] | imp(eratori) Caesari Augus[to Tutelae?] | eius senati populi[que Romani] | et gentibus nono [anno?] | introeunte felic[iter] | C. Caesare L. Pau[llo cos.] | L. Lucretius L. l(ibertus) Zethus | iussu Iovis aram Augustam | Salus Semonia posuit populi Victoria

The marble tablet, now incomplete and in three fragments, was found in 1890 on the left bank of the Tiber near to the Via de Monte Brianzo.[34] *Mercurio*, in the first line, and *Salus Semonia* and *populi Victoria*, in the last line, are by a different hand or by two different hands and were clearly added at a later date or dates. Mercurius, important in the Augustan pantheon, may have been added before the death of Augustus. However, palaeographically, the additions need be close in time neither to the original dedication nor to each other.[35]

It has been suggested that the freedman, L. Lucretius Zethus, who was responsible for the original dedication of this 'Augustan altar', may have been one of the *vicomagistri* among whose responsibilities was the preservation of local cults.[36]

It may be that the additions represent a further three deities whom at some stage it was desired to add to the deity-list of the dedication, though *Salus Semonia* and *populi Victoria* are in the nominative case.

The inclusion here of Salus represents the earliest evidence, and the only epigraphic evidence, attesting this epithet for her. Later, the epithet is attested, though ostensibly with reference to an earlier period, in Macrobius (c. AD 400. *Apud veteres quoque qui nominasset Salutem Semoniam Seiam Segetiam Tutilinam ferias observabat.*), and an association is implied in Festus (late second century, epitomizing Verrius Flaccus of the Augustan period).[37] The connection, though, may indeed be an ancient one, and it may indicate two ancient functions of Salus: one being connected with the overseeing of sowing ("granting welfare in the sphere of sowing"[38]), the other as a deity in whose name oaths were taken.

Modern scholars have generally accepted that both *Semonia* in this context and the deities called the *Semunis* (plural) in the archaic

'Hymn of the Arvals'[39] (for which name there may be a parallel in an inscription of the first century BC from Corfinium in the Paelignian dialect: sacaracrix Senunu[40]) are connected with the function of sowing (Seia, Segetia and Tutilina preside over other aspects of the life of the semina.).[41]

Indeed K. Latte has suggested that the Dea Dia, the patron deity of the Arvals, may represent a personalization of one of the Semones.[42] Another such personalization may be represented in Semo Sancus who emerges in historical times with the certain function of guaranteeing oaths and perhaps treaties and is usually conflated with Dius Fidius who was certainly also a god of oaths. After much debate there remains uncertainty as to the original significance and development of the cult, or cults, of Semo Sancus Dius Fidius and, in particular, as to whether or not there were originally two separate entities.[43]

Thus, the epithet Semonia may indicate an archaic relationship between Salus and Semo Sancus,[44] and it may then be that Salus derived from this connection a function of overseeing oaths. S. Weinstock has speculated that there may have been an early oath in the form per tuam salutem (which may not at first have implied the goddess) by analogy with the attested oath per tuam fidem.[45] As we have already noticed, we know from Cassius Dio that in 44 BC a public oath was introduced by the hygieia of Julius Caesar.[46] Weinstock also suggested that Salus Semonia may have originated in archaic times as a female version of Semo Sancus in a development analogous to that postulated of Fides out of Dius Fidius.[47]

Circumstantial indications of this postulated relationship between Semo Sancus and Salus have been seen in the geographical proximity of their respective temples on the Quirinal Hill: on the Collis Mucialis and Collis Salutaris, respectively.[48]

Whatever its origin, the word sancus appears to be connected with the Latin sancire, and, moreover, near to the temple of Semo Sancus Dius Fidius was the Porta Sanqualis (which name embodies the word sancus) which was one gate along from the Porta Salutaris.[49]

A Sabine origin for the deity, and in particular for the name Sancus is indicated by the evidence of the ancient authors. Though that of Varro may be suspect as he had an interest vested in this theory of a Sabine origin, as he believed the Quirinal to have been the site of a Sabine settlement in pre-historical times. Hence, perhaps, derives his assertion of a Sabine origin for Salus.[50]

Propertius' assertion of an identification of Semo Sancus Dius Fidius with Hercules may be incorrect, but an association with Jupiter, and in with particular in respect of Jupiter's function in overseeing the taking of oaths, seems certain (this seems to apply particularly to Dius Fidius), though it is not yet clear whether this was as an entity absorbed by Jupiter or as a specialized aspect of him which became separate.[51] It has also been suggested as a possibility that a deity of sowing had been absorbed by Jupiter.[52]

The name Dius Fidius resembles that of the archaic Umbrian patron-deity of Iguvium ('Fisius Sansios', 'Fisouios Sansios', or 'Fisovius Sancius') as attested in the bronze tablets found there describing the procedure of the purification of the town.[53] The Quirinal temple of Semo Sancus Dius Fidius, though only officially dedicated in 466 BC, was, traditionally, founded by the last Tarquinius, and it came to house several important items from Rome's past including the ancient treaty with Gabii and a deposit of talismanic bronze rings in which has been recognized a possible parallel to the ring or disk held by the officiating priest in the ritual at Iguvium.[54]

It is also from the Quirinal Hill that one of the five known dedications to Semo Sancus Dius Fidius derives.[55] This and two other dedications, one from an uncertain find-spot in Rome, the other from, and attesting a cult-centre on, the Tiber Island, are all on behalf of a priesthood called the decuria sacerdotum bidentalium.[56] The bidentales were priests whose function was the carrying out of the appropriate sacrifice (of a two years old sheep) at the places (bidentales) where a lightning-bolt had struck the ground. Herein lies a further connection with Jupiter, for this college of priests was, evidently, closely associated with the cult of Semo Sancus Dius Fidius, and, among the attributes which at least the Dius Fidius aspect of the deity shared with Jupiter was the ability to hurl lightning-bolts.[57]

Finally, we may note H.H. Scullard's remark that the cult of Semo "thus long continued in Rome and may have been more important in public life than its minor character suggests".[58] As G. Wissowa wrote, though an ancient cult-connection between Salus and Semo Sancus Dius Fidius seems certain, the evidence is too sparse to allow us to perceive with certainty the meaning of this connection.[59]

D. Salus as the Equivalent of Hygieia

In nine of these inscriptions Salus is the companion of Aesculapius. At Brigetio Salus as Hygieia is firmly indicated despite the absence of Aesculapius. The identity of Salus in the second text from Pergamum, attesting a priesthood of Roma and Salus, remains uncertain. Her identity as Salus-Hygieia in the Tibur monument to Mens Bona and Salus seems likely.

K. Latte assumed that the ministra Salutis attested at Preturo (Section I, nr. 2) related to Salus-Hygieia.[60] G. Wissowa regarded Salus as Hygieia where Salus is addressed, though alone, as a deity of health as she seems to have been in parts of Spain and probably at Baden bei Wien.[61] However, it seems more useful to include these dedications in the section concerned with the private cults of Salus (Section H: I, nr. 4 and II, nos. 1-19; compare also Section E: I, nr. 2 and III, nos. 9 and 10.). The imperial dedication of the Lambaesis temple of Aesculapius of Salus (below) could be regarded as essentially military, and the dedication at Timacum Minus is quite likely to have been that of a soldier or an ex-soldier.

1 and 2. <u>Lambèse, Algeria; LAMBAESIS, NUMIDIA</u>

1. <u>Iovi Valenti | Aesculapio et Saluti | Silvano | imp. Caes. M. Aurelius Antoninus Aug. pont. max. et | imp. Caes. L. Aurelius Verus Augustus | has aedes | per leg. III Aug. fecerunt</u>

The three large inscribed blocks, forming part of a curving frieze, were found before or in 1847 in and near the three principal sanctuaries of the temple of Aesculapius, near the Capitol in the civilian quarter of Lambaesis.

Together with two supplementary dedications they form the unified dedication of the principal sanctuary (of Aesculapius and Salus) and of the two adjacent sanctuaries, of Jupiter Valens and Silvanus (Pegasianus) respectively.[62] The stones evidently formed part of an elevated frieze carried by a colonnade above the entrances to the original three sanctuaries to which they relate. The curving colonnade framed an elongated paved court at its western end. Early excavations in the principal sanctuary revealed a mosaic floor and the cult-statues of Aesculapius and Salus-Hygieia.[63]

The date of the dedication by the emperors Marcus Aurelius and Lucius Verus is more precisely indicated by the ancillary dedications of the sanctuaries of Jupiter Valens and Silvanus Pegasianus which name the dedicant as D. Fonteius Frontinianus L. Stertinus Rufinus <u>leg. Augustor. pr. pr. cos. desig.</u> This man was designated for the consulship in AD 162 or 163.[64] As legate of Numidia he was also the commander of <u>legio III Augusta</u> which, as we know from our dedication, built the sanctuaries.

The temple of Aesculapius became one of the town's most splendid buildings. The complex formed by the temple, the forum (with its temple of the Capitoline Triad) and the Via Septimiana evidently became an important religious centre for both the military and civilian communities of the Lambaesis area. In its final form the temple precinct included a further eight ancillary sanctuaries, added on the northern side of the elongated court and a large bath-house added on the southern side, doubtless to facilitate the water-therapy practised at the shrines of Aesculapius.[65]

Apart from that of Aurelius Decimus (below) the other dedications to the associate of Aesculapius found in and around the temple employ (in Latin) her Greek name Hygieia, the latest being one of AD 320.[66] (See further below, p. 94.)

2. <u>diis bonis numi|nibus praesenti|bus Aesculapio| et Saluti sacrum | Aurel(ius) Decimus | v(ir) p(erfectissimus) p(raeses) p(rovinciae) Numidiae| ex principe pe|regrinorum | votum solvit</u>

This limestone base, found in 1959 to the north-east of the Capitol, dates from the years AD 283 to 285 which represent the maximum possible period in office for M. Aurelius Decimus as the equestrian praeses of Numidia.[67]

Four other dedications of this man attest his application of the epithet praesens to describe his 'Deus Patrius Praesens Numen Jupiter Bazosenus'.[68] He employs the epithet dii boni in his dedication to Mars Gravidus and Victoria Sancta.[69] Praesens is used elsewhere only rarely as a divine epithet: it is known to have been applied to Caelestis, Silvanus and Fortuna, all at Rome.[70] The office of princeps peregrinorum was that of commander of the castra peregrinorum in Rome.[71] (See further below.)

3. Dougga, Tunisia; THUGGA, AFRICA PROCONSULARIS

dis Aug(ustis) sacr(um)	Genio Thug(gae)	
Aescula[pio]	Saluti Victoriae	Ti. Claudius
Abascantus	suo et sodalium nomine	s. p. f.

The altar was found in or just before 1913 "to the south of the forum".[72]

In the context of suo of the fifth line the final formula is perhaps to be expanded as s(uo) p(ecunia) f(ecit). The opening dedication may suggest that the unnamed sodalitas, on behalf of which Abascantus is partly acting, was one of those devoted, nominally at least, to the imperial cult; the opening bears some resemblance to that of the Rome dedication by the collegium salutare.[73] G.C. Picard regarded the appearance of Victoria here as indicative of a military influence.[74] The dedicant's gentilicium may indicate a date after or within the period of the reigns of Tiberius and Claudius.

Aesculapius, as worshiped in the northern parts of Proconsularis and in Numidia, had become syncretistically conflated with the Punic Eshmoun of Sidon, a process which had begun in the Phoenician homeland under Hellenistic influence.[75] It has been thought, though, that the cult at Lambaesis was of a purely military character with no connection with the native African-Punic deity. However, in the view of Picard, though the conception of Aesculapius in the minds of those dedicating the temple (the emperors and legate) would have been purely that of the Roman god of medicine, the arrangement of the temple indicates that "the syncretism had already operated at the time that the legionary legate presided at the dedication".[76] Thus, he argued, for the mass of devotees visiting the temple, there would be no distinction between their deus patrius, Aesculapius-Eshmoun, and the Roman Aesculapius. It may be that the priesthood serving the new temple would have observed the vows of the old Punic priesthoods as they apparently did at Thuburbo Maius.[77]

There is ample evidence attesting both the importance of the priesthoods of Aesculapius, from at least as early as AD 42 and continuing into the third century, in the municipal life of Roman Africa and their close relationship with the imperial cult,[78] a relationship which is perhaps indicated in the Thugga dedication.

4. Rome

	Numini domus Aug. sacrum	Aesculapio et Saluti
	Aug. collegium salutar(e)	loco adsignato ab
	proc(uratore) patr(imonii) Cae(saris) n(ostri)
	a solo	fecerunt Felix ver(na) Aspergus Regianus
(sic)	Vindex	ver(na) vilici prediorum Galbanorum et
(sic)	pleps	imm(unes) Actalis Ianuarius Ulpius Sextianus
	Cluturius Secundus

There follow five columns recording fifty-three names, of both men and women, some of which indicate servile status in the imperial household. The marble tablet in fragments was found in 1885 during road-works near the site of the ancient Mons Testaceum (the Prati di testaccio).[79]

This collegium salutare is presumably a funeral and social club, in this case for the freedmen and slaves, of both sexes, employed on part of the imperial estates, the praedia Galbana.[80] The third line indicates that the site for a new (a solo) building, which was presumably a shrine or meeting place dedicated to Aesculapius and Salus, had been assigned by the procurator of the imperial patrimonium.

J.P. Waltzing considers the dedication to be of Hadrianic date on the grounds of the lettering, the gentilicia of the freedmen and the presence of the forumula Caesaris nostri.[81]

The cult of Aesculapius and Salus is firmly associated with the imperial cult in the Aug. epithet as well as in the opening dedication to the Numen Domus Aug(ustae).[82]

We know of at least a further eighteen collegia which are either called salutaris or are dedicated to a deity with this epithet.[83] None of these are known to have been dedicated to Salus, though at Aquincum there was a collegium Salutis.[84]

5. Ó-Szöny, Hungary; BRIGETIO, PANNONIA SUPERIOR

Although Aesculapius is not included in this dedication, the dedication to Apollo and Hygieia and the association with a water-source suggests that it is Salus Hygieia who is implied in the 'fons Salutis' (lines 4 to 5).

	Apollini et Hygiae	Q. Ulpius Felix Aug(ustalis)
	m(unicipii)	Brig(etionis) porticum	a portis
	II ad fon	tem Salutis a	solo inpendi(i)s	suis
	fecit et	ad epulas privileg(io) colleg(ii)
	centon(ariorum)	haberi iussit praef(ecto)
	Iul(io) Sabino	q(uin)q(uennale) Pr(a)esente et
(AD 217)	Extric(ato) co(n)s(ulibus) noni(s) No(vembribus)

The limestone tablet, decorated with an elaborate "baroque-motif" flanking the epigraphic field, was found re-used in the late Roman cemetery near the legionary fortress in 1912. An alternative restoration of the last line would produce a calendar date of June 5.[85]

From his membership of a college of serviri Augustales at Brigetio it is evident that Felix was a freedman. The two portae of the fourth line are taken to refer to the double gates of the porta decumana of the fortress. A temple of Apollo Grannus is known to have stood at the confluence of two water-supply channels some two hundred metres south of the fortress gates, and this dedication is understood to record the addition to this temple of a portico. The portico, paid for by Felix, is described as ad fontem Salutis, which could mean "near the fountain of Salus". Alternatively, it has been taken to refer to a shrine of Fons Salutis, in which case its position would have been remarkably analogous to the shrine of Fons at Rome extra Portam Fontinalem.[86]

In the eighth and ninth lines we are told that the portico is to be used for the banquets of a collegium centonariorum (workers and dealers in cloth), of which Felix was probably a member. Elsewhere centonarii were combined in joint collegia with the fabri and dendrophori, and a collegium of the latter dedicated a schola to Salus Aug. at Heddernheim.[87]

The praefectus Julius Sabinus quinquennalis (lines 9 to 10) is almost certainly the college's president or acting-president.

6 and 7. PERGAMUM, ASIA

6. [N]ummius Primus | lictor proxum[us] | [S]ex. Non. Quinctilian[i] | pro cos, | Asclepio et Saluti | v. s. l. m.

The small votive altar of white marble was found in 1931 amongst debris in the library of the temple of Asclepius.

Sex. Nonius Quinctilianus, the proconsul of Asia, whose senior lictor Primus is, is identifiable as either the consul designate of AD 8 or the suffect consul of AD 38. The letter-forms confirm the general period.[88]

7. Tullia M. f. | Viva fecit sibi et suis | M. Tullio M. f. Cor(nelia tribus) Cratippo | fratri suo | sacerdoti Romae et Salutis | T. Aufidio T. f. Ani(ensis tribus) Balbo f. suo | tr(ibuno) mil(itum) Alexandr. ad Aegypt. | leg. XXII ann. VIIII | T. Aufidio T. f. Ani(ensis tribus) Spinteri viro suo | tr(ibuno) mil(itum) in Hispania | leg. IIII an. V

The text, now lost, was found in 1446 amongst ruins in the city and is described as inscribed on an altar (which seems inappropriate) of white marble.[89]

96

M. Tullius Cratippus is a <u>sacerdos</u> of the joint cult of Roma and Salus. A. O'Brien Moore, on the basis of the movements of the legions mentioned and on that of the date of documents thought to relate to Aufidius Balbus, has assigned Cratippus' tenure of this priesthood to the 30s or 20s BC. However, it is thought unlikely that the priesthood would have continued in this form after 29 BC in which year permission was granted for the establishment at Pergamum of a cult of Augustus and Roma, which would have displaced that of Roma and Salus.[90]

G. Wissowa suggested that Salus could be understood here as Salus Augusti.[91] However, the existence at Pergamum of one of Aesclepius' most prestigious temples and the long-established veneration of Hygieia at Pergamum makes an identification with Hygieia likely.[92] The altar of Primus confirms that Hygieia could be worshipped here under her Roman name. However, a strict distinction between Salus Augusti and Salus-Hygieia may not always be necessary. We have already noted the Greek dedication at Alabanda, in Caria, attesting a priesthood of the 'Hygieia and Soteria Αὐτοκράτορος Καίσαρος' which probably refers to Augustus.[93] Now there is a dedication from Aphrodisias in Caria, 'Υγήαν Καίσα[ρι Σεβα]στῷι, which may refer to Augustus' illness of 23 BC.[94]

However, in the light of the practice of Greek cities, of awarding to benefactors, whether outstanding individuals or Rome herself, the trappings of cult, and to individuals the title of <u>soter</u>, perhaps it is possible to regard the goddess here as Roman Salus, perhaps equivalent to Soteria rather than to Hygieia.[95]

8. <u>Pozzuoli, Italy; PUTEOLI, CAMPANIA</u>

<u>Asclepio et Saluti sacrum ex voto Callistus d.</u>

This votive offering, which may come from Puteoli and has been known since the eighteenth century, is in the form of a bronze snake with the text inscribed in ligatured letters.[96]

Another dedication by this man, to Asclepius and Hygieia, informs us that he is a <u>medicus</u>.[97] Callistus, almost certainly a Greek or of Greek origin, may be a slave or a freedman[98] or, most likely, a free Greek who immigrated to Puteoli, itself a Greek foundation, to practice medicine.

9. <u>León, Spain; LEGIO, HISPANIA TARRACONENSIS</u>

(sic)	[Ae]sculapio	Saluti	Serapi Isidi	L. Cassius
(sic)	Paullus	Augustanius Alpinus	Bellicius Sollers
et M. Cassius Agrippa	Sanctus Paullinus
Augustanius Alp(i)n[us]	[...

The white marble dedication-slab with "very good lettering" and broken at the bottom was found re-used in the walls of León in 1963.[99]

The dedicants, probably either brothers or cousins, are thought to be of senatorial rank, probably connected, as is indicated by the coincidence of names, with a family of Cisalpine Gaul.[100] A. Garcia y Bellido has suggested that the dedication is actually to one divine pair, Aesculapius and Salus, and that Serapis and Isis, respectively, have been assimilated to them.[101] Both Serapis and Isis had significant healing attributes, and their separate cults were well established in the Spanish provinces by the late second century AD, the suggested date for the dedication.[102]

10. Chester, England; DEVA, BRITANNIA

> Fortunae Reduci | [A]esculap(io) et Saluti eius|
> libert(i) et familia | [T.] P[o]mponi T. f. Gal(eria
> tribu) Mamilian[i] | Rufi Antistiani Funisulan[i]|
> Vetton[i]ani leg(ati) Aug(usti) | d(ederunt)
> d(edicaverunt)

This impressive, though now slightly damaged altar, was found in 1779 during the digging of foundations on the north side of Watergate Street near its junction with Walls Road. It was found among the ruins of two or more hypocausted rooms which are assumed to have belonged to a bath-house situated outside the legionary fortress.[103] The altar is decorated with elaborate mouldings, and there are reliefs on the sides depicting inter alia Fortuna's rudder and the snake-wreathed staff of Aesculapius. In addition sacrificial utensils are depicted on both sides.[104]

Salus is here 'Salus Eius', which form is unique in the dedications, and which, as suggested by G. Wissowa, may refer to the personal health of the legatus Augusti.[105]

The dedicants are the legate's slave household and freedmen. The form of Salus together with the inclusion of Fortuna Redux perhaps supports the suggestion that the legate had been ill, had gone away and had returned with health restored.[106]

The British evidence leaves no doubt that Fortuna had a special association with bath-houses.[107] The extra-mural bath-house at Chester may have been reserved for the troops and for the less privileged members of the community, whilst that now identified inside the fortress would, according to this view, have been for the officers.[108]

Pomponius Mamilianus leg. Aug. is certainly to be regarded as the legate of legio XX. He has been identified, with almost complete certainty, as the suffect consul of AD 100 (in preference to the suffect consul of 121). Thus, he would have held his legionary command in the early 90s.[109] However, the lettering of our dedication has been regarded as of second century date.[110]

11. Ravna, Yugoslavia; TIMACUM MINUS, MOESIA SUPERIOR

   Aesculapio et | Saluti T. Fl. Adi|...]tus[...

The dedication, inscribed on the upper part of an altar, was presumably found in or near the site of the Roman fort or its civilian settlement.[111]

It is likely, because of the nature of the civilian settlement here, that the dedicant (male and a Roman citizen), if he was not a serving member of the fort's garrison, would have been a veteran or a descendant.[112] His gentilicium, if indeed Fl(avius), indicates a date of, or later than, the Flavian period when he or an ancestor probably received the citizenship. The fort was established in or before the Flavian period and was occupied into the third century.[113]

12. Tivoli, Italy; TIBUR, LATIUM

   A. Menti Bonae Saluti | Q. Caecilius Q. l. Philadelphus|
       P. Aquillius P. l. Dacus | mag(istri) quinq(uennales)
       ex pec(unia) conl(egii) f(aciendum) c(uraverunt)|
       idemque signum dedicarunt

   B. [con]leg(ium) teibeic(inum) Ro[m(anorum)] | Menti
       Bonae Saluti

Inscription A, first recorded in about 1585, is a marble tablet on which representatives of lictors are carved in relief.[114]

Inscription B, found in about 1930 in debris next to the church of Santa Maria Maior, is a fragment of a marble base, broken on all sides and similarly ornamented with the figures of lictors in relief.[115]

A collegium teibeicinum Romanorum is also attested at Rome in another dedication by magistri quinquennales which lists ten freedmen.[116] (The flute-players were employed to play during sacrifices to obscure ill-omened noises[117]).

Philadelphus' name may indicate a Greek origin, while that of Dacus is thought to indicate a Dacian origin.[118]

The discovery of B makes the given expansion more likely than conl(ata) in the fourth line of A.

Of the other ten known certain dedications to Mens, only two are not from central Italy, and only that from Lugdunum was definitely not erected by slaves, or freedmen, or both.[119] Seven out of the total of eleven are certainly the dedications of slaves or freedmen or both,[120] and four of these and one other indicate the activity of collegia.[121] Furthermore, that from Cales indicates that the collegium's primary ostensible function was the worship of Mens Bona.

At Aquileia the dedication Bonai Menti was found in the proximity

of an altar to Bona Valetudo, and it has been suggested that the two
were associated on the grounds of indications in the literary evidence
of an association between the two deities.[122] We have already seen
that Valetudo could be regarded as the equivalent of Hygieia,[123] and
the latter was venerated at Aquileia.[124] K. Latte has doubted that the
freedmen's and slaves' cult of Bona Mens would have had much in common
with the state cult of Mens.[125] Perhaps then, in the light of the
assocation with Mens, and taking into account Philadelphus' probable
Greek origin, we may be justified in suggesting that Salus-Hygieia is
indicated in the Tibur inscriptions. Latte regards the central Italian
dedications to Mens as belonging to the imperial period. The Lugdunum
dedication dates from the Severan period, and its dedicant is a
legionary legate.[126]

E. <u>Salus as Qualified by the Imperial Epithet</u>

This section is divided into three parts: I contains the two
dedications to Salus Augusta; II contains the four dedications to Salus
Augusti or its equivalent; and III includes the thirteen inscriptions
which either definitely or possibly attest the ambiguous Salus Aug. as
well as those where the imperial epithet is present but is
insufficiently extant to distinguish its intended form.

The Lambaesis dedication is quite possibly military in origin (II,
2).

I. <u>Salus Augusta</u>

1. <u>Terni, Italy; INTERAMNA NAHARS</u>

    A. <u>Saluti Perpetuae Augustae | Libertatique Publicae |
populi Romani</u>

    B. <u>Genio municipi anno post | Interamnam conditam |
DCCIIII ad Cn. Domitium | Ahenobarbum [M. Furium] |</u>
(AD 32) <u>[Camillum Scribonianum] cos.</u>

    C. <u>Providentiae Ti. Caesaris Augusti nati ad
aeternitatem | Romani nominis sublato hoste
perniciosissimo p(opuli) R(omani) | Faustus Titius
Liberalis VIvir Aug. iter | p(ecunia) s(ua) f(aciundum)
c(uravit)</u>

This impressive marble talet, inscribed in large and fine
lettering, is the earliest dated epigraphic attestation of Salus as
qualified by an imperial epithet.[127]

The dedication is evidently a municipal commemoration of the
downfall of Sejanus in AD 31 (line C.2). The establishment of the
priesthood of Providentia Aug. and Salus Publica at Corinth may be
connected with the same episode.[128]

It is notable that whereas Salus is qualified, as she is on the dupondius of AD 22 or 23,[129] by Augusta, Providentia is followed by the genetival form and Libertas is still Publica.

The dedicant, Faustus, is almost certainly a freedman in that he is a member of a local college of seviri Augustales, and, though he is paying for the tablet himself (line C.4), he is perhaps acting in an official capacity as a member of the college. According to Cassius Dio, in addition to the setting up of a statue to Libertas in the forum at Rome, the Senate had decreed that the occasion should be commemorated by annual horse-races and wild-beast hunts to be held under the direction of the four principal state priesthoods and the Sodales Augustales. This dedication by a sevir Augustalis can then perhaps be seen as a municipal counterpart to these celebrations.[130]

2. Esteppa, Spain; OSTIPPO, CONV. ASTIGITANUS, H. BAETICA

> Saluti | Augustae | L. Sempronius L. f. | Gal(eria
> tribu) Atticus d. s. d.

The dedication, by a Roman citizen, is well-inscribed upon a marble base (found in 1730).[131] The final abbreviation is perhaps to be expanded as d(e) s(uo) d(edicavit) (or d(edit)), thus making the dedication to be on behalf of Atticus' family. The dedication, one of three similar Spanish dedications manifesting an imperial epithet for Salus, is certainly to be understood as a further example of the sixteen, at least, other dedications from Baetica and Lusitania attesting a particular local interpretation of the deity.[132]

II. Salus Augusti and its Equivalents

1. Henchir B'laiet, Tunisia; OPPIDUM TEPELTENSE, AFRICA PROCONSULARIS

> Saluti | Augusto|rum | civitas | Tepelten|sis
> d. d. | p. p.

The dedication, of unknown form, was found in the urban centre of the civitas.[133] In the sixth line, d. d. can be confidently expanded to d(ecreto) d(ecurionum), whilst in the last line p(ecunia) p(ublica) is one of several expansions which would be consistent with the public nature of the dedication. The plural epithet Augustorum indicates a date during one of the joint reigns, AD 161 to 169, 177 to 180, or 198 to 212. All are possible, as the community was still of civitas status in the reign of Gordian III.[134]

2. Lambèse, Algeria; LAMBAESIS, NUMIDIA

> Saluti d(omini) n(ostri) | imp. Caes. M. Au|reli
> Severi | Alexandri | Augusti et Iul|iae Mame|ae
> Augustae matr|i(s) Aug. n. castror. | et exercitus|
> [...

The stone, presumably an altar, and damaged at its base, was found in 1933 re-used in a wall one hundred metres north of the northern angle of the court of the temple bordering the capitol on its eastern side.[135]

Lines three to seven have been erased, presumably on the accession of Maximinus in 235, and then re-carved, though less regularly, at some time after 238. Normally we would expect the titles of Julia Mamaea to continue with et senatus et patriae. However, here the titles have been regarded as complete on the grounds of the absence of et between matri(s) Aug(usti) n(ostri) and castror(um) and its presence before exercitus. It has been suggested that this arrangement reflects an intention on the part of the dedicant to distinguish between, on the one hand, the troops and organisation of the fortress (castrorum), and, on the other hand, troops posted elsewhere in the command-area of legio III Augusta (exercitus).[136]

The elaborately expressed title of Salus is strikingly similar to that employed for her in the Bonn dedication, also of the reign of Severus Alexander, set up by the army of Lower Germany.[137]

3. OSTIA

> Saluti Caesaris August(i) | Glabrio patronus coloniae
> d(ono) d(edit) f(aciendum) c(uravit)

This impressive statue-base, comprising a block of marble on top of two steps in Travertine stone, was found in situ during the excavations of 1907 to 1910 at the side of the Via Ostiensis (the Rome road) and just outside the Porta Romana (the main gate of the town).[138]

The dedication must post-date 27 BC when Octavian became Imperator Caesar Augustus. On archaeological grounds it is certain that the monument must pre-date the rebuilding of the Porta Romana under Domitian or Trajan.[139] The lettering has not proved susceptible to a closer dating than this, though the title Caesaris August(i) would imply the reign of Augustus, Tiberius, Claudius or Nero.

The dedicant is one of the Manii Acilii Glabriones who maintained a long association with the colony.[140] Among several possible identifications, that with M. Acilius Memmius Glabrio, who was Curator of the Tiber under Tiberius, is now thought the most likely.[141] The title patronus was the highest honour that the colony could confer.[142]

The occasion for the statue's erection is thought likely to have been an imperial visit. Its form may have been that of Salus-Hygieia as depicted upon the reverses of the four denarius issues of the moneyer ancester.[143] The coin-issues refer to a tradition maintained by the gens Acilia that the family assisted in the establishment at Rome of the first professional medical practice, that of Archogathus who, having emigrated from the Peloponnese in 219 BC, was granted Roman citizenship and established by public funds in campito Acilio.[144] It has been suggested that the pose of the goddess as depicted on

Glabrio's <u>denarii</u> may have been copied from the famous statue of Hygieia by Nicertus (accompanying his statue of Asclepius) which was still standing in the temple of Concordia in the time of the elder Pliny.[145] Thus <u>Glabrio patronus</u>, in the form of his gift to the colony, may have been recalling his family's purported association with the introduction of Greek medicine to Rome.

4.   Rome

<u>Saluti domus A[ugusta / ugusti]</u> | <u>collegium thurarior[um et]</u> | <u>unguentarior(um) cura a[gente]</u> | <u>Novio Successo quaes[tore]</u>

This part of a marble tablet was found in 1911 "in the area between the continuation of the Via Giovanni Branca, the Via Benjamino Franklin and the Tiber".[146]

Salus' title is unique, though in an abbreviated way it expresses the same conception as that contained in the Bonn dedication: <u>Saluti ... domus divin(a)e eius</u>.[147]

The college, of purveyors of frankinsense (for religious rituals) (<u>thurarii</u>) and makers and sellers of perfumes and perfumed olive-oil (<u>unguentarii</u>) was, presumably, ostensibly a burial club but probably had other social functions as well. Sussessus is probably a freedman and, if not a Roman citizen, then is perhaps of Junian Latin status. His office of quaestor is common among <u>collegia</u>: perhaps he managed the finances.[148]

III.   Salus Aug.

1.   Rome

The dedication to Aesculapius and Salus Aug. has been included above (D.4).

2.   <u>Henchir ed-Duâmes, Tunisia; UCHI MAIUS, AFRICA PROCONSULARIS</u>

<u>Saluti Aug. sacrum</u> | <u>C. Pacuvius C. f. Felix suo et</u> | <u>Tulliae Primulae uxoris suae</u> | <u>[nom]ine s(ua) p(ecunia)</u> <u>fecit itemq. d(onum / ono) d(edit) dedic(avit)</u>

The dedication, of unspecified form, was found in 1891 incorporated into the town-walls fifty metres north of the mosque of Sidi Messaud.[149] It is the private dedication of a Roman citizen on his own behalf and that of this wife. From the same town there is a fragmentary dedication, <u>Aesculapio Augusto sa[crum...] ... sua pecunia fecit</u>, which may indicate an identification of Salus with Hygieia in our dedication.[150] At Lambaesis the people of Gemellae, at some time during or after the reign of Commodus, made a dedication

Hygiae Aug. sac., and there is the dedication at Rome to Aesculapius et Salus Aug.[151]

3. Djemila, Algeria; CUICUL, NUMIDIA

Saluti | Aug. | [...

The dedication is that of an alter[152] and is among many indicating a diligent observance of the imperial cult at this colonia (founded under Nerva) into the second half of the fourth century. The presence among them of those to Victoria and Concordia, both at times qualified here by Augustorum, perhaps indicates a more traditionally Roman conception of Salus rather than one of her as Salus-Hygieia.[153]

4. Heddernheim, West Germany; NIDA, GERMANIA SUPERIOR

Salu[ti] Aug. | dendrophori Aug(ustales) | consistentes Med(...) | it(em)q(ue) Nidae scolam | de suo fecerunt | loc(o) adsig(nato) a vic(anis) Nide(nsibus)

The dedication, with letters well carved and originally picked out in red, is in the form of a marble plaque. Part of the ti of Saluti is traceable on a separate fragment. Traces of rust attest the former presence of metal fittings. The editors date the stone to c. AD 150 or earlier on the basis of the letter-forms and ligatures.[154]

The plaque, overturned and broken into pieces, was discovered during excavations to the north-west of the vicus of Nida in 1961 in a small cellar assumed to be that of the schola. The coins and pottery enabled the cellar's fill to be dated to the third century and provided a terminus post quem for the destruction represented by the fill.

The collegia dendrophorum perhaps originated as, and certainly came to have the characteristics of, trade guilds, that is burial and social clubs, in this case for woodworkers. At some stage, however, they had become involved with the Cybele-Magna Mater cult. These collegia dendrophorum Matris Magnae Idaeae et Attis were regulated by a decree of the Senate, probably under Antoninus Pius, but perhaps earlier, their cult activities being henceforth under the overall supervision of the quindecemviri sacris faciundis. The epigraphic evidence attests their official character and association with the imperial cult in various ways. This plaque is one of at least four which refer to the members as dendrophori Augustales.

Apart from their activities associated with the Magna Mater cult, we know of the members' gathering to honour the dead with remembrance meals and sacrifices, for administrative purposes, and to arrange burials.[155] Their scholae could be luxuriously equipped. That at Nida was used by the dendrophori of that vicus and also by those from a nearby place whose name began with Med (line 3). The land for the schola had been designated for the purpose by the inhabitants of Nida (line 6).

The editors suggest that Salus is here concealing Sirona, a Celtic deity of healing springs, an identification which would imply a perception of Salus as Hygieia.[156]

5 - 8. Italy

5. GABII, LATIUM

> Agusiae T. f. Priscillae | sacerdoti Spei et Salutis Aug. | ex d(ecreto) d(ecurionum) Gabini statuam publice ponendam curaverunt quod post | inpensas exemplo inlustrium feminar(um) | factas ob sacerdotium etiam opus portic(us) | Spei vetustate vexatum pecunia sua refectu|ram se promiserit populo cum pro | salute principis Antonini Aug. Pii | patris patriae liberorumque eius | eximio ludorum spectaculo edito | religioni veste donata | universis satis fecerit| (sic) cuius statuae honore contenta inpensam populo remiserit| l(ocus) d(atus) d(ecreto) d(ecurionum)

The marble statue-base was found in 1792 next to the Via Praenestina. An urceus and a patera are carved, respectively, to the left and right of the text.[157]

The statue is that of the priestess of a joint municipal cult of Spes and Salus Aug. in recognition of past and present benefactions. The cult is the clearest evidence for the association of Spes and Salus which is implied in the literary evidence and in a number of coin-issues.[158]

The ludi commemorated here could have been one of the regular festivals of the municipal calendar which essentially would correspond to the public calendar of religious observances at Rome. They could, on the other hand, represent a spontaneous event prompted by an imperial occasion or by an occasion in the life of the priestess.[159] Though in lines eleven and twelve there may be an indication of a fixed festival by the apparent implication of fulfilled religious obligation (religioni ... satis fecerit). Whilst the ludi need not have been connected with cult of Spes and Salus, it is notable that the dedication of the ludi, pro salute principis Antonini Aug. Pii (lines 7 to 9), goes on to specifically include the imperial children (in whom the Spes Augusta was vested[160]). The annual public festivals of Spes and Salus were within five days of each other (August 1 and 5). The priestess had also refurbished the portico of Spes (lines 5 and 6) which would perhaps have been joined to a temple of Salus.

Line thirteen records the distribution of some kind of clothing, and, though distributions of other kinds (of corn, money and oil) were common on the part of the holders of municipal offices, this particular form of communal gift seems to be unparalleled.[161]

Notably, here again there is a potential association of Salus with water: there were natural springs at Gabii, and these presumably supplied the baths which were famous in the early imperial period.[162]

6. **Pinquente, Provincia di Pola; PINQUENTUM, HISTRIA**

(sic) Saluti Aug. | pro incolu|mitate Piquent(inorum)| L. Ventinaris | Lucumo | adiect(a) iunic(e) | v. l. l. s.

The limestone tablet was first recorded in 1689 re-used in the church of St. Thomas in Goricizza.[163] T. Mommsen regarded the name Lucumo as indigenous to Histria and thus as indicating Celtic or Illyrian origin, but it now seems that both Ventinaris and Lucumo are Etruscan names.[164]

The dedication "for the safety of the inhabitants of Pi(n)quentum" is in fulfilment of a vow following the aversion of some unnamed danger and is unique among dedications to Salus in specifying a sacrifice, that of a calf (adiect(a) iunic(e)).

C.B. Pascal assumes that the goddess is here perceived as Hygieia as the cult of Aesculapius and Hygieia was particularly popular in Cisalpine Gaul, and he suggests that the cult derives directly from Greece. On dedications at Aquileia both these deities receive the epithet Aug.[165]

7. **Urbisaglia; URBS SALVIA, PICENUM**

A. Vitelliae | C. f. Rufillae | C. Salvi Liberalis cos.|
(sic) flamini Salutis Aug. matri | optumae | C. Salvius Vitellianus vivos

B. M(arci) Att(i) Fabati | Salutis Aug. Salvien(sis)

The first text is inscribed upon a gravestone or other monument and was found in or before 1524 in the church of St. Lawrence.[166] The second is the stamp upon at least forty roof-tiles, most of which were found in the excavations, up to 1979, of the "cryptoporticus enclosing the sacred area of a temple".[167]

The apparent agreement in case of flamini (A.4) with Vitelliae ... Rufillae and with matri optumae requires us to interpret the word as flamini(ca) which may indicate that the woman was the wife of a flamen (who would be C. Salvius Liberalis) of the local cult of Salus Aug. (Salviensis) and who would thus have assisted in the cult. In B the genitive Salutis Aug. Salviensis implicitly depends upon the building, presumably a temple, from which the tiles derive.

The consulship of C. Salvius Liberalis (Nonius Bassus), during or after which the dedication to his wife was set up, is known to have been held in the years AD 81 to 85. He may have had an equestrian military career before he entered the Senate in AD 73 or 74, after which he enjoyed a successful senatorial career including membership of the Arval priesthood. He was also chief magistrate (quinquennalis) of his home town, Urbs Salvia, possibly for fifteen years or more, depending upon the interpretation of the inscription from Urbs Salvia bearing his cursus.[168] Liberalis' son, C. Salvius Vitellianus, who is responsible for the monument to his mother, may also have held this magistracy.[169]

A local epithet for Salus is attested in two other inscriptions, both from Spain.[170]

8. San Vittore; (Roman name unknown) PICENUM

   [Salu]ti Aug[...|...]ssicus[... | [ex test]amen[to...| ...imm]unitas[...

The stone, broken on the left and right sides, was found in the same place as two other equally fragmentary inscriptions which may belong to the same monument.[171]

9 and 10. HISPANIA BAETICA, CONV. HISPALENSIS

9. Jerez de los Caballeros, Badajoz, Spain; SERIA / FAMA JULIA

    Saluti | Aug. | Livius | Secundus

10. Matanegra, Badajoz, Spain; (Roman name, if any, unknown)

    Saluti Aug. L. Petronius L. lib(ertus)

Number 9 is a marble base, found in 1840, in the chapel of Santa Lucia outside the modern town.[172] Number 10, is the offering of a freedman.[173]

These dedications belong to a group of at least seventeen dedications found in Lusitania and Baetica which manifest a particular local significance for the cult of Salus. One other, from Esteppa in southern Baetica, has an imperial epithet but, in this case, the unabbreviated Augusta.[174]

11 - 13. PANNONIA

11. Stein am Anger / Szombathely, Hungary; SAVARIA, PANNONIA SUPERIOR

    Salut[i...| August[...| sac[...

The form of this dedication, found in the bishop's castle and now lost, is not recorded.[175]

Savaria was, at least prior to the division of Pannonia in AD 106, an important centre for the imperial cult.[176]

12. Rusovce, Czechoslovakia; GERULTA(?), PANNONIA SUPERIOR

> [I(ovi)] O(ptimo) M(aximo) Dolichen‹n›o | [Sa]l(uti)
> Aug. | [ae]dem cum sui[s] | [or]namentis et | [po]rticu
> pro salu[te] | [.]aroni Agathang[eli] | [m(unicipii)]
> A(elii) d(ecuriones) G(e)r(ulatenses) l(ocum) d(ederunt)
> Cl(audius) mul(ieris) l(ibertus) | [M]aronius legus
> l(ibertus) p(ecunia) s(ua) [f(ecit)]

The limestone altar, broken in two places and with damaged sides, was found in 1967, in situ but re-used, in the same circumstances as the military dedication which is thought to be honouring the same two deities and is assigned to the later second or first third of the third century.[177]

The restoration of lines seven to nine is essentially that of R. Hošek and is extremely tenuous as is the restoration in favour of Sal(uti), the plausibility of which depends greatly on the slightly more certain interpretation of the military dedication.

That an aedes with its equipment and a portico has been dedicated seems certain as it is that this dedication is for the salus of a man, the beginning and end of whose name has to be restored (line 6). Line eight contains the name of another man in the nominative case who has the same nomen and who, presumably, commissioned the work "with his own money".

If, as Hošek suggests, line seven states that the town councillors of the municipium of Gerulata have designated the land for the aedes, then the situation is reminiscent of that at Nida in Germania Superior where the vicani assigned land for a schola dedicated to Salus Aug.[178] The last name of the dedicating freedman, which, in full, is suggested to be Claudius [M]aronius Legus, may indicate a Dalmatian origin.[179] The [M]aronius Agathang[elus] for whose salus the temple is dedicated would then, presumably, be a close relative.

13. Budapest, Hungary; AQUINCUM, PANNONIA INFERIOR

> L. Vepintania l[...] | lib(rario?) Serg(ia) Aq[uinco] |
> an(norum) LXX h(ic) s(itus) e(st) co[llegia] | to
> Salutis Au[g.....] | Agrippi[nenses Tra]nsalpi[ni
> posuerunt]

Approximately two-thirds of a gravestone, elaborately ornamented in bas-relief and broken on the right hand side, was found in 1931 during the excavation of a late Roman cemetery in a suburb of Óbuda and near the site of the legionary fortress. Though found in situ, the stone, with three others, had been re-used to form a coffin.[180]

Vepintania may be the Celtic native name of the deceased. The meaning of the first two lines containing the name of the deceased and probably indicating his or her freed status is not clear. The

108

deceased, though, is clearly a Roman citizen (from the citation of tribe) and is perhaps indicated as a citizen of Aquincum. It may be that the contribution of the <u>Agrippinenses Transalpini</u> towards the burial is explicable by the fact that the freedman's patron, whose name does not survive, was a citizen of Colonia Agrippinensis (Cologne) and thus a member of this guild of Rhineland immigrants. The <u>cives Agrippinenses Transalpini</u> are attested as functioning at Aquincum from at least as early as the reign of Trajan.[181]

The deceased's origin and tribe indicate that he was a citizen of the <u>municipium Aelium Aquincum</u> (two kilometres north of the fortress and its associated settlement) which received its municipal charter from Hadrian and was assigned to the Sergian tribe.[182] Thus, as the stone has already been assigned on stylistic and other grounds to the early second century AD, then perhaps it actually dates from shortly after Hadrian's grant.[183]

The third and fourth lines are problematic, but, if the restoration is correct, then the deceased is a member (<u>collegiatus</u>) of a <u>collegium Salutis Aug</u>. Whether or not this is to be taken as synonymous with the guild of the <u>cives Agrippinenses Transalpini</u> is not clear, but an indication to the contrary may be that the two other inscriptions attesting this guild do not mention the <u>collegium Salutis</u>.[184] This <u>collegium</u> may simply be a burial and common interest club, mainly or exclusively comprising freedmen whose chosen patron deity was Salus Aug. On the other hand, perhaps its function was more closely related to the observance of the imperial cult like that of the colleges of <u>severi Augustales</u>.[185]

F. Salus Publica or Her Equivalent

This section is divided into two parts: I comprises the five inscriptions definitely attesting cult-acts in honour of Salus Publica or, as in one case, Salus Populi Romani; and II comprises the three inscriptions in which Salus as Salus Publica is firmly implied, the last of the three being the monument to the emperor Carus as the <u>auctor Salutis Publicae</u>.

I. <u>Inscriptions Definitely Attesting Salus Publica</u>

1 and 2. <u>Corinth, Greece</u>

1. | Callicrateae | Philesi fil(iae) | sacerdoti in |
    | perpet(uum) | Providentiae Aug. | et Salutis Publicae |
    | tribules tribus Agripp[i]ae | bene meritae |

2. | Callicrateae | Philesi f(iliae) | sacerdoti in |
    | perpet(uum) | Providentiae Aug. | et Salutis Publicae |
    | tribules trib(us) Claudiae | bene meritae |

Both dedications are inscribed upon limestone bases and were found in the course of excavations. The first was found in 1901 near the church of St. John's Theologos.[186] The second was found near Isthmia in 1969 re-used in a pavement in the north-east of the 'Fortress of Justinian' which is attached to the Isthmian Wall.[187]

Neither Callicratea, who is priestess for life, nor her father are Roman citizens. The dedicants are the members of, respectively, the tribus Agrippia and the tribus Claudia, two of the twelve known Corinthian voting tribes whose existence derived from the reorganisation of the city under Augustus.[188]

The establishment of a joint cult of Providentia Aug. and Salus Publica appears to be a manifestation of the municipal thanksgiving following the downfall of Sejanus in AD 31 which is also attested in the dedication at Interamna of AD 32 to Salus Perpetua Augusta, Libertas Publica, the Genius of the municipium and Providentia Augusti. In any case the emphasis given to the cult of the imperial Providentia under Tiberius suggests a date in this reign.[189]

3. Tolmeita, Libya; PTOLEMAIS, CYRENAICA ET CRETA

...]oq[...	...]a quae[...	...]futurum[...	...]m
verba b[...	...]quae in v[...	... fut]urum quo[d...
...]m verba b[...	...]blica populi[...	...Sal]us Public[a...

The fragment of a marble panel was found in 1955 "during ploughing an unexcavated area in the north-east part of the site". The letter-styles may indicate a second century date.[190]

The text has been restored with reference to the formulae used in the records of the Arval brothers.[191] Thus line eight would have been [Salus Pu]blica populi [Romani quae in verba I(ovi) O(ptimo) M(aximo)], thus completing the prayer to Salus Publica. Line nine would then be a stone-cutter's error in repeating the previous line. The anomalous position of oq on the first line led the editor to suggest either a local variant of the form of the vows taken on January 3 for the welfare of the emperor, or that the fragment instead records vota extraordinaria which might account for exceptional wording.

The text may tentatively be taken to indicate not only that vows for the emperor's welfare were taken throughout the empire, a fact for which we already have evidence,[192] but further that the form of the vows, their fulfilment, recording and public display was, in the provinces (including the Greek-speaking provinces), the same as or similar to that pertaining to the acts of the Arval Brothers at Rome.

Two further fragments of similar records have been found at Ptolemais, one possibly dating from the reign of Vespasian, the other perhaps from that of Marcus Aurelius.[193] A similar fragment was found at Cyrene,[194] and at Sarmizegetusa a fragment found there appears to record vota extraordinaria, perhaps connected with a military crisis.

The editors of the Dacian fragment accept the suggestion of J.M. Reynolds that the missing fourth deity would have been Salus Publica P. R. Q. They suggest that the fragment records the activities of the provincial concilium III Daciarum perhaps under or later than the reign of Marcus Aurelius.[195]

The likely assumption is that the Cyrene and Ptolemais records refer to civic activity. However, the possibility has to be allowed that the fragments record military religious activity.[196]

4. Tiaret, Algeria; (Roman name unknown) MAURETANIA CAESARIENSIS

Saluti populi Romani | Victorinus aedilis po[n] | derarium sua p. p. d. q.

The details of the find-circumstances and form of this dedication are not available.[197]

Victorinus, apparently not a Roman citizen, is presumably a municipal aedile, though ponderarium (indicating his responsibility for the public weights office) seems to be an inappropriate form to qualify aedilis.[198]

In the last line sua invites the expansion, for the first p, of p(ecunia) which would suggest a private dedication despite the public nature of Salus. Thus, for the final letters p(osuit) d(edicavit)que or a similar expression seems the most likely interpretation. The dedication must at least post-date the constitution of the Mauretanian provinces under Claudius.

5. Ferentino, Italy; FERENTINUM, LATIUM

[S]aluti Publicae |[s]acrum Quintius C. f.|
[P]alatina | Cestianus | Duceniu[s]| Procul[us]

The form of the dedication, known since 1565, is not recorded. The restored letters were once clearly visible.[199]

E. Groag has identified the man as the C. Ducenius Proculus who was suffect consul in AD 87.[200] In any case he is probably a near relative of a man who held a legionary legateship under Trajan and some of whose names certainly derive from those of the dedicant.[201]

I have discussed above the inference possible from Tacitus that a temple of Salus was founded at Ferentinum following the failure of the Pisonian conspiracy in AD 65.[202]

II. Salus Publica Implied

1. Splitska, (island of) Brač, Yugoslavia; (Roman name unknown) BRATTIA, DALMATIA

(AD 211, March 1)

[dominis nostris M. Aurelio Antonino et P. Septimio Get]ae et Iu[liae Domnae Augus][ta]e matri Augg.[et castrorum] [Io]vi Optimo Max. Iu[noni Reg. Minervae] [Sa]luti Mar. Patri [Mar. Victori] [Vic]toriae Augg. F[ortun. Red. devic][tis] host. voto sol[uto dedicavit] Hermes Gent[iano et Basso] co[s...] cal(endis) M[artis]

The dedication, of unknown form, was found in 1884 on the north coast of the island. M[aiis] is an alternative restoration of the last word.[203]

Hermes, presumably a Greek, must be either a slave or a freedman. A slave of the same name, and belonging to a praefectus vehiculorum et conductor publici portorii, is attested at Vratnik on the mainland.[204] If an identification is possible, then perhaps Hermes was on an official visit to the important marble quarries on Brattia.[205]

The dedication, in fulfilment of a vow and in honour of Caracalla, Geta and Julia Domna, is assumed to refer to the victories won in Britain in AD 211. The choice of deities, their order and epithets (apart from Victoria's imperial epithet), are strikingly reminiscent of those included in the records of the Arval Brothers. The deity list is particularly similar in these respects to that recorded for the Arval sacrifices in celebration of the return of Trajan from Dacia (AD 101).[206]

2. Várhely in Siebenbürgen, Romania; SARMIZEGETUSA, DACIA APULENSIS

[I.] O. M. | Iunoni [M]inervae | Diis [C]onsentibus
Saluti Fortunae | [R]educi Apollini | Dianae
V[ict]rici Nemesi Me[rc]urio | Herculi Soli Invicto
Aesculapio Hygiae diis | deabusq. immortalib.
P. Aelius Hammonius | [I]un. proc(urator) Aug.

The dedication, a marble altar, was found by chance in 1930.[207] Hammonius Junior is almost certainly the son of P. Aelius Ammonius, who after holding several equestrian military commands in the Danube area was procurator of Lower Moesia and is identified as the recipient of an imperial rescript of AD 240. Hence, our dedicant will have been the procurator of Dacia Apulensis at some time in the period AD 244 to 260.[208]

In its list of deities his dedication reflects both the archaism which is particularly observable in dedications of the second and third centuries in the Danube area,[209] as well as the more widely prevailing religious syncretism, here expressed in conventional polytheistic form. Also, and apart from any manifestation of Hammonius' own predilections, his choice of deities may have been influenced by a desire to include locally and regionally important deities. Sarmizegetusa was an important religious as well as an administrative centre.[210]

We have already noted the possibility that Apollo and Diana may represent regional native deities in Roman guise with regard to the dedication at Apulum (c. AD 200) by another imperial (though military) official.[211]

Thus, local importance may account for the inclusion here, among others, of Aesculapius and Hygieia whose cult was well established in Dacia as a whole, as well as at Sarmizegetusa where a <u>flamen coloniae</u> made a dedication to "Pergamene Aesculapius and Hygieia".[212] They come at the end of the list, and after Apollo, Diana Victrix, Nemesis, Mercury, Hercules and Sol Invictus, who may perhaps be included primarily by virtue of their local or regional significance.

Salus' position (as well as her appearance <u>in addition</u> to Hygieia), in fifth place, after the Capitoline Triad (and only separated from them by the archaistic Dii Consentes) and followed by Fortuna Redux, seems to firmly imply her presence here as one of the group of deities included here by virtue of their importance to the state and therefore as Salus Publica.

3. <u>Pozzuoli, Italy</u>; PUTEOLI, CAMPANIA

auctori Salutis	Public(a)e genitori	principum
Divo [Caro]	Rutilius Crispinus	v(ir) c(larissimus)
curator rei p(ublicae)	Puteolanor(um)	

The marble tablet was found in about 1960 in the course of excavations at the crossing of the Via Vecchia S. Gennaro by the Via Vigna. The name of Carus has been deliberately erased (after the defeat of Carinus by Diocletian in 285) but is still legible.[213]

The dedication is to the deified emperor Carus (AD 282-283) who is addressed as "the <u>auctor</u> of Salus Publica": thus it is uncertain whether or not the deity is referred to. The inscription has to date from the period between Carus' apotheosis and the death of Numerianus, whom the phrase <u>genitori principum</u> (lines 2-3) tells us is still alive, in November 284.

Rutilius Crispinus, of senatorial rank and here acting in his capacity as imperial <u>curator</u> of Puteoli, is perhaps the grandson of Rutilius Pudens Crispinus who was consul in about the years AD 235 to 237. He may be identifiable as the <u>praeses</u> of Syria-Phoenicia in the years 292 to 293.[214]

The tablet is perhaps to be seen as a demonstration of allegiance, on the part of the municipal authorities of Puteoli, to the dynasty of Carus following receipt of the news of Carus' death and deification. It has been suggested that the dedication would have been accompanied by two others honouring Carinus and Numerianus and that it would have stood in the forum of the <u>colonia</u>.[215]

G. The 'Augurium Salutis'

Rome

	auguria maximum quo salus p(opuli) R(omani) petitur quod actum est
(AD 3)	L. Aelio Lamia M. Servilio cos.
(AD 17)	L. Pomponio Flacco C. Caelio cos.
	quae acta sunt
(AD 1)	[C. Caesa]re L. Aemilio Paullo cos.
(AD 2)	[P. Vini]cio P. Alfenio Varo cos.
(AD 8)	[M. Fur]io Camillo Sex. Nonio Quinctiliano cos.
(AD 12)	[Germ]anico Caesare C. Fonteio Capitone cos.
(AD 17)	[C. Cael]io L. Pomponio Flacco cos.

The marble cippus, found in the Via Marforio on the Capitol in 1910, may once have supported a bronze statue. The text is inscribed on the side: that once inscribed on the front has been worn away. The inscription seems to have been completed on one occasion and that perhaps in AD 17.[216]

It seems certain that this augural ceremony did not involve the cult of Salus.[217] The text refers to the augurium salutis in its revived and probably modified form following Augustus' revival of it in 29 BC, when, as we are told, it was in a state of disuse.[218] The only observance prior to this, of which we know, is that of 63 BC, when it took place after a "very long interval".[219] It took the form of an annual augural inquiry of Jupiter as to whether or not it was a fas to seek the salus of the Roman people. It could only take place at a time when no military campaigns were either under way or imminent. This may have been a debased form of the ceremony which may originally have taken place early in the year, just after the consuls ordinarii had assumed office, and was perhaps analogous to auguria concerned with activities such as sowing and harvesting.[220] According to Tacitus it was revived again in AD 49 after an interval of twenty-five (depending upon a manuscript emendation) years.[221]

Among the problems of interpretation posed by the text is that of the division of the auguria (also apparent in Festus) into greater ones (the first two) and those which, by implication, were in some way incomplete.[222]

H. The Private Cults of Salus

These inscriptions are not all of those indicating private or non-official cult-acts. The others are included as appropriate in the sections above in those cases where a particular perception of Salus by the dedicant is indicated. The dedications from Ariminum, Civitella and Napoca in the next section may be essentially or entirely acts of private piety. Three other dedications from Hispania Baetica, those from Esteppa, Jerez de los Caballeros and Matanegra, differ in kind from those included under II below only in that Salus is qualified by the imperial epithet.

In most cases the inscriptions here indicate their private nature in the terms of the dedication, but some are included simply in view of their brevity. The dedicants, where recorded, are all acting only as private individuals.

The section is divided into three parts: I comprises the dedications from Asseria, Lugdunum, Asculum Picenum and Baden bei Wien (Aquae); II comprises the twenty-one inscriptions from Spain and Portugal not all of which certainly relate to Salus; and III is the unique dedication to Salus Generis Humani.

I. The Dedications from Asseria, Lugdunum, Asculum Picenum and Baden bei Wien (Aquae)

1. Podgradje (near Benkovac), Yugoslavia; ASSERIA, DALMATIA

    Rubria | Ceuni f(ilia) Pola | Saluti | v. s.[l. m.]

The fragment of limestone altar was found at some time between 1960 and 1970.[223]

The form of her name should mean that Rubria Pola is a Roman citizen. The Rubrii were an aristocratic family of the native Liburni, an Illyrian people, and its members were among those holding important positions in the *municipium* founded at Asseria in or after the reign of Claudius.[224] The name of Rubria's father, Ceunus, is peculiarly Illyrian and is perhaps Celtic.[225] There are local parallels for the unusual word-order of her votive-dedication.[226]

2. Lyon, France; LUGDUNUM, GALLIA LUGDUNENSIS

    ...]|[S]everus | [u]ti voverat | Marcella | sua | Salutis| (aram) dedicavit

The altar, broken at the top, was found in 1849 in the garden of the "Hospice of the Antiquailles". In the last line *causa* would be an alternative expansion.[227] A man whose name is or ends in Severus is fulfilling a vow either in the company of (*cum*) or on behalf of (*pro*) his wife Marcella.

3. Ascoli Piceno, Italy; ASCULUM PICENUM

    | coniugis Firminae | bono reddito dea | Salutis| |
    | Frontinius | A(uli) l(ibertus) Acer h(a)ec | tibi |
    | dona dedit |

The fragment of Travertine stone, thought to be of an altar, was found in or just before 1972 built into the foundations of the church of San Venanzo.[228]

The meaning is rendered ambiguous by the incorrect case-endings. As it stands there seems to be nothing, understood or in the text, for <u>bono reddito</u> to qualify. A tentative translation might be:-

> "For the happy return of his wife, Firmina, Frontinius Acer, freedmen of Aulus, gave these gifts to you, O goddess (of) Salus."

It seems possible that here the freedman, who could be of either Roman citizen or Junian Latin status, has, unusually, adapted for his <u>gentilicium</u> (Frontinius) his patron's <u>cognomen</u>.[229]

4.   <u>Baden bei Wien, Austria; AQUAE, PANNONIA SUPERIOR</u>

<u>Saluti | P. Gemini|[us]</u>

The dedication, of uncertain form but apparently complete, was found in or shortly before 1906.[230] Its brevity and discovery at the site of a healing spring imply Salus' association with a healing cult, a situation which finds analogy in parts of Spain.[231]

II.   <u>Inscriptions from the Spanish Provinces</u>

Three dedications from Baetica of the same type as most of those below are included above, as in them Salus is qualified by the imperial epithet.[232]

1 - 4.   <u>HISPANIA BAETICA</u>

1.   <u>Campillo de Arenas, Spain; MUNICIPIUM FLORENTINUM ILIBERRITANUM, CONV. CORDUBENSIS</u>

           <u>L. Valeri Laeti | M. Valeri Vetusti | libertus verna|</u>
           <u>M. Valeri Vetusti | Prima vernae ux(or) | v. s. l. m.</u>
(March 1, <u>Saluti | posita k. Mart. | Cn. Cornelio Gaetulic[o]|</u>
 AD 26) <u>C. Calvisio Sabino c[o]s.</u>

The small base was found in 1822 near the village which, reputedly, is the site of a salutiferous spring.[233]

The relationships manifested in this votive dedication are not completely clear. The dedicants are a freedman, whose name is not obvious and who still designates himself as servile, and his wife Prima who is still the slave (<u>vernae</u> apparently in the wrong case) of M. Valerius Vetustus. As it stands the first two names could be those of the patrons of the freedman.

2. Coria del Rio, Spain; CAURA, CONV. HISPALENSIS

> Saluti | Secunda | pro sa|lute ELV Severia|ni ex votu|
> a(nimo) lib(ens) aram posuit

This votive dedication for the salus of Severianus by Secunda, perhaps his wife, is of a small marble altar. If, in the fourth line, E should be P, then P. Lu(...) would be a possible interpretation.[234]

3. Marchena, Spain; (Roman name uncertain) CONV. ASTIGITANUS

> ara Sal(utis) | pro redit(u) | L. N. P. | Celsus f.

The form and find-circumstances are not recorded. L. N. P. presumably represents the person whose return (notably) is being either asked for or commemorated. The final f could be either f(ilius) or f(ecit).[235]

4. Zafra, Spain; (Roman name unknown) CONV. HISPALENSIS

> Saluti | s. ex v(oto) | M. Marius | Caesianus

This votive dedication is that of a small altar with a patera and a praefericulum carved in relief on the sides. For s in the second line, s(acrum) or s(olvit) are the most probable expansions.[236]

5 - 8. CONVENTUS PACENSIS, HISPANIA LUSITANIA

5. Loulé, Portugal (Roman name unknown)

> d(eae) S(aluti) s(acrum) | Fonteius | Philomu|sus
> ex vo|tu anim[o]| libens | posuit

This votive cippus was found built into the tower of the church of San Clemente. The letter-forms have been assigned to the late second or early third century.[237] The ex votu animo libens posuit is, apart from abbreviation and aram before posuit, the same formula which ends Secunda's dedication at Coria del Rio (above).

6. San Romao do Sado, Portugal (Roman name unknown; near Colonia Pax Julia)

> Saluti | pro G. Atilio | Cordo N. Cat|tulus ser(vus) |
> votum s(olvit) a(nimo) l(ibens)

(AE assigns the inscription to Pisões in Beja region, ends the first line after pro, has no t beginning the fourth line and has serv(us).) The small votive altar of the slave Cattulus was found in a villa. In the third line, N could represent Cattulus' first name or perhaps N(epote) as a second cognomen for G. Atilius Cordus, the beneficiary of the votum, who is thought to be the owner of the villa.[238]

7. Serros Altos, Portugal (Roman name unknown)

    S(aluti) s(anctae) d(eae) | votum | posuit | aram| Peculiaris

This votive dedication is described as "a small cippus in the form of an altar".[239]

8. Villa Viçosa, Portugal (Roman name unknown)

    Saluti | pro salu|te Acili Ru|fini Canie|ius m. a. l. | v. s.

The abbreviations might be expandable as m(erito) a(nimo) l(ibens) v(otum) s(olvit).[240] The votive dedication displays a notable similarity to that borne by the altar of the slave Cattulus at San Romao do Sado (above).

We may note an analogous votive dedication from the same place, Fontano et Fontanae pro salut(e) Albi Fausti Albia Facina v. s. a. l.,[241] which may imply the presence of a salutiferous spring.

9 - 18. CONVENTUS EMERITENSIS, HISPANIA LUSITANIA

9 and 10. Baños de Montemayor, Spain (Roman name unknown)

    9. Saluti | Valeria | Privata | l. a. v. s.

    10. Salu[ti] | Rufi. | libe(n)s | vot. s|olv. VS| [...

The two votive altars were found (in or before 1894) at the "springs of the Nymphae Caparensium", the former inside the bath-building there.[242]

The state of the second altar renders much of the reading uncertain. However, the dedication is clearly of a votive nature and probably in honour of Salus.

The two altars are thought to be likely to date from the late second or early third century on the basis of the dates assigned (on the basis of their letter-forms) to most of the other, mainly votive, dedications (of which there are over twenty) found at the site of the baths. The baths are fed by the springs which gave Roman Baños its significance.[243] It is suggested that both Salus altars, as well as another seven of the twenty-one small votive altars found at Baños, were the products of a workshop in Capera, twenty-five miles to the south-west.[244] Thirteen out of the twenty-two, including that of Valeria Privata to Salus, were found in the baths themselves.[245] Fifteen of the altars are, with certainty, dedicated to the Nymphae,[246] and of these eight invoke them as the Nymphae Caparensium.[247] Two of the altars from the bath-house, both thought to have been produced at the Capera workshop and both thought to date from the late second or early third century, are dedicated to Fontana, the personification of the springs.[248]

Five of the altars have been dated, on the basis of their letter-forms, to the late second century.[249] Another two, apart from the Salus and Fontana dedications, are dated to the late second or early third century.[250] Two others have been assigned to the third century and early third century respectively,[251] whilst the remaining two to which dates have been assigned, are thought to be of the late first century and the late first or first half of the second century respectively.[252]

11. Coria, Spain: CAURIUM (?)

Saluti

Although an altar bearing this dedication is recorded at Coria (in Estremadure) in 1944, it appears neither in ILER nor CPIL.[253]

12. Ibahernando, Spain (Roman name unknown)

S(aluti) s(acrum) C|l. M.[f.]| Sam[...]|is a[ram]| p(ro) s(e) [suisque]

This fragmentary and equivocal dedication is borne by a small altar known since at least 1904. Its letter-forms have been assigned to the late second century. For the dedicant's gentilicium (lines 3-4) Sam[n]is and Sam[mal]is have been suggested.[254]

13. Madrigalejo, Spain (Roman name unknown)

[......]| Saluti | p. m.

On this fragmentary altar there is at least one line missing above the extant part of the dedication. P(osuit) m(erito) is suggested as an expansion for p. m.[255]

14. Montánchez, Spain (Roman name unknown)

   Caturo | Sa(luti) Bidie(n)|si v. a. l. | s.

   The dedication, inscribed on a small altar, was found in or prior to 1901 near the town and en el castillo Olappa.[256] The letter-forms have been assigned to the late second century.[257]

   'Bidia' has been suggested as the nominative of a place-name giving rise to the locally designated Salus Bidie(n)sis.[258] The name of the dedicant, Caturo, and others of the same root are frequently attested in Spain in general and in Lusitania in particular.[259]

15. Oliva de Plasencia, Spain (Roman name unknown)

   Saluti | Vicinia | Capere|nsis

   The dedication, inscribed on stone but of unrecorded form (presumably an altar) was found in the palace of the Count of Oliva. It is assigned, in CPIL, presumably on the basis of the letter-forms, to the early third century.[260]

   It is assumed, in both CPIL and CIL, that the stone had been transported from Capera (modern Cáparra: perhaps, we may add, from the same workshop which is thought to have produced the votive altars found at Baños de Montemayor[261]) to the find-spot some three miles to the south-west along the main Roman road.

   Vicinia Caperensis, the dedicant or dedicating body, could represent the name of a female municipal slave of Capera or, alternatively, it could refer to the locality of Capera. In the latter case, the name could be reflected in the modern Las Ventas de Cáparra.[262] However, the former interpretation is preferred in CPIL as it is for the Vicinia Clunensium attested on another inscription from Oliva de Plasencia.[263] Vicinia occurs elsewhere as both personal name and as a reference to a locality.[264]

   In CPIL it is assumed that Salus is here the genius of a salutiferous spring, perhaps though for no other reason than that she seems to fill this role elsewhere in the region.

16. Santa Ana, Spain (Roman name unknown)

   L. Norb|anus | Tancin|us Aida|ni f(ilii) S(aluti)| ara b(ene) f(ecit)

   The altar, "with pedestal and cornice", found in about 1900, is assigned on the basis of its letter-forms to the third century AD.[265]

   The dedicant's gentilicium and cognomen are among the commonest in Spain generally and in Conventus Emeritensis in particular.[266]

17.   Torreorgaz, Spain (Roman name unknown)

        Laneanae | S(aluti)

The text, inscribed on a granite altar, was found in or before 1965.[267]

18.   Valencia de Alcántara, Spain

        Saluti sa(crum) | f.[.....]SOM | Tongiu[s .]| IT[....]

The small granite altar, much damaged, was found in or before 1966 in the vicinity of the Fuente Blanca.[268]

Two editors have assumed that a complete line has to be restored after the first which would have completed sacrum.[269] The name Tongius is well attested in the area.[270]

It is assumed on the basis of the modern name of the place of the altar's discovery that Salus is here, again, the genius of a salutiferous spring.[271]

In CPIL it is noted that sala is a Celtic word meaning 'river' and that nearby is the Rio Salor. Thus, it is suggested that this coincidence may account for the local choice of Salus as the Roman equivalent for the native deity of springs.[272]

19 - 21.   HISPANIA TARRACONENSIS

19.   Caldas de Montbuy, Spain; AQUAE CALIDAE, CONV. TARRACONENSIS

        S(aluti)| s(acrum) C. Iroc. Zoticus | v. s. l. m.

The find-circumstances and form of this now lost dedication are not recorded.[273]

The ancient name implies the presence of salutiferous springs, and the likelihood of a healing cult here is strengthened by the presence of three dedications to Apollo and one to Isis, both of whom had significant healing attributes.[274]

20.   Castro Urdiales, Spain; FLAVIOBRIGA (?), CONV. CLUNIENSIS

        Salus Umeritana | L. P. Corneliani III   ΧI   (sic)

The first line is inscribed in "gilded" letters inside the bowl of a silver patera which was found in 1826 at Castro Urdiales (thirty

121

kilometres north-west of Bilbao) which is a site identified as possibly that of the colony of Flaviobriga. The second line is picked out in points on the outside of the patera.[275]

One surface of the patera is ornamented with scenes in bas-relief: in the middle of the scenes is a recumbent nymph beneath two trees who pours a liquid from an urn; below her a man in a toga who is pouring from a patera is visible above an altar; a young man pours water (?) into a large vessel; a bearded man accompanied by a boy is performing a sacrifice; a little lower down another young man is pouring water for a seated man who seems to be ill; and, in the lowest scene, two mules draw a cart in which is a very large wooden vessel into which a young man pours water from an amphora.

The implication is that at a place with a name like Umeri there was a healing-cult associated with a spring. As may have occurred in parts of Lusitania and perhaps Baetica, a native deity associated with a spring has come to be called Salus.[276] The patera was perhaps the gift to the deity of L.P. Cornelianus who was perhaps giving thanks for, or seeking a cure.

21. Cartagena, Spain; NOVA CARTHAGO, CONV. CARTHAGENSIS

...]|[...]BL SP[...]|[...] Salus[...]|[...] SO [......] IS [...]|[...

The stone, perhaps a gravestone, was found in 1782 during excavations for the embankment of a new castle-wall.[277]

A. Hübner regards 'Salus' here as likely to be a personal name.[278]

III. 'Salus Generis Humani'

St. Paulien, France: RUESSIUM, GALLIA AQUITANICA

On the front:-

Saluti Ge|neris Hu|mani| Sergius | Primus | posuit| merito

On the back:-

Saluti Gene|ris Humani | L Sergius Pri|mus meri|to posuit | deae S[aluti]

The dedication, inscribed negligently on a marble tablet, was found "at a placed called Marchadial" in 1896.[279]

According to CIL the letter-forms, despite the negligence of their execution, are assignable to a period which would be consistent with a putative date for the tablet's erection shortly after Galba whose coins were the first to bear the legend SALUS GENERIS HUMANI.[280]

The legend borne by Galba's coins (both before and after his accession in June AD 68) may reflect the words of the appeal of Julius Vindex, both to Galba, as conveyed by letter, and to the Gauls in his speech launching the rebellion against Nero.[281] However, there may be a more direct connection between the dedication and the rebellion. Vindex, who was of royal Aquitanian ancestry, was governor of one of the Gallic provinces, probably Lugdunensis, when he raised his revolt in March AD 68,[282] and Ruessium, in the far east of Aquitania and only sixty miles south-west of Vienne, which city had declared for Vindex,[283] may well have been in the disaffected area.

Later, coins of Trajan, Commodus and Caracalla also carried the legend.[284]

I. Inscriptions Attesting Cults of an Uncertain Nature

No common feature characterizes these six inscriptions except that in none of them is the nature of Salus or her implied cult discernible with certainty. All, though, except the gravestone, have at least one characteristic which potentially makes them more than simply private acts of piety. The gravestone is that of a ministra Salutis, perhaps of a cult of Salus-Hygieia. The five other inscriptions are dedications, two by imperial procurators and three by municipal officials. The aedile of Ariminum and the quinquennalis of Venusia are dedicating aedes, the latter by virtue of a decree of the council, the former in fulfilment of a vow but probably specifying that the aedes (which has been assumed to be of Salus Aug.) was to be administered according to the canon of the Aventine temple of Diana.

1 - 4. Italy

1. Rimini; ARIMINUM, GALLIA CISALPINA

Saluti ex voto	Q. Plautius Iustus aedil(is)
Arim(inensium)	n(omine) s(uo) et Cassiae Thretes
c(oniugis) s(uae) et	Q. Plauti Verecundi f(ilii)
s(ui) aedem S(aluti) A(ug.) ded(icavit)	h(aec)
a(edes) S(aluti) A(ug.) h(abet) l(eges) q(uas)	
D(ianae) R(omae) in A(ventino)	

The tablet of local marble has been known since the seventeenth century.[285] The interpretation of the last line, which is adopted in CIL and accepted by R.E.A. Palmer, is plausible, in the light of circumstantial evidence.[286] However, some doubt must remain concerning the attribution to Salus here of the imperial epithet.

The dedication of an aedes is in fulfilment of a vow by an aedile of the colonia on behalf of himself and his family. The temple, however, perhaps as Iustus' gift to the colonia, is, presumably, to be a public one.

If the interpretation is correct, then the dedication stipulates that the new aedes and its cult are to be administered with the same leges as those attaching to the temple of Diana on the Aventine Hill.

These leges were a canon of religious law regulating cult-practice with regard to "the donation, consecration and dedication of temples, sculptures, and utensils, and like instruments destined for a divinity".[287] There are parallels elsewhere for its adoption for the regulation of cults.[288] The significance of the Aventine canon (as opposed to other canons) for cults at Ariminum and elsewhere may, it has been suggested, derive ultimately from Rome's attempts to achieve hegemony in the Latin League from the sixth century BC onwards, and thus from the supposed transference of the cult centre of the league from the shrine of Diana at Aricia to the Aventine temple. The Aventine canon, then, may be a development from a body of regulations formulated to govern the meetings and festivals of the Latin cities belonging to a newly-formed alliance under Roman leadership.[289]

The sacral canon of Diana's Aventine temple may later have been extended to regulate cults in the Latin colonies (one of which was Ariminum), which may have had Diana as their special protectress. There is evidence indicating that Ariminum may also have had a special relationship directly with the original shrine of Diana at Aricia.[290] There are also firm indications that there was a special relationship between the colony and Diana's Aventine temple.[291]

It is, thus, perhaps understandable why this canon would have been chosen for the regulation of Iustus' new temple of Salus in preference to the leges apparently attaching to an ara Salutis (perhaps sited on the Quirinal Hill) which were, as we know, adopted for the cult of Hercules at Praeneste, though at a much earlier date.[292]

The two other inscriptions which refer with certainty to the Aventine canon date from the years AD 11 to 13 (Narbo) and from AD 137 (Salonae, Dalmatia) respectively, a fact which may reinforce the general impression given by the dedication of a date in the imperial period.[293]

2. Preturo; AGER AMITERNINUS

| Dis Man. | sacrum | Plaetoriae | Secundae | ministrae |
| Salutis | ann. XIII vixit XXX |

The epitaph inscribed upon a "four-sided coffin" was found in 1874 three kilometres south-south-west of Amiternum.[294] Secunda was seventeen years old when she became a ministra in a local cult of Salus (perhaps at Amiternum), an office she held for thirteen years. She is identifiable as the woman of the same name who appears with two men, perhaps relatives, C. Plaetorius Cnidus and C. Plaetorius Acratus, on an inscription from Trebula Mutuesca.[295] This inscription attests the freed status of the three, and the men's names indicate Greek origin which is what perhaps led K. Latte to assume that Secunda was a ministra of a cult of Salus-Hygieia.[296]

3. Civitella; RESPUBLICA AEQUICOLORUM

> Saluti | Fortunatus [rei publ(icae)]| arcarius

The form of the dedication, broken on the right hand side and found incorporated into the steps of the parish church, is not recorded.[297]

The respublica, of which Fortunatus is the treasurer, is presumably the respublica Aequicolorum which was constituted as a municipium probably in 90 or 89 BC.[298]

Fortunatus is presumably a slave. Three dedications from the vicinity (one dating from AD 172) attest another arkarius reipublicae Aequicolorum, one Apronianus, who is a slave.[299] Furthermore, Fortunatus is a common servile name.[300]

4. Venosa; VENUSIA, APULIA

> ...]| quinq. aedem | Saluti d(e) d(ecurionum) s(ententia) d(edit)

The inscription, found in a ditch near the castle, is broken above the extant text.[301]

The first word, which is almost certainly quinq(uennalis), makes the given expansion of d. d. s. d. very probable. Quinq(uennales) would also be possible as it is that duumviri or duumvir would have been the last word in the missing portion. In any case there need be little doubt that the first word refers to one or both of the colonia's chief magistrates and, furthermore, to their tenure of office in a quinquennial or census year. The procedure of holding the potestas censoria is attested as occurring at Venusia in 29 BC, and it has been suggested that this year saw the establishment of the practice at Venusia and elsewhere coinciding with Augustus' holding of a census at Rome in that or the following year.[302]

Perhaps then this dedication of an aedes to Salus, by decree of the colonial council, took place at some date after this. At Urbs Salvia, as we have seen, C. Salvius Liberalis, who seems to have held the office of quinquennalis in four separate census years, was probably the flamen of the municipal cult of Salus Aug. in or after the years AD 81 to 85.[303]

5 and 6. Dedications of Procurators

5. Martigny, Canton Wallis, Switzerland; FORUM CLAUDII VALLENSIUM, ALPES ATRECTIANAE ET POENINAE

> Saluti sacrum | Foroclaudien|ses Vallenses | cum
> T. Pomponio | Victore| proc(uratore) [Augusto]|rum

The altar was found in the course of excavations in 1896 in a large building adjacent to the forum.[304]

The Foroclaudienses Vallenses may refer simply to the inhabitants of Forum Claudii which, since the formation of the procuratorial province at some time between the reigns of Claudius and Marcus Aurelius, had been the administrative centre for the province. Vallenses, however, was also now the common name for the inhabitants of the four previously distinct civitates of the Vallis Poenina for whom Forum Claudii was the principal urban centre.[305]

Whichever constituency is implied by the name, the Foroclaudienses Vallenses, or their officials, are here acting in concert with the procurator, the highest imperial official of the province. Augustorum indicates a date during a joint reign and that of AD 161 to 169, reasonably, but for no compelling reason, has been preferred.[306] The inscribed rustic poem addressed by Pomponius Victor to Silvanus (and also assigned to AD 161-169), found at another tribal centre and procuratorial seat, Forum Claudii Ceutronum (Aîme en Tarantaise), indicates the procurator's Italian origin and ostensibly manifests an ingenuous religiosity.[307]

6. Cluj, Romania; NAPOCA, DACIA POROLISSENSIS

Salu[ti]| M. Aur[e]|lius Apol[l]ina[ris] | proc(urator) Aug(usti) cum suis

The dedication is described simply as a limestone block and was found, presumably, in or prior to 1973.[308]

The dedicant, acting on behalf of his family, is presumed to be the procurator of Dacia Porolissensis, the administrative centre of which was Napoca. He has been identified as the tribune of the praetorian guard who participated in the assassination of Caracalla (AD 217). His post may have been a reward from Macrinus (217-218).[309] His cognomen need no longer be assumed to indicate a Graeko-oriental origin.[310]

J. Seals and a Graffito (or Stamp)

1. Seville, Spain: HISPALIS, CONV. HISPALENSIS, H. BAETICA

Salus

The word is scratched or stamped upon a small vessel of white clay, which need not be of local origin.[311]

2. NUMIDIA (place of discovery unknown; now in Timgad museum)

Salus Pesi[...

A leaf-decoration divides the words which are inscribed upon an earthenware seal or stamp (eight centimetres in length).[312]

3. <u>Volterra, Italy; VOLTERRAE, ETRURIA</u>

<u>Salus</u>

The word is inscribed upon a bronze seal <u>in planta pedis</u>.[313]

K. <u>Conclusion</u>

1. <u>The Early Evidence</u>

The view of G. Wissowa that the Pisaurum, Horta and Praeneste evidence indicates an early distribution of the cult of Salus in central Italy[314] may need some qualification. The cult indicated by the Pisaurum <u>cippus</u> was presumably introduced as a result of the establishment of the citizen colony in 184 BC or perhaps of that of the pre-colonial <u>conciliabulum civium Romanorum</u> as early as the last third of the third century. The Horta <u>patera</u> or <u>poculum</u> was probably made in Latium if not actually in Rome, though perhaps as early as the late fourth century. The inscribed base of the statue of Hercules, though only twelve miles distant from Rome at Praeneste, may indicate that a cult-centre of Salus, probably that of the Quirinal Hill at Rome, was, before the middle of the second century and perhaps in the third century, prestigious enough, at least in Latium, for its <u>leges</u> to be adopted, without specification beyond "of the altar of Salus" for the regulation of apparently unrelated cults.

Whilst noting the difficulty in discerning the meaning of 'Salus' in the early evidence, K. Latte suggested that the above evidence and the earlier <u>dipinto</u> dedication at Pompeii indicated a cult in republican Rome distinct from that which resulted from the identification, occurring at about the same time, of Salus with the Greek Hygieia. He supposed that the existence of Salus Semonia indicated an original connection with a cult of crop-fertility from which this cult of Salus alone had become detached.[315] Thus, among the Pompeii evidence, which seems to indicate a modest public street shrine, it is interesting to note the depiction of two <u>cornucopiae</u>.

Salus Semonia may also have been a deity who oversaw the taking of oaths, although the meaning of her probable connection with Semo Sancus Dius Fidius remains obscure.

The <u>Saluti sacrum</u> altars of Herculaneum and Tarracina are perhaps of late republican date.

2. Salus-Hygieia

In addition to those inscriptions in which Salus-Hygieia is asociated with Aesculapius, she may be identifiable in other instances: as the deity associated with Roma in the joint cult attested at Pergamum in about 30 BC; as the deity associated with Mens Bona in the monument of the collegium teibeicinum Romanorum at Tibur; and as the deity implied in the fons Salutis at Brigetio, assuming, in the last case, that Salutis is not simply a none-divine epithet for Fons. Latte assumed Salus-Hygieia to be the deity of the cult of which the freedwoman attested in the Preturo epitaph was a ministra Salutis. G. Wissowa regarded Salus as Hygieia wherever she appeared alone but as a healing deity, as in parts of Spain and at Aquae (Baden bei Wien) in Pannonia, and this view may be at least partially correct (see below).

It may also be that in some cases Salus Aug. can be equated with Hygieia. In the Rome dedication of the collegium salutare, of about the time of Hadrian, Salus Aug. is the companion of Aesculapius. However, there is circumstantial evidence to suggest Salus-Hygieia in the ostensibly private dedications to Salus Aug. at Uchi Maius and Pinquentum. The statue outside the main gate at Ostia of Salus Caesaris Augusti may well have depicted her in the form of Hygieia.

In the Chester dedication to Fortuna Redux, Aesculapius and Salus Eius, of the late first century AD, the perception of Salus-Hygieia seems to have been altered by the personalization of Salus in favour of the beneficiary of the dedication.

The dedication, assigned to the late second century AD, of two relatives, thought to be senators, at Léon (Tarraconensis), may manifest the assimilation of Serapis and Isis, respectively, by Aesculapius and Salus.

3. Salus as a Local Deity

In Spain, in particular in Lusitania and Baetica, Salus was the object of a strikingly intensive veneration. There are seventeen certain (and a further five less certain) dedications, all of a manifestly personal nature. Notably, none of the dedicants indicates his or her tenure of any office, whether imperial, municipal, collegiate or priestly. Though the perception, by the inhabitants, of Salus as Hygieia seems probable in explaining their favouring of Salus, it seems certain that here Salus represents a regional Celtic deity of healing springs who has been given the name of the Roman deity perceived by the inhabitants as performing an equivalent function. In three of these dedications, all from Baetica, Salus is, moreover, qualified by the imperial epithet, once in the form Augusta which otherwise occurs only once, in the Interamna dedication of AD 32. A dedication from Lusitania (Montánchez) and the Castro Urdiales patera provide Salus with a local designation: Salus Bidiensis and Salus Umeritana, respectively. The only one of this group which is dated, that from Campo de Arenas in Baetica of AD 26, is also somewhat exceptional in that it is not either very brief or brief. Otherwise, on the basis of their letter-forms, three have been assigned to the late second or early third century AD, two to the late second century, one to the early third century and one simply to the third century.

In the case of the tablet at Heddernheim in Upper Germany recording the dedication (dating from the mid-second century) of the schola of the local college of dendrophori Augustales to Salus Aug., here too Salus may have been perceived as Hygieia in that she may represent a Celtic deity of healing springs (Sirona) in Roman guise.

4. The Private Cult of Salus outside the Spanish Provinces

Private piety accounts for the dedication to Aesculapius and Salus of the praeses of Numidia at Lambaesis (AD 283-285), for that of the proconsular lictor at Pergamum (first half of the first century AD), for that of the Greek medicus at Puteoli and for that of the freedmen and slave household of the legionary legate at Chester (in the 90s AD).

Apart form the three dedications from Baetica, only three other dedications to Salus as qualified by the imperial epithet represent private acts: that at Pinquentum (pro incolumitate Pinquentinorum), that at Uchi Maius and, if the rather speculative interpretation is accepted, that of Rusovce (Pannonia Superior) where it may have been an aedes of Jupiter Dolichenus and Salus Aug. which was dedicated for the salus of another individual by a freedman.

Salus Publica is apparently the object of private worship at Tiaret in Mauretania Caesariensis and at Ferentinum, though, perhaps significantly, the former is the dedication of a municipal aedile and the latter, of the late first century AD, is that of a senator. At Splitska in Dalmatia and Sarmizegetusa in Dacia, Salus Publica is implied in the personal dedications of, in the first case, a slave or freedman celebrating a victory of Caracalla in AD 211 and, in the second case, an imperial procurator in the middle of the third century AD.

Of the unambiguously private dedications to a Salus of an unspecified nature at Asseria in Dalmatia, Lugdunum, Asculum Picenum and Aquae in Pannonia, the last two provide indications of a function as a healing deity with a freedman giving thanks for the restoration of his wife at Asculum Picenum and in the place of discovery of the last, at the site of a healing spring.

Salus Generis Humani is commemorated by a private individual at Ruessium in eastern Aquitania perhaps in the context, or in the aftermath, of the rebellion of Julius Vindex (AD 68).

At Ariminum, an aedes, presumably representing a gift to the colonia, is dedicated ex voto by an aedile to Salus (possibly implying Salus Aug.). Brief dedications to a Salus of an unspecified nature are recorded at Civetella by a municipal, perhaps servile, arcarius and at Napoca in Dacia by an imperial procurator acting cum suis.

5. **The Public Cult of Salus**

a. **Collegia**

The altar at Thugga, dedicated to the Dii Augusti, the Genius of Thugga, Aesculapius, Salus and Victoria was set up in the name of a sodalitas. At Rome, in about the time of Hadrian, a collegium salutare, whose members, freed and servile, were the workforce of the imperial praedia Galbana, dedicated a shrine or schola to the Numen Domus Aug. and Aesculapius and Salus Aug. on land assigned by the procurator of the imperial patrimonium. At Tibur, a collegium teibeicinum Romanorum, probably of freedmen, erected a monument to Mens Bona and Salus. At Rome a collegium thurariorum et unguentariorum honoured the Salus Domus Aug., and at Heddernheim in about the middle of the second century AD a local college of dendrophori Augustales dedicated their new schola to Salus Aug. At Aquincum there was a collegium Salutis Aug. in the early second century AD.

b. **The Municipal and Provincial Cult**

At Pergamum in the 30s or early 20s BC there was a joint cult of Roma and Salus which may have had both a municipal and a provincial significance and which would have been superseded after 29 BC by that of Augustus and Roma. In AD 32 a sevir Augustalis was responsible for a monument at Interamna to Salus Perpetua Augusta, Libertas Publica, the Genius of the municipium and Providentia Augusti, probably in celebration of the failure of Sejanus' conspiracy. In a joint reign the civitas Tepeltensis, by a decree of the council, honoured Salus Augustorum. At Ostia, possibly during the reign of Tiberius, the patronus of the colonia, erected, perhaps on the occasion of an imperial visit, as an imposing gift to the colony, a statue of Salus outside the main gate. At Gabii there was, in the reign of Antoninus Pius, a joint municipal cult of Spes and Salus Aug., and, at Urbs Salvia in the late first century AD, there is attested a temple and cult of Salus Aug. Salviensis. The ostensibly private dedication to Salus Aug. at Pinquentum is pro incolumitate Pinquentinorum.

The uncertain Rusovce dedication may record that the council had assigned the land for an aedes of Jupiter Dolichenus and Salus Aug. Similarly, the vicani of Nida (Heddernheim) assigned land for the schola, of the dendrophori Augustales, dedicated to Salus Aug.

At Corinth, almost certainly in the reign of Tiberius, there was a joint cult of Salus Publica and Providentia Aug. whose establishment may be a further manifestation of municipal reaction to the events of AD 31. At Ptolemais in Cyrenaica evidence, which may also indicate a much wider phenomenon, attests public cult activity in honour of Salus Publica which, if civilian in nature, may manifest municipal or even provincial cult activity analogous to that of the Arval Brothers at Rome. In AD 283 or 284 the imperial curator of Puteoli set up a statue glorifying the now deified Carus as the auctor Salutis Publicae.

At Ariminum the aedes, whose leges were to be those of Diana's Aventine temple at Rome, though dedicated by the aedile as a private act, may be presumed to have been a gift to the colony. Under a joint reign, perhaps that of Marcus and Verus, at Forum Claudium Vallensium, the praesidial procurator in cooperation with the <u>Foroclaudienses Vallenses</u> set up an altar to an unqualified Salus. At Venusia, probably after 29 BC, the chief magistrate, by a decree of the council, dedicated an <u>aedes</u> to Salus. The extensive temple complex at Lambaesis, its principal sanctuary having been dedicated by the emperors Marcus and Verus, to Aesculapius, Salus, Jupiter Valens and Silvanus, and built by <u>legio III Augusta</u> in AD 162 or 163, became an important religious centre for both the military community and for civilians in the Lambaesis region.

c. Priesthoods of Salus

In the 30s or early 20s BC M. Tullius Cratippus was <u>sacerdos</u> of the cult of Roma and Salus at Pergamum. At Gabii in the reign of Antoninus Pius, Agusia Priscilla, a wealthy local woman, was <u>sacerdos</u> of Spes and Salus Aug. Vitellia Rufilla, whose husband, of consular rank, was one of the town's chief magistrates, is attested at Urbs Salvia in the late first century as the <u>flaminica</u> of the cult of Salus Aug. Salviensis.

Aquincum furnishes the only evidence, probably of the reign of Hadrian, for a <u>collegium Salutis Aug.</u>, perhaps essentially comprising freedmen.

At Corinth, probably in the reign of Tiberius, a peregrine woman, Callicratea, was <u>sacerdos in perpetuum</u> of the cult of Providentia Aug. and Salus Publica. Plaetoria Secunda, a freedwoman, probably of Greek origin, is attested at Preturo near Amiternum as having served as a <u>ministra Salutis</u> for thirteen years.

6. The Augurium Salutis

There is no evidence at present to connect this augural inquiry with the cult of Salus.

NOTES

1. Latte, 234.

2. CIL, X, 8167.

3. CIL, I^2, 1626; CIL, IV, 3774; ILS, 3822; ILLRP, 253; Mittheilungen des kaiserlich deutschen archaeologischen Instituts, Römische Abteilung, IV, 121-122, nr. 16.

4. Latte, 234.

5. CIL, X, 6307.

6. CIL, I^2, 373; ILS, 2975; ILLRP, 18; Imagines, 12 (with photograph).

7. CIL, I^2, 368-381; ILLRP, 13-26; Imagines, 7-20, with photographs on pp. 9, 11, 13, 15; ILS, 2970-2983.

8. T. Mommsen, CIL, I^1, pp. 32-33.

9. ILLRP, p. 47; E. Lommatzch, CIL, I^2, p. 406.

10. As previous note; cf. I. Zicari, RE, Suppl., XI (1968), 1092 ('Pisaurum').

11. T. Mommsen, CIL, I^1, p. 33; E. Lommatzch, CIL, I^2, 407.

12. CIL, I^2, 378, 379; ILS, note 8 on nr. 2980; ILLRP, p. 50, note on nr. 23.

13. CIL, I^2, 375, 377; ILS, 2977, 2979 with notes 4, 5, 6; T. Mommsen, CIL, I^1, p. 32; ILLRP, p. 47.

14. CIL, I^2, 450; CIL, XI, 6708 (10); ILS, 2967; ILLRP, 254.

15. Pulgram, 191; cf. Ryberg, 138.

16. Ryberg, 136; J.D. Beazley, Etruscan Vase-Painting, Oxford, 1947, 209-210; W.V. Harris, Rome in Etruria and Umbria, Oxford, 1971, 172; Imagines, p. 40, under nr. 56.

17. Beazley, op. cit. (note 16), 209-216; Ryberg, 135-140.

18. CIL, I^2, 448; Ryberg, 135-136.

19. Ryberg, 136-140.

20. Ibid., 137; Beazley, op. cit. (note 16), 215.

21. Ryberg, 135-137; G.C. Picard, Revue archéologique, Ser. 6, XII (1938), 106-107.

22. Ryberg, 137-140; Beazley, op. cit. (note 16), 215; Harris, op. cit. (note 16), 172.

23. CIL, I^2, 442, 446, 439, 444, 445, 447, 451, 453, 440, 452, 2495, 443, 441, 449, respectively.

24. Ryberg, 138-139; ILS, 2957, 2960.

25. Beazley, op. cit. (note 16), 207-210.

26. Ryberg, 136; Picard, op. cit. (note 21), 105.

27. CIL, I^2, 62; CIL, XIV, 2892; ILS, 3419; Degrassi, Imagines, 48-49, nr. 70 (with photograph); Palmer, 59; ILLRP, 132; E. Vetter, Handbuch der italischen Dialekte, Heidelberg, 1953, I, 355, nr. 509.

28. Palmer, 59.

29. Pulgram, 191.

30. Pulgram, 179-180, 183, 185, 189, 201.

31. Ibid., 191, 201; Imagines, 48; cf. Wissowa, Lex, 295-296; Wissowa, RK, 132.

32. CIL, XIV, under 2892; Palmer, 59-60; above, 5, for an indication in Julius Obsequens.

33. Palmer, 59-60, and 57-58 for other such canons; below, 123-124, for Diana's Aventine canon adopted for an aedes of Salus at Ariminum.

34. Gordon, I, 35 and pp. 48-50; pl. 21b; CIL, VI, 30975; ILS, 3090.

35. Gordon, I, p. 49.

36. Ibid., p. 48.

37. Macrobius, Saturnalia, I.16.8; Festus, p. 404, lines 18 and 20 (ed. W. Lindsay, Hildesheim, 1965).

38. Fears, 867.

39. CIL, I^2, ii, 2 (p. 369), verse 4, lines 36-37.

40. Vetter, op. cit. (note 27), I, p. 145, nr. 213, line 5; G. Radke, Die Götter Altitaliens, Münster, 1965, 286.

41. Radke, op. cit. (note 40), 285-286, 303; Dumézil, 228, 231; Fears, 867; Latte, 51, 65, 234; cf. Scullard, 147. The late writers, Martianus Capella (II.156) and Fulgentius (11: ed. R. Helm, Stuttgart, 1970, p. 115, lines 5-10) both, by a mistaken etymology, characterize the Semones as demi-gods.

42. Latte, 65.

43. Scullard, 146-147, 170; Palmer, 152; Weinstock, 168-169; Dumézil, 180, 198-200; G. Radke, KP, V (1975), 97 ('Semones'); Latte, 126-128; Wissowa, RK, 131-132.

44. Radke, op. cit. (note 40), 278, 286; Fears, 867; Wissowa, RK, 131-132.

45. Weinstock, 168-169.

46. Above, 6.

47. Weinstock, 168; cf. Norden, 213.

48. Wissowa, RK, 131.

49. Scullard, 147; Radke, op. cit. (note 40), 279-282.

50. Propertius, IV.9.74; Varro, De Lingua Latina, V. 66 and 74; Ovid, Fasti, VI. 213-218; Dion. Hal., II.49.2 and IV.58.4.

51. Palmer, 152; Scullard, 147; Dumézil, 180, 198-200; cf. Wissowa, Lex, 297; Radke, op. cit (note 40), 279-281; on Varro, above, 4-5.

52. H.J. Rose, OCD^2, 973 ('Semo Sancus Dius Fidius').

53. J.W. Poultrey, The Bronze Tables of Iguvium, Baltimore and Oxford, 1959, eg. pp. 252-258, VIb, 3-16; Scullard, 147; Dumézil, 180.

54. Scullard, 147.

55. CIL, VI, 568; Palmer, 152-153.

56. CIL, VI, 30994 and 567; cf. 30995 and CIL, XIV, 2458.

57. Palmer, 152-153; Scullard, 147.

58. Scullard, 147.

59. Wissowa, Lex, 297.

60. Latte, 227, note 3.

61. Wissowa, RK, 308, note 8.

62. CIL, VIII, 2579 a-e (a = my lines 2, 4 and 5; b = lines 1 and 6; c = lines 3 and 7), 18089; ILS, 3841, 3034, 3539. leg. III is a deliberate erasure but is still legible.

63. R. Cagnat, Lambèse (Guides en Algérie à l'usage des touristes et des archéologues) Paris, 1923, 37 (drawing), 52-56; M. Janon, Antiquités africaines, VII (1973), fig. 25 (pp. 252-253) and fig. 2 (facing p. 202); G.C. Picard, Castellum Dimmidi, Paris and Algiers, 1944, 132-133; L. Leschi, Études d'épigraphie, d'archéologie et d'histoire africaines, Paris, 1957, 15; G. Boissier, Roman Africa: Archaeological Walks in Algeria and Tunis, London, 1899, 126-127.

64. PIR^2, III, p. 199: F. 472.

65. Picard, op. cit. (note 63), 133.

66. CIL, VIII, 18218, 2590, 2589, 2624; AE, 1915, 30 (AD 320).

67. J. Marcillet-Jaubert, Zeitschrift für Papyrologie und Epigraphik, IV (1974), 249-250 and Taf. XIIIc; AE, 1973, 630; H.G. Kolbe, Die Statthalter Numidiens von Gallien bis Konstantin (268-320), München, 1962, 21-28.

68. Kolbe, op. cit. (note 67), 21, nos. 4, 5, 6, 10 (from Lambaesis).

69. Ibid., 21, nr. 11.

70. Latte, 356-357.

71. Kolbe, op. cit., (note 67), 24.

72. AE, 1914, 166; R. Cagnat, A. Merlin, L. Chatelain, Inscriptions latines d'Afrique (Tripolitanie, Tunisie, Moroc), Paris, 1923, nr. 546.

73. Below, 95.

74. Picard, op. cit. (note 63), 134.

75. G.C. Picard, Les religions de l'Afrique antique, Paris, 1954, 56-72, 109-125.

76. Picard, op. cit, (note 63), 133-134, 146, 159; Ferguson, 216; F.R. Walton, OCD^2, 19 ('Aesculapius'); S. Raven, Rome in Africa, London, 1969, 114.

77. Raven, op. cit. (note 76), 114.

78. H.G. Pflaum, Afrique romaine, (Scripta varia, 1) Paris, c. 1980 (undated), 266-267, 303, 310, 337, 340-341.

79. CIL, VI, 30983; ILS, 3840; R. Lanciani, NS, 1885, 156-157.

80. Platner-Ashby, 261, 432.

81. Waltzing, III, 314.

82. Cf. the Thugga dedication, above, nr. 3.

83. Waltzing, IV, 202-203.

84. Below, 108-109.

85. RIU, II, 377 and p. 280 and Taf. LXII; Oliva, 330-331, note 69.

86. See under RIU, II, 377; K. Póczy in Lengyel, Radan, op. cit. (above, 83, note 32), 258-259; Scullard, 192.

87. Jones, LRE, II, 858-864; 1358-1360, notes 83-95; Oliva, 211-214, 328-334; Alföldy, 189-190; Mócsy, 125, 160-161; Wilkes, 236; below, 104.

88. C. Habicht in E. Böhringer (ed.), Altertümer von Pergamon (Deutsches Archäologisches Institut), VIII, 3, Die Inschriften des Asklepieions, Berlin, 1969, nr. 67, cf. nr. 68; AE, 1962, 13.

89. CIL, III, 399; A. O'Brien Moore, YCS, VIII (1942), 25-38.

90. O'Brien Moore, op. cit. (note 89), 25-38; D. Magie, Roman Rule in Asia Minor, Princeton, 1950, 1321, note 34.

91. Wissowa, Lex, 299.

92. O'Brien Moore, op. cit. (note 89), 31.

93. Above, 18, note 57; A. Laumonier, BCH, XXXVIII (1934), 300-303.

94. AE, 1980, 869.

95. Above, 8-9.

96. CIL, X, 1547.

97. Ibid., 1546; above, 72-73, for his military counterparts.

98. Solin, II, 670-673.

99. A. Garcia y Bellido, Les religions orientales dans l'Espagne romaine, EPROER, 15, Leiden, 1968, 166; J. Maria Blazquez, ANRW, II. 3 (1975), Taf. IX, Abb. 15 (between pp. 512-513); AE, 1968, 235.

100. AE, 1967, under 223; AE, 1977, under 811.

101. AE, 1968, under 235.

102. Garcia y Bellido, op. cit. (note 99), 106-139.

103. RIB, 445; W.T. Watkin, Roman Chester or a Description of Roman Remains in the County of Chester, Liverpool, 1886, 174-175; Webster, 199-200; F.H. Thomson, Deva, Roman Chester, Chester, 1959, 34, 39, and fig. 1 (facing p. 5) and fig. 8 on p. 29.

104. Watkin, op. cit. (note 103), fig. facing p. 173.

105. Wissowa, Lex, 300-301.

106. Watkin, op. cit. (note 103), 174; cf. A.R. Birley's explanation, that "the legate's household may have been suffering from the effects of their stay in Britain"; A.R. Birley, 1979, 148; cf. the Obernburg dedication, above, 71-72.

107. Birley, 1978, 1534-1535.

108. Webster, 199-200.

109. A.R. Birley, 1981, 234-235.

110. RIB, under 445; R.G. Collingwood, J.N.L. Myres, Roman Britain and the English Settlements, Oxford, 2nd ed. 1937, 120.

111. AE, 1934, 186.

112. Mócsy, 97, 98, 195, 225, 231, 241.

113. Ibid., 51, 97-98, 231.

114. II, IV, 1, 64; CIL, XIV; ILS, 3821.

115. II, IV, 1, 633.

116. CIL, VI, 36756 and cf. 3877.

117. Scullard, 23.

118. Kajanto, 203 (Dacus).

119. CIL, IX, 3910, 3911 (Alba Fucens); CIL, X, 6512, 6513 (Cora); 4636 (Cales), 472 (Paestum), 1550 (Puteoli); CIL, XI, 1327 (Luna); CIL, XIII, 1673 (Lugdunum); A. Calderini, Aquileia romana, ricerche di storia edi epigrafia, Rome, 1972, 111 (Aquileia); cf. CIL, X, 6514 (Cora).

120. CIL, IX, 3190, 3911; CIL, X, 1550, 4636, 6512, 6513; cf. CIL, X, 6514.

121. CIL, X, 472, 1550, 4636, 6512, 6513.

122. Calderini, op. cit. (note 6), 111; E. Marbach, RE, XV, 1 (1931), 937 ('Mens'); R. Peter, Lex, II, 2, 2800 ('Mens'); Petronius, 61 and 88; Seneca, Epistulae, I.10.4.

123. Above, 1, 22.

124. Below, 106.

125. Latte, 240.

126. Ibid., 240; CIL, XIII, 1673.

127. CIL, XI, 4170; ILS, 157.

128. Weinstock, 172; below, 109-110.

129. Above, 22.

130. Cassius Dio, LVIII.12.4-5; R. Duthoy, ANRW, II.16.2 (1978), 1266, 1293, 1306.

131. CIL, II, 1437; ILER, 468.

132. R. Thouvenot, Essai sur la province romaine de Bétique, Paris, 1940, 288; cf. below, 107, 116-122.

133. CIL, VIII, 12247.

134. Ibid., 12250.

135. Leschi, op. cit. (note 63), 170.

136. Ibid., 170-171.

137. Above, 75.

138. D. Vaglieri, NS, 1910, 60 and fig. 3; AE, 1910, 189; CIL, XIV, 4324; Meiggs, 206, 432, 508.

139. Meiggs, 66-67, 508; cf. L.R. Taylor, The Cults of Ostia, Pennsylvania, 1912, 50-51.

140. Meiggs, 206, 507-509.

141. Ibid., 508; PIR^2, I, p. 13: A.75.

142. On the functions of a patronus, Meiggs, 179, 206.

143. Above, 22.

144. Pliny, Nat. Hist., XXIX.12; H.A. Grueber, Coins of the Roman Republic in the British Museum, I, London, 1910, p. 497, note 3; E. Babelon, Historique et chronologique des monnaies de la république romaine, I, Paris, 1885, pp. 100-101, 105, and 107, nr. 11.

145. Pliny, Nat. Hist., XXXIV.80; Grueber, op. cit. (note 144), 497.

146. CIL, VI, 36819; AE, 1912, 38; G. Mancini, NS, 1911, 443-445.

147. Above, 75.

148. G.H. Stevenson, OCD^2, 256 ('Clubs, Roman'); cf. above, 94-96, 127, and below, 104, 108-109; M.I. Finley, OCD^2, 582 ('Latini Iuniani'); Waltzing, IV, 419-423.

149. CIL, VIII, 15448.

150. *Ibid.*, 15446.

151. *Ibid.*, 18218; above, 95.

152. CIL, VIII, 8305.

153. CIL, VIII, 20156; 8300, 8303.

154. AE, 1962, 232; U. Fisher, W. Schliermacher, Germania, XL (1962), 73-84 with Taf. 16, facing p. 76.

155. F. Cumont, RE, V, 1 (1903), 216-219 ('Dendrophori'); A. Garzetti, From Tiberius to the Antonines, A History of the Roman Empire, AD 14-192, London, 1974, 140, 602-603; cf. the centonarii of the Brigetio dedication, above, 95-96.

156. Fisher, Schliermacher, op. cit. (note 154), 83; cf. - Keune, RE, III, A, 1 (1927), 354-360 ('Sirona'). Cf. the situation in Spain; below, 116-122. An altar from Mainz, dated stylistically to AD 200-210, depicts four divine pairs, two of which, interpreted as Grannus and Sirona, are in the guise of Apollo and Hygieia; A. von Domaszewski, Abhandlungen zur römischen Religion, Leipzig and Berlin, 1909, 130 (Fig. 22, C), 132-133, 137; Bauchhenss, 1984b, 61-63 and Taf. 101.

157. CIL, XIV, 2804; ILS, 6218. I am grateful to Dr. G.P. Burton who assisted greatly in the interpretation of this dedication.

158. Above, 12-13, 25, 28-30.

159. J.P.V.D. Balsdon, Life and Leisure in Ancient Rome, London, 1969, 329-332.

160. Fears, 862, note 146.

161. A.R. Hands, Charities and Social Aid in Greece and Rome, London, 1968, 89-95, 100-115.

162. T. Ashby, PBSR, I(1902), 181-182; E.T. Salmon, OCD^2, 451 ('Gabii').

163. II, X, iii, 103 and photograph on p. 51; CIL, V, 428; ILS, 3824.

164. CIL, V, p. 44-45; cf. A. Degrassi, II, X, iii, p. 51.

165. C.B. Pascal, The Cults of Cisalpine Gaul, Bruxelles, 1964, 36-38; CIL, V, 730, 731.

166. CIL, IX, 5534; ILS, 1012.

167. CIL, IX, 5530 (= 6078, 1); AE, 1979, 201; the reference to an excavation report is erroneous.

168. A.R. Birley, 1981, 211-213; CIL, IX, 5533; cf. the dedication of an aedes to Salus by another quinquennalis at Venusia, below, 125.

169. E. Groag, RE, I, A,2(1920), 2056 ('Salvius', nr. 22).

170. Below, 120-122.

171. CIL, IX, 6379-6381.

172. CIL, II, 6338; ILER, 470.

173. AE, 1962, 741; ILER, 469 (find-circumstances and form not given).

174. Below, 116-122; above, 101.

175. RIU, I, 24; CIL, III, 4162.

176. N. Vulić, RE, II, A,1(1921), 249 ('Savaria'); RIU, I, 31, 39, 71.

177. Hošek, op. cit (above, 82, note 31), 307-310 and pl. 30; AE, 1972, 445; above, 76.

178. Above, 104.

179. Hošek, op. cit. (above, 82, note 31), 309.

180. L. Nagy, Germania, XVI (1932), 288-290 and Taf. 16,2; AE, 1933, 111; AE, 1952, 10; Oliva, 221-222, note 254; A. Mócsy, Die Bevölkerung von Pannonien bis zu dem Markomannenkriegen, Budapest, 1959, 253, nr. 186/25.

181. Nagy, op. cit. (note 180), 290; L. Nagy, Germania, XV (1931), 261-264; Oliva, 221-222; Mócsy, 125.

182. Mócsy, 139-143; Mócsy, op. cit (note 180), 70, note 379.

183. Nagy, op. cit (note 180), 288-290; Nagy, op. cit. (note 181), 264; Oliva, 221-222, note 254.

184. CIL, III, 10548; AE, 1932, 38.

185. On collegia salutares, above, 95.

186. A.B. West, Corinth, VIII,2, Latin Inscriptions (Results of Excavations Conducted by the American School of Classical Studies at Athens), Cambridge (Mass.), 1931, nr. 110.

187. J.P. Michaud, BCH, XCIV (1970), 946, 949, 951 (fig. 135); AE, 1974, 607; AE, 1978, 778.

188. J. Wiseman, ANRW, II.7.1(1979), 497-498.

189. Above, 100-101; West, op. cit. (note 186), 90-91; Weinstock, 172.

190. J.M. Reynolds, PBSR, XXX (1962), 34-35.

191. Ibid., 34.

192. Above, 10.

193. J.M. Reynolds, PBSR, XXXIII, 1965, 52-54, nos. 2a and 2b.

194. Reynolds, op. cit. (note 190), 33-34.

195. L. Mărghitan, C.C. Petolescu, JRS, LXVI (1976), 83-85.

196. Reynolds, op. cit. (note 190), 35.

197. AE, 1912, 156.

198. P.G.W. Glare, Oxford Latin Dictionary, VI, Oxford, 1977, 1400.

199. CIL, X, 5821; ILS, 3826.

200. PIR^2, III. p. 65: D.202.

201. PIR^2, I. pp. 240-241: A.1207.

202. Above, 3-4.

203. CIL, III, 10109.

204. Wilkes, 229, 407-409.

205. Ibid., 201, note 1; CIL, III, 13283; cf. the centurion in CIL, III, 3096.

206. Speidel, 1969, 69-70; above, 47.

207. IDR, III, ii, 246; AE, 1930, 135; AE, 1933, 13.

208. PIR^2, I, pp. 20-21: A.135, 136; Pflaum, Carrières, II, 854-855: nr. 329, and p. 1066.

209. Latte, 334, note 4; 159, note 2.

210. N. Vulić, RE, II, A.1 (1921), 25-26 ('Sarmizegethusa').

211. Above, 82, note 19.

212. CIL, III, 1417a; cf. ibid., 1417, 1427, 7896-7898.

213. AE, 1977, 203.

214. A.H.M. Jones, J.R. Martindale, J. Morris, The Prosopography of the Later Roman Empire, I, Cambridge, 1971, 232; Crispinus, 2.

215. AE, 1977, under 203.

216. CIL, VI, 36841; ILS, 9337; A. Pasqui, NS, 1910, 132-134.

217. K. Abel, KP, IV, 1523 ('Salus'); A.S. Pease, University of Illinois Studies in Language and Literature, VI, nr. 3, part 2 (M. Tulli Ciceronis, De Divinatione, I), 288, note 3; H. Mattingly, OCD², 948 ('Salus'); Wissowa, RK, 133; Wissowa, Lex, 298.

218. Cassius Dio, LI.20.4; Suetonius, Aug., 31.

219. Cassius Dio, XXXVII.24. 1-2; Cicero, De Divinatione, XLVII.105; cf. Cicero, De Legibus, II.21.

220. Dumézil, 596; Latte, 67, 140-141; Wissowa, RK, 133, 525-526.

221. Tacitus, Annales, XII.23.

222. Festus, p. 152, lines 30-33 (ed. W. Lindsay, Hildesheim, 1965); Pease, op. cit. (note 217), 288, note 3; Latte, 140; F. Blumenthal, Hermes, XLIX (1914), 246-252.

223. A. and J. Šašel, Inscriptiones Latinae Quae in Jugoslavia inter Annos MCMCLX et MCMLXX Repertae et Editae Sunt, Ljubljana, 1978, nr. 868.

224. Wilkes, 160, 214-215.

225. Ibid., 161; A. and J. Šašel, Inscriptiones Latines Quae in Jugoslavia inter Annos MCMCXL et MCMLX Repertae et Editae Sunt, Ljubljana, 1963, under 207; Holder, I, 1002-1003.

226. Šašel, op. cit. (note 223), nr. 870; CIL, III, 13993.

227. CIL, XIII, 1782. There may not have been lines before those extant.

228. P. Bonvicini, Atti della accademia nazionale dei Lincei anno CCCLXIX, Rendiconti, 8th ser. XXVII (1972), Roma, (1973) 195 and tav. 1, fig. 1 (facing p. 206); AE, 1975, 350.

229. Bonvicini, op. cit. (note 228); Cagnat, 83; P. Garnsey in B. Levick (ed.), The Ancient Historian and his Materials, Farnborough, 1975, 176; cf. CIL XIII, 1902; M.I. Finley, OCD², 582 ('Latini Iuniani').

230. AE, 1907, 141.

231. Below, 116-122, cf. also Salus-Sirona(?), above, 104-105. This dedication and that from Brigetio (to Apollo and Hygieia, of AD 217) which mentions a "fountain of Salus" or a deity called Fons Salutis (above, 95) perhaps implies a situation similar to that obtaining in parts of Spain where Salus seems to have been the local choice as the Roman equivalent (probably perceived as Hygieia) of the native deity of springs. In this context it has been suggested (below, 121) that this choice may be accounted for in the light of the similarity of 'Salus' to the Celtic word for river (sala). The situation in Pannonia is far less

indicative (above, 76, 107-109, for the other Pannonian evidence for the cult of Salus), but it is at least noteworthy that a river flowing in the area south of the Danube and west of the present Lake Balaton (thus, approximately 130 km south-west of Brigetio) was called Sala (or Salla: the present day Zala, or Szala) (Holder, II, 1297). The Hadrianic municipium called Sala (or Salla), attested in the area, is perhaps to be identified with modern Zalalövö in the Zala valley (Mócsy, 144; CIL, III, 4321).

232. Above, 101, 107. CIL, II, 338 (=5230; ILER, 975, from Collipo, Lusitania) is not included, as it now seems unlikely that it refers to Salus.

233. CIL, II, 2093; ILER, 472.

234. ILER, 476; EE, IX, 212.

235. CIL, II, 1391; ILER, 480.

236. ILER, 5963; AE, 1968, 208.

237. CIL, II, 5136; ILER, 479.

238. ILER, 6781; AE, 1970, 213.

239. ILER, 477; CIL, II, 5138 (quoted).

240. ILER, 5962.

241. CIL, II, 150.

242. CPIL, 63, 64; ILER, 474, 473; EE, VIII, 78, 79.

243. CIL, II, p. 110.

244. CPIL, under 63 and 64.

245. CPIL, 57, 59, 60, 62, 63, 65-71, 73.

246. CPIL, 57-60, 62, 67-74, 78, 79.

247. CPIL, 57-60, 62, 70, 71, 73; on the epithet, CIL, II, p. 110.

248. CPIL, 65, 66.

249. CPIL, 57, 59, 73, 74, 77.

250. CPIL, 68, 69.

251. CPIL, 60, 67.

252. CPIL, 70, 71.

253. AE, 1952, 118.

254. CPIL, 290; ILER, 471.

255. CIL, II, 653; CPIL, 322.

256. CPIL, 336; ILER, 699; EE, IX, 1, 99; AE, 1902, 2.

257. CPIL, under 336.

258. EE, IX, 1, under 99.

259. ILER, p. 677 (indices); CPIL, p. 365 (indices).

260. CIL, II, 806; CPIL, 357; ILER, 475.

261. Above, 118-119.

262. CPIL, under 357.

263. CPIL, 362.

264. CIL, VIII, 14743; CIL, XIII, 3652; cf. RIB, 2.

265. CPIL, 447.

266. ILER, pp. 725, 753 (indices); CPIL, pp. 369, 371 (indices).

267. CPIL, 510.

268. CPIL, 592; ILER, 5961; AE, 1968, 217.

269. ILER, 5961; AE, 1968, 217.

270. CPIL, p. 372 (indices).

271. CPIL, under 592; AE, 1968, under 217.

272. CPIL, under 592.

273. CIL, II, 4493; ILER, 478.

274. CIL, II, 4487-4489, 4491.

275. CIL, II, 2917 and p. 397; ibid., Suppl., p. 934.

276. J. M. Blasquez, Imagen y mito: estudios sobre religiones mediterraneas e ibericas, Madrid, 1977, 376-377.

277. CIL, II, 3517; cf. 3485.

278. CIL, II, p. 1091 (indices); cf. 'Salut(ius)' in CPIL, 479.

279. CIL, XIII, 1589; AE, 1896, 94.

280. Above, 23.

281. Cassius Dio, LXIII.22.6 (the speech); Suetonius, Galba, 9.2 (the letter); above, 18, note 57, and 10, for similar expressions in the literature used of Augustus, Domitian and Trajan; cf. also the language of the Arval records under Domitian, above, 40-41.

282. Garzetti, op. cit. (note 155), 186.

283. Tacitus, Historiae, I.65.

284. Above, 24, 26.

285. CIL, XI, 361.

286. Palmer, 58, 61; cf. Cagnat, 433.

287. Palmer, 58.

288. Ibid., 58-60.

289. Ibid., 58, 62, 72, 77.

290. Ibid., 62, 76-78.

291. Ibid., 62.

292. Ibid., 59, 61-62; above, 89-90.

293. Palmer, 58; CIL, XII, 4333; CIL, III, 1933.

294. CIL, IX, 4460; ILS, 3828.

295. CIL, IX, 4929.

296. Latte, 227, note 3.

297. CIL, IX, 4111.

298. A.J. Toynbee, Hannibal's Legacy, Oxford, 1965, I, 114, note.

299. CIL, IX, 4109, 4110, 4112; cf. CIL, II, 4187; CIL, III, 1996 and 6077; CIL, VI, 678.

300. Kajanto, 13, 29, 72, 273.

301. CIL, IX, 427.

302. Ibid., p. 45; Meiggs, 174-175; II, XIII, 1, p. 254, line 56 and p. 256.

303. Above, 106-107; CIL IX, 5533; A.R. Birley, 1981, 211.

304. AE, 1898, 98; ILS, 3823; Em. Espérandieu, Inscriptiones latines de Gaule (Narbonaise), Paris, 1929, nr. 20; G. Walser, Römische Inschriften in der Schweiz, Bern, 1979, III, n. 271 and photograph p. 57. H.G. Pflaum, Les procurateurs équestres sous le haut-empire romaine, Paris, 1950, 313, regards the stone as a statue-base.

305. P. Goessler, RE, XVII, 2 (1937), 1872-1875 ('Octodurus'); E. Meyer, KP, IV, 234-235 ('Octodurus'); A.N. Sherwin-White, The Roman Citizenship, 2nd ed., Oxford, 1973, 372-373; Garzetti, op. cit. (note 155), 593-594.

306. Pflaum, op. cit. (note 304), 311; Espérandieu, op. cit. (note 304), p. 9; PIR¹, III, p. 81: P. 569; Walser, op. cit. (note 304), p. 56.

307. Pflaum, op. cit. (note 304), 229, 310-315.

308. AE, 1974, 544.

309. Ibid., Cassius Dio, LXXIX.5.2; PIR², I, p. 295: A.1452.

310. Kajanto, 20, 53-55, 107.

311. CIL, II, 6257 (171).

312. CIL, VIII, 22646.

313. CIL, XI, 6712 (390).

314. Wissowa, Lex, 295-296.

315. Latte, 234.

CHAPTER EIGHT: CONCLUSION

This chapter aims especially to indicate those significant or potentially significant characteristics and developments of the cult of Salus which are manifested in more than one of the main categories of evidence or in more than one of the preceding chapters.

A. The Early Cult

The earliest epigraphic evidence and that of Varro has been taken as indicative of an antiquity for the cult of Salus at Rome greater than that of the Quirinal temple, vowed in the war-time emergency of 313 BC, and the previous existence on the same site of a more modest fanum has been postulated. However, none of the epigraphic evidence necessarily pre-dates the Quirinal temple, though the Horta patera may do so. Furthermore, the early geographical extent of the cult may have been quite restricted: the Horta patera and the cult attested by the cippus, perhaps of the late third century BC, at Pisaurum are both likely to be of Latin, indeed of Roman, origin. The Praeneste statue-base may indicate a significant prestige for the Quirinal cult-centre in the third or early second century BC, at least in Latium. The indications corroborating Varro's assertion of a Sabine origin for Salus are circumstantial and indirect.

The question of an origin for Salus as a deity of crop-fertility though not without some positive indications remains inconclusive: there are the later coin-types depicting Salus holding corn-ears (of AD 81-83 and 96-97) and that of AD 258 bearing the legend SALUS ITAL(IAE) and depicting the goddess offering fruits to the emperor; there are the cornucopiae depicted at the street shrine at Pompeii (perhaps of the late republican period); and, most significantly, there is the later (after AD 1) attested epithet 'Semonia' perhaps indicating, along with circumstantial evidence, an archaic connection with the, perhaps also originally Sabine, Semo Sancus Dius Fidius. This connection may indicate a function for Salus as a deity of oaths, a function which may be indicated later by the oath by the health of Caesar and that by the salus of the emperor(s).

However, it remains possible that the public cult of Salus owes its establishment to a need perceived during the Second Samnite War, with the foundation of the temple coming in fulfilment of Bubulcus' vow and thus commemorating the act of salvation. The inspiration for this could have come from the contemporary Hellenistic practice of soteria, though the Romans themselves may have taken the initiative of personifying the concept of salvation inherent in these Greek festivals. Alternatively, it is possible, though perhaps less likely, that both the inspiration and a model for the innovation, if such it was, had been provided by a cult of Soteria which may already have been established at Metapontum in Greek southern Italy in the late fourth century BC. In either case the increased contact between Rome and the Greek cities of the south, brought about by the Second Samnite War, would have provided a context for the introduction to the Romans of Greek concepts and practices such as these. The same context may account for the introduction of the related Greek concept of <u>soter</u>. In any case the Hellenistic practice of granting this title to both gods and mortals must have had an impact upon Roman thought in the succeeding period as Rome's contacts with the Greek east increased.

Though the idea of <u>soter</u> was to have important consequences in the sphere of public cult, its initial impact was upon the private aspect of the cult of Salus. S. Weinstock assumed that this aspect of Salus would have been much older than the foundation of the Quirinal temple,[1] although, with the possible exception of the Horta <u>patera</u>, there is no direct indication of this. Its existence in the late third century is clearly indicated in the comedies of Plautus, where the effect of Hellenistic influence upon the concept of personal Salus is apparent. She is, though, still clearly here a deity of general salvation and thus distinct from Hygieia whose introduction at Rome occurs, by implication, shortly after 293 BC with that of the cult of Aesculapius.

This transformation of the private cult, in association with the Roman practice of awarding the <u>corona civica</u> (which also underwent a significant transformation) occurring in the context of the upheavals of the last decades of the Republic had consequences which were brought to fruition by the actions of the followers of Julius Caesar. Increasingly, the <u>salus</u> of the state was regarded as dependent upon outstanding individuals. At the same time the personal health of individuals, such as Livius Drusus, Pompey and Caesar, came to be of paramount importance for the state. The two republican coin-issues can be interpreted as reflecting the change in attitude during the period separating them (91 to 49 BC). If a cult of Salus Caesaris was not actually established, and almost certainly one was intended to be, the developments towards that end nevertheless provided the context for the establishment of those of Salus Augusti and Salus Augusta which took place, if not under Augustus, then certainly under his successor.

B. <u>Salus Augusta and Salus Augusti</u>

Salus Augusta first appears in the legend borne by the <u>dupondius</u> of AD 22 or 23, with a type probably depicting the head of Livia, and thereafter in the municipal dedication of AD 32 at Interamna commemorating the failure of Sejanus' conspiracy. Salus Augusti also may be first attested under Tiberius, in the Ostia dedication to Salus Caesaris Augusti where the accompanying statue, perhaps erected on the occasion of an imperial visit, probably portrayed the goddess as Hygieia as on Glabrio's coin of 49 BC. She is portrayed as Hygieia when she first appears in a securely dated context, that of Galba's coin issue of AD 69. Thus she may represent 'The Health of the Emperor'.

Notably, when SALUS AUGUSTA reappears as a coin-legend, under Galba, it is with a distinctive type: the goddess, enthroned, holding patera and sceptre. The type, though without the sceptre, had already appeared under Nero but with the unqualified SALUS, perhaps commemorating Nero's survival of the Pisonian conspiracy. A possible interpretation of the meaning of Salus Augusta might be that of 'The Beneficial Power of the Emperor'. However, if any distinction between Salus Augusti and Salus Augusta was originally intended by the minting authorities, and this is possible, it had disappeared by the time of Trajan on whose coins the fusion of the types is complete, although it is only under Hadrian that the fused type is associated with the unambiguous SALUS AUGUSTI (as opposed to SALUS AUG under Trajan). Thus, it has been suggested, is the beneficial power of the emperor (Salus Augusta) unambiguously combined with the health of the emperor (Salus Augusti).

Only in the reign of Antoninus Pius, though, is the fused Salus-type first combined with SALUS PUBLICA. In other media articulating imperial ideology, however, the closer identification of the person of the emperor with the public salus was manifested earlier. Under Domitian, in the January 3 vota of AD 91, the Arval Brothers had honoured Salus Augusta Publica P.R.Q. This and other innovations, manifested in the Arval records for the reign of Domitian and in both the Panegyricus of Pliny and his reports from Bithynia-Pontus under Trajan, presumably reflect a deliberate imperial policy. The emperor is now the mediator through which the Salus Publica operates and upon whose health it depends. Furthermore, the emperor is now projected as the guarantor of the salus of all the people of the empire, citizen and non-citizen. Thus, on Trajan's aurei, probably commemorating his decennalia of AD 108, is proclaimed the SALUS GENERIS HUMANI. In AD 283 or 284 the imperial curator of Puteoli erected a statue of Carus with the dedication hailing the deified emperor as the auctor Salutis Publicae.

Of the seven dedications where the imperial epithet is provided in full, five of these honour an equivalent of Salus Augusti. These include that of the patronus of Ostia (mentioned above), that by the civitas Tepeltensis during a joint reign, that at Rome of the collegium thurariorum et unguentariorum to the Salus Domus Aug. and that at Bonn of the army of Lower Germany in the reign of Severus Alexander.

Apart from the Interamna dedication by a sevir Augustalis, mentioned above, Salus Augusta is attested in one other dedication, that a private one at Ostippo in Baetica. After Vespasian, Salus Augusta occurs unambiguously only on a sestertius issue of Marcus (AD 170-171), in the legend SALUTI AUGUSTAE.

SALUS AUGUSTI appears regularly in the coin-issues until the tetrarchy, either in full or implied in the plural as SALUS AUGG (or AUGGG). The appearance of SALUS AUGG implies that SALUS AUG, which is the predominating Salus legend, represents the genetival form. Approximately as many issues as those bearing a Salus legend bear a type of Salus unaccompanied by a Salus legend. In the vast majority of issues the types are variations on the theme established under Trajan: the goddess, enthroned or standing, feeds from a patera the snake which is usually coiling around an altar. Sometimes, and when appropriate, she holds either a sceptre or a rudder. Under the tetrarchy the legend SALUS AUGG ET CAESS NN also appears (AD 285-311). Thereafter the imperial epithet qualifies Salus only on the coins of Magnentius (AD 351-353: including those struck by him in the name of Constantius II) which bear a type depicting the chi-rho flanked by alpha and omega.

In the sphere of municipal cult a female sacerdos of Spes and Salus Aug. is attested at Gabii under Antoninus Pius, and a temple and flaminica of Salus Aug. are attested at Urbs Salvia in the late first century AD. Furthermore, the town-council at Rusovce in Pannonia Superior may have assigned the land for an aedes of Salus Aug. and Jupiter Dolichenus (late second or first third of third century AD). Certainly the vicani of Nida in Germania Superior, in the middle of the second century, assigned land for a schola, of the local dendrophori Augustales, which was dedicated to Salus Aug. who may here conceal a Celtic deity in Roman guise. Also in the sphere of collegiate cult, the collegium salutare at Rome, probably under Hadrian, dedicated a new schola or shrine to the Numen Domus Aug., and to Aesculapius and Salus (-Hygieia) Aug. on land assigned by the procurator of the imperial patrimonium, and a collegium Salutis Aug. is attested at Aquincum, probably in the same reign. In two of the private dedications, that at Pinquentum (though here the dedication is pro incolumitate Pinquentinorum) and that at Uchi Maius, Salus Aug. may represent Hygieia. Salus Aug. may also be the object of the two uncertain, but presumably private, dedications at Rusovce both to Jupiter Dolichenus and, perhaps, Salus Aug.: one is certainly that of two or more military officers, the other is that of a freedman dedicating the aedes mentioned above.

C. Salus-Hygieia

Salus' identification with Hygieia may be presumed to have developed as a result of the transplantation of the cult of Aesculapius to Rome shortly after 293 BC. It is manifested in the public cult-act of 180 BC as we know from Livy and is established in popular perception by 165 BC as we know from Terence. From the beginning she seems to have provided the imagery associated with Salus Augusti.

With Aesculapius she is honoured in at least nine dedications. Four are those of medici, with three of these being those of military medical officers, one dating from AD 82, another from the late second or early third century. The dedication by the freedmen and slave household of a legionary legate at Chester dates from shortly after AD 90. We have noted the dedication of the collegium salutare at Rome, probably of the reign of Hadrian. Otherwise an unspecified sodalitas honoured Aesculapius and Salus and the Dii Augusti at Thugga.

The principal sanctuary of the important temple at Lambaesis, built by legio III Augusta, was dedicated by the emperors Marcus and Verus in AD 162 or 163. Presumably from that temple came the dedication of the praeses of Numidia dating from AD 283 to 285. The votive dedication of the legionary tribune at Apulum, of about AD 200, and that of the beneficiarius at Ammãn, of AD 245 to 246, may also honour Aesculapius and Salus.

Salus-Hygieia may also be the deity honoured with Bona Mens by the collegium teibeicinum Romanorum at Tibur and that implied in the joint cult of Roma and Salus attested in about 30 BC at Pergamum.

She was probably the deity perceived by the inhabitants of Lusitania and Baetica as the nearest Roman equivalent to their native Celtic deity of healing who is represented under Salus' name in seventeen or more private dedications. It is the connection with water-sources and healing-springs which indicates Salus-Hygieia in the Baden bei Wien (Aquae) dedication and perhaps also in the early third century AD dedicatory poem of the centurion at Bu-Ngem. Salus may also have been perceived in her healing aspect in the centurion's dedication to Jupiter Dolichenus, Caelestis, Brigantia and Salus, probably of the early third century AD, at Corbridge and, though perhaps less probably, in the dedication of the praefectus legionis, of AD 198 to 209, to Salus Regina at Caerleon. The private dedication by a freedman at Asculum Picenum is for the restoration of his wife, perhaps from illness, and at Preturo, Salus-Hygieia may be implied in the epitaph of a ministra Salutis. Salus' healing aspect may be perceivable at Heddernheim in the schola dedication to Salus Aug. who may here represent the Celtic Sirona.

D. Salus Publica

Salus Publica is the name given in the imperial period to the deity of the Quirinal temple. Cassius Dio records that Augustus honoured her with a statue in 11 BC. The form Salus Publica, or an expanded version of it, is that used almost invariably for the deity in the records of the Arval Brothers (appearing for the first time in AD 38). Here she invariably accompanies the Capitoline Triad and almost invariably is invoked in fourth place after the Triad in the order of deities receiving vows or sacrifices or both. The Brothers' activities involving Salus, both annual and extraordinary, are exclusively those pertaining to the activities, welfare, health and occasions of the emperor and his family. She is last attested in the record of the vota of January 3, AD 231.

Although the epithet Publica is first attested in the coinage on one of the unattributed denarii of Galba (AD 68) accompanying the type of a laureate bust, she can undoubtedly be understood as the deity celebrated as SALUS on the obverses of the denarii issues of 91 BC (with the type of a diademed head) where she is accompanied by a type of Victoria and sometimes the legend ROMA on the reverses. She is presumably the deity on the Salus issues of Nero where she is depicted as enthroned and holding a patera. Presumably also, Salus Publica was the deity to be honoured with one or possibly two new temples, by a decree of the Senate, in thanksgiving for Nero's preservation from the Pisonian conspiracy.

Although not named as such, she is the deity whose anniversary, the natalis of the Quirinal temple, is listed for observance in the civilian calendars and the Feriale Duranum and which is alluded to in the Menologica Rustica. She may be securely inferred as the deity included in the thirteen dedications by members of the equites singulares Augusti and dating from AD 118 to 141.

She is perhaps the deity who, in a joint cult with Roma, had a sacerdos at Pergamum in about 30 BC. Combined with Providentia Aug. she had a female sacerdos in perpetuum at Corinth, where the cult may have been established as part of the same municipal reaction to the events of AD 31 as is attested at Interamna, though there, as mentioned above, Salus Augusta was the form of the deity honoured. She is the recipient of the dedication by a senator at Ferentinum in the late first century AD and of the private offering (to Salus Populi Romani) of a municipal aedile at Tiaret in Mauretania Caesariensis. It is possible to infer from Tacitus that a temple had been founded at Ferentinum, by decree of the Senate, following the Pisonian conspiracy.

Her next appearance in the coinage, after Galba, that on all the Salus issues of Nerva (AD 96-97) with the type of the enthroned goddess holding corn-ears, may reflect a reaction to the policies of Domitian. Under Hadrian her accompanying type, depicting the goddess standing, holding patera and rudder, and with her foot on a globe, is still distinct from those accompanying SALUS AUGUSTI and SALUS AUG. However, as mentioned above, from the reign of Antoninus Pius onwards, SALUS PUBLICA is accompanied by variations of the fused type previously only associated with SALUS AUGUSTI and SALUS AUG.

This apparent hesitancy on the part of the minting authorities in overtly associating SALUS PUBLICA with the type of the imperial Salus is interpreted by K.H. Schwarte as reflecting the exceptional prestige attaching to the concept of Salus Publica deriving from the republican tradition.[2]

She does not now reappear in the coinage until the reign of Macrinus during which SALUS PUBLICA represents the only Salus legend (AD 217-218). Thereafter, and prior to Constantine I, the legend appears on seven issues of Severus Alexander, on one issue each of Valerian and Gallienus (AD 257), on five issues of Tacitus and Florian (AD 275-276) and on the one issue of Magnia Urbica (AD 283-285) after whom it appears only on two issues of Carausius (AD 286-293).

The Ptolemais fragment (possibly of the second century AD) may indicate a regular observance of her cult on a municipal or even provincial basis, the performance and recording of which was apparently analogous to that of the acts of the Arval Brothers.

As the object of ostensibly private piety she is clearly implied in the dedication at Splitska (Dalmatia, dated to AD 211) by a slave or freedman, and in that by the imperial procurator at Sarmizegetusa (of the mid-third century AD).

We have noted above the manifestations in the Arval evidence, in Pliny's evidence and, tentatively in the coinage, of a developing imperial policy under Domitian and Trajan of projecting Salus Publica as dependent upon the mediation and health of the emperor. As a later reflection of this concept, we mentioned above the statue of the deified Carus, erected by the curator of Puteoli in AD 283 or 284, the dedication of which hails the emperor as auctor Salutis Publicae.

In the fourth century the coins, apart from those of Magnentius mentioned above, always proclaim SALUS REIPUBLICAE (often combined with

SPES). There was perhaps now a deliberate distancing of the "Salus of the State" from the person of the, now Christian, emperor. The female figure with two children depicted on the folles of Fausta (AD 324-327) may represent Salus, but certainly after Constantine I no imagery of Salus remains. By the reign of Valentinian I and Valens the concept of Salus is firmly part of the ideology of the Christian emperors (AD 364-378).

However, the calendar of AD 354 may, in view of circumstantial evidence, indicate the continued observance (despite the existence of laws intended to repress paganism) of the festival of Salus on August 5, at least at Rome, though perhaps with its religious aspect now diminished or absent. The festival had since at least as early as the reign of Severus Alexander, as we know from the Feriale Duranum, been celebrated, at least at Rome, with ludi circenses.

E. Salus Generis Humani

Salus Generis Humani appears as a legend on the coins of Galba, Trajan, Commodus and Caracalla and as the object of a private dedication. The literary evidence suggests that in the coinage of Galba the legend may reflect the sentiments expressed by Julius Vindex to the Gauls and to Galba when raising his revolt in AD 68. Similarly, the dedication, which is from Ruessium in eastern Aquitania, may relate to the revolt or its aftermath.

On the aurei of Trajan[3] the legend is accompanied by a type, which may recall one of those borne by the coins of Galba, of a goddess, perhaps Fortuna, with foot on globe, sacrificing with a patera over an altar and holding a rudder. The type on the issues of Commodus and Caracalla depicts the goddess holding a snake-wreathed staff and raising a kneeling figure.

F. Irregular Forms of Salus in the Coinage

An antoninianus of Gallienus (AD 258) bears the legend SALUS ITAL(IAE) accompanied by a type of the goddess offering fruits to the emperor who is holding a spear. Among the idiosyncratic features of the Salus coinage of the Gallic empire (AD 259-274) are the legends SALUS EXERCITI and SALUS PROVINCIARUM. The first accompanies a type of Aesculapius, and the second accompanies types depicting the personified River Rhine. An antoninianus of Probus bears the legend SALUS MILITUM accompanying a traditional type (AD 276-282).

G. Salus of Uncertain Nature

The epigraphic evidence includes five dedications in which there is no clear indication of the perceived nature of Salus, either by virtue of an epithet or circumstantially. Two of these are the dedications of a private nature at Asseria in Dalmatia and at Lugdunum.

The dedication by the aedile at Ariminum of his votive aedes, which he specified was to be administered according to the canon attaching to Diana's Aventine temple, has been inferred as implying Salus Aug. There is the brief dedication of a municipal, perhaps servile, arcarius at Civitella, and at Venusia an aedes was dedicated by decree of the council, probably after 29 BC. At Forum Claudii the procurator of the Alpes Atrectianae et Poeninarum, probably in the reign of Marcus and Verus, joined with the inhabitants of the town, and perhaps of the region, in a public dedication. At Napoca in Dacia Porolissensis in the early third century another imperial procurator dedicated simply cum suis.

H. Divine Associations with Salus of Potential Significance (Apart from that with Aesculapius)

1. Spes

The most persistent association, apart from that with Aesculapius, is that with Spes. Most notably it occurs in Plautus, in Velleius Paterculus' description of Tiberius' adoption, in the joint cult of Spes and Salus Aug. at Gabii under Antoninus Pius and in the coinage. Perhaps coincidentally, Salus and Spes, along with Diana and Vulcan, are the deities whose anniversaries are selected for August in the Menologia Rustica (AD 36 - 121). The anniversary of Spes was August 1. In the coinage the association occurs in the three issues of Commodus (AD 183-186) where Spes appears in the type along with a mass of other symbolic detail. Under Claudius II the legend SPES PUBLICA accompanies a type of Salus and Aesculapius. Medallions of Constantine I and Constantius Caesar and a gold issue of each of Constantius, as emperor, and Constans proclaim SALUS ET SPES REIPUBLICAE.

2. Concordia and Pax

The literary evidence hints at an association, which may be more than fortuitous, between Salus, Concordia and Pax. The legends borne by the local coins of Buthrotum (c. 10-1 BC) and those borne by an aureus associated with the revolt of Civilis (AD 69-70) indicate a relationship between Salus and Concordia. The legend PAX AUG(G) occurs with types of Salus on three issues of the Gallic empire (AD 259-274), and there is a pronounced association between the two in the coinage of Carausius (AD 286-293).

3. Fortuna

Fortuna is associated with Salus in two references in Plautus. What may be a type of Fortuna appears on some of the SALUS GENERIS HUMANI issues of Galba and also on the aurei bearing the same legend which are thought to commemorate Trajan's decennalia (AD 108). Thereafter until the reign of the Philippi (AD 244-247) and then again in issues of the Gallic empire, Salus appears intermittently with the Fortuna attribute of the rudder, sometimes set on a globe, as a held attribute replacing the sceptre. Fortuna occurs alone with Aesculapius and Salus in the Chester dedication by the freedmen and slave household of the legionary legate of about AD 90 and with Jupiter Optimus

Maximus, Apollo, Aesculapius and Salus in the Obernburg dedication of the medicus cohortis. In the legionary tribune's dedication at Apulum, of about AD 200, and in that of the procurator at Sarmizegetusa, of about AD 250, she occurs adjacent to Salus (who perhaps represents Hygieia in the former and probably Salus Publica in the latter), though, in both cases, as one in a long list of deities.

4. Felicitas

The dedications of the equites singulares Augusti manifest a, perhaps superficial, association between Salus, Felicitas and the Fata. Felicitas receives sacrifices after Salus on three occasions in the Arval records, and a silver medallion of Salonina (AD 260-268) bears a type depicting Pudicitia, Salus and Felicitas.

5. Isis

A type of Isis accompanies SALUS AUG on two issues of Claudius II (AD 268-270). Isis, who had a significant healing attribute, may be assimilated to Salus in the Léon dedication, dating from the late second century, by two senators to Aesculapius, Salus, Serapis and Isis.

NOTES

1. Wissowa, <u>RK</u>, 132.

2. Schwarte, 244, 246.

3. And see above under B.

ADDENDUM: THE MAINZ JUPITER COLUMN

This imposing public monument, found in 1904 and 1905 in Sömmeringstrasse, Mainz, originally consisted of eight principal parts: an upper and a lower pedestal, five column-drums, an ornate capital (with acanthus-leaf carving) surmounted by a square, ornately carved statue-base, and a bronze statue of Jupiter.[1] (Its height to the top of the statue-base was approximately 9.1 m.) As found, smashed (in antiquity) into over a thousand fragments, all but the statue (of which five fragments remained) had substantially survived. Reconstructed, it suffered significant damage in the Second World War.[2]

The column-drums and both pedestals bear relief carvings which, as far as can be interpreted, exclusively, or almost exclusively, depict members of the Roman state pantheon.[3] Not all the twenty-eight deities depicted can be identified with certainty.

According to the inscription (carried on the front of the upper pedestal), the column was dedicated to Jupiter Optimus Maximus for the safety of Nero (pro salute Neronis).[4] It was erected at some time betwen AD 59 and 67 by or on behalf of the inhabitants of the canabae at Moguntiacum. The approval, co-operation or perhaps even the initiative of the governor of the province, P. Sulpicius Scribonius Proculus, is indicated by the inclusion of his name in the dedication.[5] The broad dating of the dedication (AD 59-67) derives from both the known and the inferred years of the governorship of Scribonius Proculus.[6] The purpose of the monument is presumed to have been the public expression of loyalty and thanksgiving for the deliverance of the emperor from a particular danger (whether actual or supposed). H.U. Instinsky has argued that the two most likely occasions for such an expression of public thanksgiving (in the years AD 58 to 67) are the supposed deliverance of Nero brought about by the assassination of Agrippina (in 59) and the failure of the Pisonian conspiracy (in 65).[7] There are fewer dating problems in associating the dedication of the column with the aftermath of the death of Agrippina.[8] As noted above, following an obsequious decree of the Senate in April, AD 59, the Arval Brothers gave thanks to the Capitoline Triad, Salus (Publica), Providentia, the Genius of Nero and the Divus Augustus for the safety of Nero.[9] In AD 65, after the failure of the Pisonian conspiracy, the Senate decreed the building of a temple to Salus in gratitude for Nero's safe deliverance. The gold and silver coins of Nero bearing a type and legend of Salus may have celebrated the same deliverance.[10]

In a new and major republication of the Jupiter column, G. Bauchhenss endorses Instinsky's interpretation of the political significance of this monument and, with some reservation, accepts earlier interpretations of the deity depicted (with Mercury) in the relief-panel on the left side of the lower pedestal as Salus

(Publica).[11] The attributes of the female deity accompanying Mercury are far from clear, and what can be detected with certainty is not unequivocally indicative of Salus; she holds in her right hand a caduceus (winged and snake-wreathed, though rather indistinct) and in her left hand a round, winged object (suggestive of the small, winged hat worn by Mercury), and between her and Mercury a snake, coiled around an object of uncertain nature (possibly an altar), makes towards her.[12]

As Bauchhenss observes, according to the coin evidence, the iconography of Salus had not yet become fixed at this date.[13] (Indeed, even after the Hygieia archetype had become established as the norm, by the reign of Hadrian, there were always departures, more and less idiosyncratic, from the traditional type.[14]) Only twice in the state coinage is Salus depicted holding a caduceus (or snake-wreathed staff), and in all of the issues concerned the accompanying legend is SAL(US) GEN(ERIS) HUM(ANI): the three such issues of Commodus (c. AD 191) and those of Caracalla (AD 199-201) depict Salus holding a snake-wreathed staff or sceptre and raising a kneeling figure.[15] Salus is, however, frequently depicted in the central state coinage from the reign of Hadrian onwards, both as Hygieia and (at the same time) as holding a simple sceptre.[16] Her earliest appearance holding a sceptre is on the coins of Galba, where she is accompanied by the legend SALUS AUGUSTA. Here she is enthroned and holds also a patera.

Other issues of Galba celebrate, for the first time, SALUS AUGUSTI accompanied by a type clearly indicating a conception of her as Hygieia - leaning on a column and holding and feeding a snake. Thus, in official contemporary ideology, as represented in the coinage, distinct conceptions are indicated respectively for Salus Augusta and Salus Augusti, with Salus Augusti perhaps representing the 'Health of the Emperor' (indicated by her depiction as Hygieia). (Salus Augusta may then be the welfare-bringing power of the emperor.[17])

The legend SALUS PUBLICA appears on coins of the same reign accompanied by a lauriate bust type.[18] As is clear from Chapter Two, Salus Publica and Salus Augusti, as depicted on the coins, both came to assume the imagery of Salus-Hygieia.[19] (Salus Augusta does not appear on the coins after AD 78.)

Although Jupiter Optimus Maximus is the only deity mentioned in the dedication, those deities depicted in the reliefs which can be identified with certainty or with probability clearly imply that, if Salus is depicted on the column,[20] then the conception of her which is most strongly suggested (leaving aside the imagery employed) must be that of Salus Publica and not that of Salus-Hygieia. Salus conceived as Hygieia is more likely to be associated either with Aesculapius, as on the dedication-slab from Binchester,[21] or with Apollo, as on the altar from Mainz[22] and the Pompeii relief-tondo.[23] Although, as Bauchhenss observes, the pairing of Fortuna and Minerva in the relief-panel on the right side of the lower pedestal indicates that we need not assume any close cultic connection between deities depicted together in the reliefs.[24]

If Salus is to be recognized in this relief, her depiction would represent the earliest depiction of Salus Publica in the guise (at least partially) of Hygieia. Salus Augusti (though not Salus Augusta) is depicted as Hygieia on the coins of Galba (AD 68-69), with a type which thus recalls for the first time on an imperial issue the type used on the coins of Acilius Glabrio (of 49 BC).[25]

NOTES

1. Bauchhenss, 1984a, Taf. 36 (replica).

2. Ibid., Vorwort.

3. Ibid., 2-9, 19.

4. CIL, XIII, 11806; Bauchhenss, 1984a, 5.

5. Instinsky, 1959, 131, 132, 138 and note 60.

6. Cf. Instinsky, 1959, 132-133: he allows AD 58 to 67.

7. Instinsky, 1959, 132-133, 136-139. Bauchhenss adds, as a third possibility, Nero's deliverance from the Vinician conspiracy (in, perhaps, 66); Bauchhenss, 1984a, 33.

8. Instinsky, 1959, 138-139; Bauchhenss, 1984a, 33. In addition, Bauchhenss prefers the earlier date on stylistic grounds; ibid., 26-29, 33.

9. Above, 43.

10. Above, 3-4, 22.

11. Bauchhenss, 1984a, 4, 11, 14-16; Instinsky, 1959, 139; cf. Bauchhenss, 1984a, table on p. 12.

12. Bauchhenss, 1984a, 4.

13. Ibid., 16; above, 22 ff.

14. Above, 24-29.

15. Above, 25, 26.

16. Above, 24-28.

17. Above, 24.

18. Above, 23, and 23 ff. for the development of the Salus types on the coins, with the fusion of the types of Salus Augusta and Salus Augusti being completed under Hadrian and this fused type being combined with Salus Publica under Pius.

19. Above, 24-25.

20. The chief alternative possibilities are Felicitas, Maia (the mother of Mercury), and Rosmerta (the native Celtic equivalent of Maia); Bauchhenss, 1984a, 12 (table), 14-16.

21. Above, 72. We may also note the joint dedications: above, 71-73, 92-99.

22. Above, 139, note 156; Bauchhenss, 1984b, 62.

23. Above, 14; cf. also above, 13, 71, 73, 95.

24. Bauchhenss, 1984a, 16.

25. Above, 22-23: cf., though, the likely form of the Ostia statue (probably depicting Salus as Hygieia) dedicated to Salus Caesaris Augusti, perhaps during the reign of Tiberius; above, 102-103.